MODERN LEGAL STUDIES

Discretion and Deviation
in the
Administration of Immigration Control

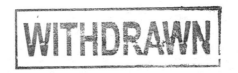

AUSTRALIA
LBC Information Services
Sydney

CANADA and USA
Carswell
Toronto – Ontario

NEW ZEALAND
Brookers
Auckland

SINGAPORE and MALAYSIA
Thomson Information (S.E.) Asia
Singapore

MODERN LEGAL STUDIES

Discretion and Deviation
in the
Administration of Immigration Control

Satvinder S. Juss
Ph.D., Barrister of Gray's Inn
Human Rights Fellow,
Harvard Law School

London
Sweet & Maxwell
1997

Published by
Sweet & Maxwell Limited of
100 Avenue Road
London NW3 3PE
http://www.smlawpub.co.uk
Typeset by LBJ Enterprises Ltd of Chilcompton & Aldermaston
Printed in Great Britain by Clays Ltd, St Ives plc

A CIP catalogue record for this book
is available from the British Library

ISBN 0421 618 302

No natural forests were destroyed to make this product,
only farmed timber was used and re-planted.

"[I]t has yet again become necessary for me . . . . as a member of what is referred to as the 'ethnic minority' in Britain to disagree . . . I feel that to fail to oppose the dismissal of this appeal would be tantamount to endorse the denial of justice to the appellants and a lack of compassion, whatever the legal arguments. The law imposed by Parliament apparently establishes equality for all. However, it seems to me that in its application, cultural differences, interpretation, prejudices, generalisation etc. . . . . leave much to be desired. . . . . It would seem to me unjust to pick and choose from the evidence what one prefers to fit into a preconceived notion. This places the appellant's side in an insurmountable situation irrespective of the truthfulness of their evidence."

A. G. JEEVANJEE
(minority Immigration Appeal Tribunal determination in
Mohammed Shaban v. Visa Officer Islamabad (1996) (unreported))

For Amrit and Ajit.

— *the source of all unalloyed joy.*

Foreword

The thrust of this scholarly and useful work is that the individual officials and courts who adjudicate upon the applications of immigrants and asylum-seekers must inform themselves of the cultural norms and practices of the applicants. Dr Juss' thesis is a great deal more than the author's submission of a weighty tome as the requirement for a higher university degree.

The author's research into the working of the Entry Clearance System — the officials who operate the system abroad (mainly in the new Commonwealth countries) and their counterparts in the United Kingdom — suggests that decision making fails to conform to the basic precepts of fairness, both in its procedural aspect and in its substantive application. "Parity, equity and justice" are lacking, simply because the process of decision making is culturally incompetent in evaluating the factual material and the inferential conclusions to be drawn from that material. Dr Juss pleads for the development of a "cultural jurisprudence" to repair the current deficiency.

"Cultural jurisprudence" is defined as a "legal agency through which principles of equity, parity and justice can be more accurately secured in an increasingly diverse and multicultural society". Such a futuristic approach can realistically be promoted only by the judges, from whom the grass-roots officials will necessarily take their cue. So long as the process of interrogation for claims of entry into the United Kingdom is, however, conducted adversarially by a "white, male, entry clearance officer interviewing an illiterate village woman in *purdah*", the result is unlikely to give satisfaction to claimants even if the decision may be objectively justified. Dr Juss distinguishes fairness in the procedures ("liberal judges" are "procedure minded") and fairness in the substantive decision ("conservative judges" are "record-oriented"). The distinction is well made in theory. Practice hardly follows suit.

When Lord Parker C.J. handed down the *locus classicus* decision in *Re HK* 30 years ago, that immigration officers have a duty to act fairly towards an aspiring immigrant, he was saying so in the climate of a barely emerging public law that was still heavily focused on the old prerogative writs and hence procedurally-oriented. Judicial review had not yet taken off. Lord Parker said specifically that the matter was entirely "for mandarins and could not be a matter for certiorari". The fact that the final decision about HK was receiving the personal attention of the Home Secretary meant that the application to the courts had achieved more than could be hoped for from judicial proceedings. (It has never been publicly stated whether HK ultimately gained entry into the United Kingdom.)

Until an administrator's or Minister's duty to act fairly encompasses the quality of the decision itself, the procedural safeguard of the manner in which the decision is arrived at will not suffice to provide any "cultural jurisprudence". Change in that direction will be slow in coming. It is no exaggeration to say that legislators and administrators are the primary law makers, not the judges. What is needed, therefore, is some legislative indicator to inculcate in immigration officers the cultural dimensions of their task.

Training and managerial supervision will provide the key, rather than occasional judicial precept. And it is not just in the field of immigration that cultural attitudes and attributes have to be imbibed by officials; the administration of the Housing Act 1995 with regard to homelessness involves a large element of the immigrant population.

It could be said of Dr Juss, in a work that eschews erudite language, that he excuses the fire of indignation at officialdom in the immigration service and the sympathy felt for aspiring immigrants unused to British habits. He renders himself as the perfect advocate for justice to immigrants and asylum seekers. He pleads for public debate in place of closeted policy making. If the advent of the new Labour Administration on May 1, 1997 encourages the belief of better treatment in the future, there is as yet only a few signs of reform.

The *Special Immigration Appeals Commission* (SIAC), introduced into the House of Lords on May 20, 1997 may be only an inheritance from the outgoing Conservative Government. Whether or not that is so, where an order of deportation, exclusion or departure from the United Kingdom is made, the departing alien will have a right of appeal in cases where the issue is "conducive to the public good". That new procedural safeguard will not enhance the cultural dimension, unless the members appointed to the SIAC by the Lord Chancellor are carefully selected. Sensitive appointments might token a new approach to highly sensitive issues.

Sir Louis Blom-Cooper, Q.C., LL.B.(London), Dr.Jur. (Amsterdam)
Master of the Bench of the Middle Temple,
Chairman of the Mental Health Act Commission 1987–1994.

cultural norms and values of the subjects of immigration law. Indeed, immigration law often directly impacts on cultural, religious and ethnic rights and values because it can be used as a tool to distinguish the "otherness" of the newcomer on that basis, and thus help preserve the culture of the host community.

The essential focus of this work is to examine the decisions of officials and official bodies that administer the entry clearance system in British immigration law. This work examines the operation of the system from its inception in 1969, when it was first instituted as a response to the 1950s–1960s New Commonwealth immigration, through to the 1980s, when concern in the manner of its operation was at its highest both amongst immigrant communities and representative organisations. It should therefore be of interest to academic and practising lawyers alike. The research contained in this book sets out to provide the first theoretically detailed and practically coherent account of the external extra-legal influences that impinge on a particular and specific substantive area of immigration law to be published. To that extent this work does not give a general account of immigration law as such which has by now been well documented in a number of books.[2]

Previous works on immigration law have alluded to the desirability of such a study. In 1987 Professor Stephen Legomsky, in his excellent *Immigration and the Judiciary*,[3] observed that given the existence of recent works that have emphasised the role of extra-legal influences on decision making, the "next logical step is to build on these works by studying, comprehensively, judicial decisions falling within a carefully limited substantive sphere". He argued that, without such a study, it is impossible to gauge either the nature or depth of the external influences that the recent writings have emphasised, since "confining the focus to a single substantive area provides

---

[2] For general accounts of immigration law, see Jackson, *Immigration: Law and Practice* (London, 1996); Macdonald, C. and N. Blake Q.C., *Macdonald's Immigration Law and Practice* (London, 4th ed., 1994); Juss, *Immigration, Nationality and Citizenship* (London, 1993); Bevan, *The Development of British Immigration Law* (London, 1987); Evans, *Immigration Law* (London, 2nd ed., 1983); Grant and Martin, *Immigration Law and Practice* (London, 1982); Dummett and Nicol, *Subjects, Citizens, Aliens and Others* (London, 1990); Spencer, *Strangers and Citizens* (London, 1994); Vincenzi and Marrington, *Immigration Law: The Rules Explained* (London, 1992). For brief summaries see Bradley and Ewing, *Constitutional and Administrative Law* (London, 11th ed., 1993), pp. 431–458; Harlow and Rawlings, *Law and Administration* (London, 1984), pp. 510–517; Turpin, *British Government and the Constitution* (London, 2nd ed., 1990), pp. 400–401.

[3] Legomsky, *Immigration and the Judiciary* (Oxford, 1978), p. 5.

Preface

Books these days are usually the product of sustained, thoughtful inquiry undertaken over many years, that is telling of one's labour in a field. Coleridge said, "Judge no man by his books", but this book will inevitably call for plenty of judgment. It follows the author's first book, *Immigration, Nationality and Citizenship* which laid the ground-work for this work.[1] Immigration is a new setting for scholarly work. Not only are scholars in this setting searching for traditions of critical inquiry to apply to this context, but scholars studying other regula-tory contexts are looking to this emerging research area for fresh comparative materials. This book is the first in British immigration law to undertake a detailed and systemic study of the exercise of official administrative discretion which determines the rights of claimants before decision-making bodies. It is the first to attempt a thorough analysis of the right to family life in domestic British immigration law. It is the first to seek to develop a theory of immigration adjudication in the context of the emerging national minorities in nation states world-wide.

It is suggested that the practice of immigration law currently fails to meet the standards of parity, equity and justice for two reasons that have been hitherto much neglected. First, immigration adjudica-tion eschews an equalitarian approach. It neglects due process rights, some relevant process values, and some relevant substantive values of public law adjudication when it deals with the rights of immigrant communities. It, therefore, fails to treat everyone equally. Even within the immigrant community, it treats immigrant women dif-ferently from immigrant men. Secondly, immigration law is culturally incompetent in that it is not culturally sensitive, in questions of proof and evidence, to the rights of national minorities principally because it does not formally recognise that it is dealing with minority peoples and their rights. Accordingly this work calls for the development of a "cultural jurisprudence" as a necessary prerequisite to the formulation of a rational theory of immigration adjudication, which requires decision making to be informed by the

---

[1] (London, 1993).

provides a measure of constancy vital to the distillation of more specific patterns". For too long now immigration law has been a political, legal, administrative and ideological backwater. He referred in his study to "the limits of internal coherence attained by public law" in this area and to the existence of "discrete substantive areas" where "systematic departures from established general norms do occur" which detract from the existence of a unified general theory. Professor Legomsky expressed the hope that his book would be useful as a starting point for developing the methodologies by which such studies can proceed.[4]

Through its particular analysis, this book also sets out to develop a sound theory of immigration adjudication. It does so not by examining judicial decision making but by examining administrative decision making in a carefully defined and limited area which is arguably more important because most immigration cases are settled before administrative bodies rather than in the courts. The scope for discretion and deviation and the interplay of legal with extra-legal influences is much greater in the adminstrative control of immigration than in judicial decision making. Furthermore, although the nature of this process is more likely to affect a larger number of people, it is at the same time also more likely to go unnoticed as it exists outside the mainstream of the legal process, by and large unnoticed and secluded from public view. It is the emerging specific patterns which this work attempts to highlight that will be of a larger and more enduring importance both to those researching within immigration law and to those researching outside it in the broader realms of public law.

The research materials contained in this book originally formed part of a doctoral dissertation submitted to the University of Cambridge, which was subsequently also used to lecture students there on the undergraduate course in immigration law, although the theoretical underpinning to this work was given subsequently during a year's leave of absence in the United States as a *Harkness Fellow*. The work undertaken originally was done by sifting through all the unreported decisions of the immigration appellate authorities over several months in the Supreme Court Library Royal Courts of Justice, that arose on the operation of entry clearance procedures between 1970 and the mid-1980s. This task had never before been undertaken. Entry clearance for the re-union of family members was the burning issue of this period in immigration law. In the 1990s the

---

[4] Legomsky, *op. cit.*, p. 4.

legal obligation to admit the wives and children of men settled here
will be slowly coming to an end, hopefully making this study now a
most timely one. However, entry certification will undoubtedly
continue to remain very important in family contexts. In July 1996

Dame Elizabeth Anson published, for example, a report on monitor-
ing visit refusals from the Indian sub-continent.[5] This report is
generally critical of family visit refusals, in particular those of elderly
parents who have sought to come for family occasions. It is more
critical than previous reports. Dame Elizabeth states that "it is in the
exercise of discretion that I have found decisions that have caused me
great concern and where most lawyers, M.P.s and applicants themselves have asked for cases to be reconsidered. . . . The posts that deal
with the greatest number of family cases are therefore subject to the
greatest criticism. That criticism is often justified when older people
are refused permission to see their families in the United Kingdom.
Every effort must be made in such cases that entry clearance officers
are seen to be acting fairly as well as firmly". So long as there is entry
certification, the exercise of discretion by entry clearance officers
(ECOs) will remain important and will call for scrutiny from those
outside the system.

Thus, Dame Elizabeth is critical of officers for "enforcing their
personal opinion". She focuses particularly on Bangladesh. She states
that "it is unrealistic in Dhaka to refuse an application for a
granddaughter's wedding on the grounds it was a 'short social visit',
or there was 'little cogent reason' for a grandparent to visit grand-
children for the first time . . . it is not for the ECO to refuse a visit
application on the grounds that the trip would 'deplete' savings. . . .
And the ECO should not just state that there was 'no reason' for the
trip especially when tourism or shopping has been given as reasons at
the interview." It is therefore clear, that in an increasingly mobile
world with large parts in upheaval, applications for entry clearance
certificates or visas are destined to reach new levels throughout the
1990s. Consequently, the patterns that emerge from this study are no
less relevant today to any critique of the use of law as a technique for
what is actually the effecting of a political policy through the forum
of an administrative agency. Ultimately, this aspect is more revealing
about the quality and efficacy of law in this sphere than any other —
a salutory thought for legal reformers as we approach the next
century and leave behind the present.

It is customary to thank family, friends and all those to whom the

---

[5] See *JCWI Bulletin* (Vol. 6. No. 1, Autumn 1996), p. 4.

writer is indebted. The writer is eternally grateful, as always to his wife, Rani without whose encouragement, assistance and faith this work would not have met the publisher's deadine. He is grateful for the year that he has spent with his wife in the United States as a Harkness Fellow, working in Washington D.C. and at Harvard Law School, where he has also held a Human Rights Fellowship. The support of Professor Henry Steiner, Director of the Human Rights Programme has been invaluable. He is grateful for his time as a Visiting Scholar at the Georgetown Law Centre, as an International Visiting Scholar at the Federal Judicial Centre in Washington D.C., and for the personal friendship that he developed with Mr. James Apple, Chief of the Interjudicial Affairs Office. The writer will remember always the generosity of all that he met during this period. Thanks are due to the publishers for their support of this work; their high professionalism in working on the manuscript has ensured its careful yet speedy publication. This work owes a special debt to Professor David Wexler of the University of Arizona Law School and to Sir Louis Blom-Cooper, just recently retired as a Justice from the High Court. Professor Wexler's constant willingness to discuss his ideas of "Therapeutic Jurisprudence" left an unmistakable mark on the writer as he was developing his own theory of "Cultural Jurisprudence". Sir Louis Blom-Cooper has kindly contributed an insightful and most thought provoking foreword to this work which stands as an enduring inspiration to all those concerned with justice in the law.

Satvinder S. Juss.
Human Rights Programme
Harvard Law School
Boston.

Contents

Tables of Cases

Table of Statutes

Table of Statutory Instruments

Table of Treaties, Conventions, Covenants and Declarations

Table of Abbreviations

CRE	Commission of Racial Equality
CSCE	Conference on Security and Co-operation in Europe
ECOs	Entry Clearance Officers
FCO	Foreign and Commonwealth Office
IASP	Immigration Advisory Service of Pakistan
IAT	Immigration Appeal Tribunal
ICCPR	International Covenant on Civil and Political Rights
IND	Immigration and Nationality Department
JCWI	Joint Council for the Welfare of Immigrants
NCCL	National Council of Civil Liberties
OSCE	Organisation for Security and Co-operation in Europe
SIAC	Special Immigration Appeals Commission
UKIAS	United Kingdom Immigrants Advisory Service
UNESCO	United Nations Educational, Scientific and Cultural Organisation

Reports and Government Documents

(1965) *Immigration from the Commonwealth*. Cmnd 2379.

(1967) *Report of the Committee on Immigration Appeals* (the Wilson Committee). Cmnd 3387.

(1969–70) *Report of the Select Committee on Race Relations and Immigration on Control of Commonwealth Immigration*. HC 17.

(1969–70) *Select Committee on Race Relations and Immigration* (Control of Commonwealth Citizens). HC 205–I, II.

(1970) *Statement of Changes in Immigration Rules for Control on Entry* (Commonwealth Citizens). Cmnd 4298.

(1970) *Statement of Changes in Immigration Rules for Control on Entry* (Non-Commonwealth Citizens). Cmnd 4296.

(1970) *Statement of Changes in Immigration Rules for After Entry* (Commonwealth Citizens). Cmnd 4295.

(1970) *Statement of Changes in Immigration Rules for Control After Entry* (Non-Commonwealth Citizens). Cmnd 4297.

(1973) *Statement of Immigration Rules for Control on Entry* (Commonwealth Citizens). HC 79.

(1973) *Statement of Immigration Rules for Control on Entry* (Non-Commonwealth Citizens). HC 81.

(1973) *Statement of Immigration Rules for Control After Entry* (Commonwealth Citizens). HC 80.

(1973) *Statement of Immigration Rules for Control After Entry* (Non-Commonwealth Citizens). HC 82.

(1977) *Report of the Parliamentary Committee on the Feasibility and Usefulness of a Register of Dependants*. Cmnd 6698.

(1977) *British Nationality Law: Discussion of Possible Changes*. (Cmnd 6795.

(1977–78) *First Report of the Select Committee on Race Relations and Immigration*. HC 303, I and II.

(1979) *First Report of the Home Affairs Committee: Proposed New Immigration Rules and the European Convention on Human Rights*. HC 434.

(1980) *Statement of Changes in Immigration Rules*. HC 394.

(1980) *British Nationality Law: Outline of Proposed Legislation*. Cmnd 7987.

(1981) *Second Report of the Home Affairs Committee: Numbers and Legal Status of Future British Overseas Citizens without Other Citizenship*. HC 158.

(1982) *Proposals for Changes in the Immigration Rules.* Cmnd 8683.

(1982) *Revised Changes in the Immigration Rules.* HC 66.

(1982) *Fifth Report from the Home Affairs Committee: Immigration from the Indian Sub-Continent.* HC 90–I and II.

(1982–83) *British Nationality Fees.* HC 248.

(1983) *Statement of Changes in Immigration Rules.* HC 169.

(1984–85) *The Immigration and Nationality Department of the Home Office.* HC 277.

(1985) *Report of a Formal Investigation: Immigration Control Procedures.* Commission for Racial Equality.

(1985) *Statement of Changes in Immigration Rules.* HC 293.

(1985) *Statement of Changes in Immigration Rules.* Cmnd 9539.

(1985) *Statement of Changes in Immigration Rules.* HC 388.

(1989–90) Fifth Report of the Home Affairs Committee Administrative Delays in the Immigration and Nationality Department. HC 319.

(1990) *Statement of Changes in Immigration Rules.* HC 251. (As amended on March 26, 1991 by HC 320, April 17, 1991 by HC 356, September 30, 1991 by Cm 1672, October 18, 1991 by HC 670, January 21, 1992 by HC 175, June 10, 1992 by HC 49, and November 5, 1992 by HC 251.)

(1990–91) *Statement of Changes in Immigration Rules.* HC 670.

(1990–91) *Statement of Changes in Immigration Rules.* Cm 1672.

(1991–92) *Home Affairs Committee: Migration Control at External Borders of the European Community.* HC 215–I, II and III.

(1992) *Income: Pensions, Earnings and Savings in the Third Age.* Folkestone: Bailey Management Services.

(1992) *Employment: The Role of Work in the Third Age.* Folkestone: Bailey Management Services.

(1993) *Statement of Changes in Immigration Rules.* HC 725.

(1994) *Statement of Changes in Immigration Rules.* HC 395.

Introduction

A Rational Theory of Immigration Adjudication

It has been the traditional concern of adminstrative law that a high degree of discretionary authority should not be placed in the hands of officials and others who have been delegated the power to apply the law through the exercise of their discretion. The concern has been centred around the potential for producing abuse.[1] However, this dilemma knows little certain answers. If low level and low visibility administrative officials are vested with discretion, there is present always the potential for arbitrary and discriminatory application of the law by some amongst them. Yet, how is this potential for abuse to be curbed? This introductory chapter aims to provide some answers. The argument developed here is that the abuse of discretionary authority can be minimised if discretionary power is culturally competent in its aims and is culturally sensitive in its exercise. This book seeks to demonstrate this in the context of immigration law and this introduction calls for a theory of "cultural jurisprudence" that can be applied to aspects of immigration control discussed in the remaining chapters. These chapters leave, it is believed, little doubt that such an approach is warranted. It is particularly warranted given the way in which immigration control disproportionately impacts on minority populations that are becoming such a distinctive part of the polity in Western European countries.

Chapter One introduces the establishment of the Entry Clearance System in 1969 and highlights the creation of a large and unstructured domain of administrative discretions upon which the exercise of statutory rights is dependent. Examples of discretionary abuse of authority are seen in Chapter Two, where there is a discussion of the so-called "discrepancy system" which is a technique of deliberate and persistent questioning that leads the interviewee to give discrepant answers to the same questions, and the marriage rules which are replete with unsubstantiated behavioural assumptions in the law. In Chapter Three we will see some of the influences on adminstrative deviance with a consideration of the legal factors, policy guidelines,

---

[1] See, *e.g.*, K.C. Davis, *Discretionary Justice* (Chicago, 1971).

concerns for administrative convenience and management, and general pressures that bear upon official governmental decision making. We will see that policy factors are dominant over legal norms leading to increased exercise of subjective discretions by officials. Chapter Four will examine the institutional context of immigration control. It will consider the role of immigration adjudicators and appeal tribunals. An important question to bear in mind here is the absence of any effective systems of political, administrative and legal accountability giving, once again, a heightened importance to discretionary decision making. It will be seen from a reading of this chapter that it is essentially the weakness of these systems that encourages a culture of unaccountability. As a result, the lack of political scrutiny of immigration guidelines and policy directions feeds into an executive-led decision making process. By the end of the chapter it will become plain that there is an internal culture of immigration officialdom which gives it essential character. Chapter Five, however, then demonstrates how a culturally sensitive and competent approach by individual decision makers has been able to produce a decidedly different result in particular cases, thus providing practical proof of how useful cultural jurisprudence is as a theoretical framework in this area of the law. Finally, Chapter Six draws together the various strands from previous discussions and concludes by giving some attention to the nature of discretion and the various creative ways in which it has been exercised.

The central problem of adminstrative law remains, however, even by the end of the book. How can the potential for administrative abuse be minimised?[2] Administrative law has, of course, devised a number of approaches.[3] Legislatures should put forth statutory standards to structure and limit administrative discretion. When, within the statutory standards, administrative practices have developed into administrative standards, these standards should be codified through administrative rule making.[4] Next, when an administrative action adversely affects anyone, some kind of administrative hearing should be provided at which that person can be given the opportunity to present his case and call his evidence. Finally, if the administrative body hearing a grievance errs in law, judicial review of administrative action will bring the matter within the jurisdiction of

---

[2] Davis has argued that the key purpose for rules is to control administrative discretion: Davis, *ibid.*
[3] Various adminstrative law models have been devised to deal with problems of police abuse: Davis, "An Approach to Legal Control of the Police" (1974) 52 *Tex.L.R.* 703.
[4] The various types of rules that governments use are discussed in Robert Baldwin, *Rules and Government* (Oxford, 1995).

the higher courts which will scrutinise administrative behaviour and strike down the illegal administrative action. Such procedures, developed by administrative law, can no doubt limit the scope for discretionary abuse of authority. However, an application of such a logical procedure has been discussed in Chapter Five in a way that makes its frailties all too plain. Indeed, one may refer here to the recent work of Professor David Jackson,[5] Vice-President of the Immigration Appeals Tribunal (IAT), which makes a major contribution to the clear and coherent exposition of the rules of immigration adjudication. Professor Jackson, referring to the well-known 1994 Tribunal decision of *R. v. Secretary of State for the Home Department, ex p. Kaja*[6] which held that the standard of serious possibility of persecution in a political asylum case is to be assessed by reference not only to the estimate of persecution in the future but the establishment also of the historical facts on which the estimate is based, draws attention to the failure of some adjudicators to accept precedent in the immigration appellate system:

> "The problems were well illustrated by the persistence of some adjudicators in refusing to follow the Tribunal majority decision in *Kaja* (11038) concerning the standard of proof in asylum cases — a persistence as curious as it was harmful. The decision was not appealed and the continued insistence of a contrary view simply led to continued remittals. It was a regettable example of failure to grasp a fundamental tenet of a hierarchical appellate system, causing a great deal of unneccessary cost."[7]

In his previous work, the author has indeed referred to this failure to follow clear guidelines as a deliberate practice of "administrative lawlessness".[8]

What is needed is a resort to a substantive understanding of the "rule of law" conception which requires every rule and practice to be applied fairly, even-handedly and non-discriminatorily so as to promote parity and equity amongst all consumers of the law. By contrast, the classical definition of the "rule of law" lacks a substantive context. The chief exponent of the doctrine in its classical form has been the nineteenth-century jurist, A.V. Dicey, who in his *An Introduction to the Law of the Constitution* in 1885 devoted a large part of his work to an exposition of the rule of law. Dicey wrote that:

> "no man is punishable or can lawfully be made to suffer in body or goods except for a distinct breach of law established in the ordinary legal manner

---

[5] Jackson, *Immigration: Law and Practice* (London, 1996).
[6] [1995] Imm. A.R. 1.
[7] See *supra*, n.5, p. 647.
[8] Juss, *Immigration, Nationality and Citizenship* (London, 1993), at p. 87.

before the ordinary courts of the land. In this sense the rule of law is contrasted with every system of government based on the exercise by persons in authority of wide, arbitrary, or discretionary powers of constraint. . . . It means the absolute supremacy or predominance of regular law . . ."[9]

However, the only equality that this reposes in the common law is the equality of treatment in the application of the law to all persons who become subject to it.[10] Equality is a formal concept that is satisfied provided that the right procedures are followed. Consequently, there is no *a priori* content of an equality code in the rule of law model as classically understood. What this work calls for, is a substantive understanding and application of a concept of the rule of law that defines due process as incorporating the relevant process values of participation, dignity and trust and the relevant substantive values of a just and accurate result, that is arrived at through the determination of a socially and culturally competent decision-making process. Fairness and even-handedness cannot just be achieved by the formal adoption of a set procedure. Judges, lawyers and administrators will have to develop an approach of substantive Equality which may be defined as an Equalitarian approach whereby immigration authorities ensure that the values of parity and equity are protected on an equal basis in a substantive sense so that they can reach fair and accurate decisions. This, in turn, can only be done by adopting an approach that is culturally sensitive to every individual in every social situation.

(1) A NEW CULTURAL JURISPRUDENCE

The 1967 case of *Re H.K. (An Infant)*[11] is a *cause célèbre*. It lies at the heart of English administrative law. In it, Lord Diplock expressed the principle that sits at the root of modern judicial review: "Good administration and an honest or *bona fide* decision must, as it seems to me, require not merely impartiality, not merely bringing one's mind to bear on the problem, but acting fairly."[12] Yet it is often forgotten

---

[9] See, *An Introduction to the Study of the Law of the Constitution* (10th ed., London, 1965), p. 188.
[10] Indeed, Professor Jeffrey Jowell has even questioned whether equality can be said to be a constitutional principle in the British system of government: see, "Is Equality a Consitutional Principle?" *Current Legal Problems* (Freeman, ed. 1994), Vol. 47, pp. 1–19.
[11] [1967] 1 Q.B. 617.
[12] *ibid.* at 630C.

that, whereas a lack of impartiality or failure to apply one's mind may be easy to discern, the absence of substantive fairness is amongst the most difficult things to pinpoint in a tribunal of inquiry. How, for example, is fairness to be judged in a legal process that is alienating of its participants? If women, the poor, the uneducated, the ethnic minorities and the unfamiliar feel intimidated by the process of the law, can a mere adherence to procedural safeguards ensure their active participation, still less, secure justice for them? Is the playing field of judicial and legal processes really level when the requirements for assessing that process are tailored to the cultural experiences of the mainstream majority; if the skills that make for success are nurtured by institutions and cultural practices from which the disadvantaged minority feels excluded; if the language and ways of comporting oneself are alien to the life experiences of groups that are forced to turn to the law to make their claims? Can affirmative action become a viable tool of social policy and, if so, by what mechanisms of affirmative action can such institutionalised unfairness and inequality be altered?

This work deals with this question by arguing for the development of a new "cultural jurisprudence" whereby the law is seen as a cultural agent through which the principles of equity, parity and justice can be more accurately secured in an increasingly diverse and multicultural society. Cultural jurisprudence aims to explore ways in which the development of the law can be informed by an understanding of culture so that values of justice can be enhanced and expanded to apply to all populations that come within the jurisdiction of the law. Cultural jurisprudence requires lawyers, courts and administrators to use social science and social facts to determine the extent to which a legal rule of practice promotes or protects the cultural expectation of a person, as an aspect of the realisation of justice. It is a jurisprudence that may be applied in innumerable different contexts where pluralist values and interests are at stake. Thus, it may be used in the criminal justice system where there is a disproportionate representation of lower socio-economic classes, ethnic minorities and women. It may be used to examine the inequality of bargaining power in the current law of contracts, as it relates to minority women in traditional family set-ups especially in the law relating to property repossessions where manipulated partners have been subjected to misrepresentation, duress, undue influence, or unconscionable bargains, leading to mortgage repossessions. It may be used to redefine the law of nullity in marriage law where a young Asian girl has been forced to marry a husband from abroad contrary to her will, as the Scottish courts have recently recognised.[13] It may be used in employment law to give clearer recognition to cases of discrimination. It is, however, in the field of immigration law that cultural jurisprudence can make its most obvious contribution. It is not as alien as may appear at first sight Indeed, such jurisprudence was used by Lord Justice Woolf in the adoption case of *Immigration Appeals Tribunal v. Tohur Ali*.[14] His Lordship observed that the general introductory rules in the Immigration Rules, r.2 state[15] (of HC 169) that "Immigration Officers will carry out their duties without regard to the race, colour or religion of people seeking to enter the U.K." and that this position "reflects the generally non-discriminatory approach adopted by the rules". On this basis, his Lordship allowed the adoption of a Moslem boy from Pakistan even though there was no adoption formally in the court of strict Moslem law. His Lordship reached this result by having regard to social science and to social facts: "Accustomed as we are now in this country to legal adoption, it is natural to think that the use of the word 'adopt' in an Act refers to some legal adoption. However, that approach loses a lot of its force when it is remembered that there are immigrants from many parts of the world where there is no legal adoption."[16] By recognising that there was *de facto* adoption of the boy Tohur Ali, his Lordship accurately achieved the standard of fairness highlighted in the 1967 case of *Re H.K. (An Infant)*.[17]

(2) A New Factfinder System

The primary advantage of cultural jurisprudence is that it allows us to find facts accurately and, therefore, to make better decisions. This is because cultural jurisprudence works within a person's reality conditions. It acknowledges and incorporates variance in normative acceptable behaviours, beliefs and values and incorporates those variables into factual assessments. It enables us to develop a rational theory of immigration adjudication by ensuring that the law in this field is based upon cultural assumptions that are accurately founded. If those laws are not founded upon accurate cultural assumptions, then cultural jurisprudence helps us to understand the negative cultural effects of

---

[13] See *Mahmood v. Mahmood* (1993) S.L.T. 589 and *Mahmud v. Mahmud* (1994) S.L.T. 599, which approved the earlier judgment of Ormrod L.J. in *Hirani v. Hirani* (1982) 4 F.L.R. 232 at 234, CA.
[14] [1988] Imm.A.R. 237.
[15] See *Statement of Changes in Immigration Rules* (1983) H.C. 169.
[16] See *supra*, n.14 at 250.
[17] See *supra*, n.11.

those laws. A rational theory of immigration adjudication would require us to be culturally sensitive at every stage of the immigration process. So that when we talk about due process we know that to be meaningful to diverse ethnic communities, this implies recognition of their participation, dignity and trust in the legal process, and the evaluation of the rightness of the eventual result achieved. This would mean a new kind of factfinder system. Let us consider how this new factfinding model applies to investigating entry clearance officers and decision-making administrative tribunals.

(a) Immigration Officials as Factfinders

As far as Entry Clearance Officers (ECOs) are specifically concerned, the knowledge that their cultural assumptions can have negative cultural effects, can mean either that they shed such assumptions where they are not scientifically verifiable, or, where they do not have such assumptions and where they employ a legal rule or carry out a particular practice, they should be aware of the cultural effects of what they are doing. In *Tohur Ali*,[18] Lord Woolf was clearly aware of the cultural effects of what he was doing. In either event, this means that ECOs should thoroughly study the facts of each case; communicate with (and not just interrogate) the applicant, family and friends who arrive at the interview to accompany the applicant; fully understand the events preceding the application for entry clearance at the post overseas; investigate the socio-cultural background of the applicants and families, including local conditions and family traditions; and explore the possible cultural implications of how the officer applies a rule or practice in the ascertainment of eligibility for entry clearance to the United Kingdom. It is immediately plain from this that an adversarial approach by a white, male entry clearance officer interviewing an illiterate, village woman in *purdah* (*i.e.* veiled), will be totally counter-productive. What is required, therefore, is an approach that increases the factual integrity of the process. This can only be done by clarifying the roles of the participants and by increasing the involvement of all players in a way that makes them feel that the finding of fact in these particular kinds of civil proceedings is a shared, collaborative process. Participants must be treated with dignity and respect. This will result in more trust being reposed in the immigration process at large. In return, the immigration service, which has for many years suffered from low morale, will be more highly esteemed as a profession. It will be highly esteemed

---

[18] See *supra*, n.14.

within the service and by ordinary people when they attend upon it. For the immigration service too, therefore, law is a cultural agent. Both the server and the served can be either alienated by the process of law or integrated within it.

(b) Adjudicators and the Tribunal as Factfinders

Equally, for the adjudicators and the tribunal the above considerations are no less applicable. They must confront some questions head-on. Does the law operate in a culturally insensitive way? If so, does it promote cognitive distortion? Or, if the law operates in a culturally competent manner, does it set the stage for cognitive restructuring? An immigration appeal hearing is an ideal setting in which to examine the cultural jurisprudence implications of the legal process. When an adjudicator or the tribunal hear a case their actions have clear cultural implications. If the bench involves the applicant and principal wit-nessess only minimally, and looks to the record and the entry clearance officer's explanatory statement to establish the factual basis of their refusal of entry clearance, an applicant from a different cultural background might not have that cultural aspect fully explored by the appeals process. On the other hand, if the bench involves the witnesses for the applicant fully at the appeal stage, and looks to them to establish the factual basis of the application by clearing up all doubts and discrepancies, then the Bench may actually be performing a culturally valuable task of cognitive restructuring of social and cultural facts. The result can lead in this way to a convergence of cultural and justice goals. It is clear the decision makers have the ability to behave in this way. Research undertaken by the legal anthropologist, Susan Philips, shows that many civil libertarian judges are "procedure oriented" and do involve a defendant heavily in the process of establishing the facts at a hearing, whereas politically conservative judges were "record ori-ented" and tended to establish the factual basis with minimal involve-ment of the defendant. Those judges often thought that a defendant would be unhelpful in contributing to an otherwise clear statement of facts in the record.[19]

Obviously, both ECOs and the appeals tribunals should perform their roles as impartial factfinders. A factfinder represents the interests of no party. A factfinder hears all witnessess, gathers all pertinent evidence and interviews as many people as is necessary. A factfinder ensures that the applicant or appellant has a forum in which to present

[19] See Philips, *Ideological Diversity in Courtroom Discourse: Due Process, Judicial Discretion and the Guilty Plea* (forthcoming in the United States).

his or her views. This procedure of treating both ECOs and the tribunal as factfinders is necessary precisely because due process is so vital. Remoulding their functions as factfinders would have some very positive effects. At the moment, Home Office Presenting Officers appearing at an appeal hearing are often unaware of the nature of their cases until the morning of the hearing. At the hearing itself, the Bench is sometimes too easily swayed by what the Presenting Officer, as a Home Office professional, has to say about the case. The decline in civility in the courts generally over the last 25 years also means that the process of representation at a hearing is unnecessarily combative and aggressive, not only against one's opponent, but also against witnesses attending, as well as the Bench. The entire process is excessively alienating and wrongly justified as an inherent aspect of the English adversarial system. The fact is that the same point can be made just as well with civility and decorum and would be far less alienating to the witnesses who are there to help ascertain the facts. What is needed is a procedure that actually helps a decision maker make the right decision. Yet, under the present immigration appellate system, counsel or the representative for the applicant, is hampered in giving the right kind of assistance to the Bench. He cannot have his client, who is denied admission to the United Kingdom from the post overseas, attend at the appeal hearing and give evidence regarding discrepancies in the answers to the interviewing officer. Under a factfinder system, the bench would assume a role that is basically responsible for gathering the facts of the case.

What is needed is a more conciliatory and collaborative process of factfinding. The traditional adversarial hearing typically takes less than half a day, but if the tribunal of inquiry's role was really to search out the facts, the due process rights properly understood may well require a higher investment of overall time by the tribunal. The tribunal, assuming a lead role in the search for facts, may well decide to dispense with legal representations from counsel. The sponsor should be allowed to pay for the applicant to travel to England to attend the appeal hearing and give evidence. This would not necessarily do a disservice to justice. By finding creative ways of crafting new legal arrangements justice can be preserved and the cultural impact of the law harnessed to good effect. An applicant who makes an unconvincing witness at the hearing can have his or her application rejected after failing to satisfy the proper standard of proof, but at least such an applicant will go away knowing why the application has been rejected. Judges, lawyers and administrators would have a special appreciation of their roles in the adjudicative process. They would be aware of the potential for promoting well-

being and minimising harm, both individual and communal, because
of the way in which they do their work. They can do this best if they
realise and appreciate the power of law as a cultural agent. This
applies to all kinds of legal and administrative officials in the
immigration process. If those involved in law making, in law
applying, and in law-related activity begin also to see themselves as
cultural agents when carrying out their duties, they can enhance
considerably the potential of law as a helpful and culturally healing
profession. What judges, lawyers and adminstrators must do is to
facilitate understanding of the law's requirements. What these professionals say to the consumers of law will have a significant impact on
their appreciation of those requirements and may help people to
adapt to them in ways that have positive effects on both their lives
and on the life of the law.

Cultural Jurisprudence and Immigration Adjudication

In the foregoing section, we have suggested that a theory of
immigration adjudication based on a cultural jurisprudence requires
an understanding of due process rights in terms of certain relevant
process values and certain relevant substantive values. In this section
we consider the implications of these values in the adjudicative
process. We will begin first by a consideration of due process rights.

(1) DUE PROCESS RIGHTS

Many commentators believe that the "procedural due process revolution" began with the 1970 American case of *Goldberg v. Kelly*,[20] where
the Supreme Court held that due process requires that welfare
recipients must be afforded an evidentiary hearing prior to the
termination of benefits. Brennan J. gave a judgment that is relevant to
the requirement that the wives and families of British settled
Commonwealth citizens should be subject to the entry clearance
procedure discussed in Chapter One, before seeking entry into the
United Kingdom, because the judgment suggests that such a requirement is a violation of due process rights. The judgment is important
because it recognises that statutory entitlements, like the right to
family re-unification for Commonwealth citizens, is not a "privilege"

---

[20] 397 U.S. 254 (1970): see also *Ridge v. Baldwin* [1964] A.C. 40, the British equivalent
which did not go as far as the *Goldberg* case.

but an undoubted "right" and that the governmental interest must be clearly defined when encroaching upon such rights. Brennan J. however, was here just dealing with welfare benefits:

"[welfare] benefits are a matter of statutory entitlement for persons qualified to receive them. Their termination involves state action that adjudicates important rights. The constitutional challenge cannot be answered by an argument that public assistance benefits are a 'privilege' and not a 'right'. Relevant constitutional restraints apply as much to the withdrawal of public assistance benefits as to the disqualification for unemployment compensation or to denial of a tax exemption or to discharge from public employment. The extent to which procedural due process must be afforded the recipient is influenced by the extent to which he may be 'condemned to suffer grievous loss', and depends upon whether the recipient's interest in avoiding the loss outweighs the governmental interest in summary adjudication."[21]

It will be argued in this book that the imposition of the entry clearance requirement to persons who have a "legal right" to join principal family members in this country, failing which they cannot even attend to give evidence at their appeal hearing, is a violation of due process rights as defined in the *Goldberg*[22] case. The Supreme Court in *Goldberg*, although primarily concerned with issues of accuracy, held that the evidentiary hearing must take place prior to the adverse decision against the applicant; an adverse decision without a hearing would be harmful to the applicant, potentially damaging feelings of security, dignity, and self-worth. It is true that an ECO undertakes an interview at the post overseas of the applicant, but as we shall see, this is not a proper hearing and a wife seeking to join her husband in the United Kingdom may moreover often not have her husband attend the interview with her. The hearing envisaged by Brennan J., "need not take the form of a judicial or quasi-judicial trial", but an applicant must have "timely and adequate notice detailing the reasons for a proposed termination, and an effective opportunity to defend by confronting any adverse witnesses and by presenting his own arguments and evidence orally".[23] Of course, a wife who is refused entry and a post overseas cannot enter the United Kingdom to give evidence at a hearing even though, as Brennan J. said, she is "condemned to suffer grievous loss", and this negates the observance of due process rights.

[21] *ibid.*
[22] *ibid.*
[23] See *supra*, n.20.

Accordingly, it is suggested that for wives and children having the right to join a sponsor in the United Kingdom, the entry clearance requirement should have been disapplied. Family members should be able to join their sponsors in this country with relative ease after having submitted the relevant papers at posts overseas. If there is an issue as to their true relation to the sponsor in the United Kingdom, this should then be ventilated at a hearing, which should take place fairly speedily, but at which the family members can have the right that we all enjoy of calling witnesses and preparing for trial. Nothing less is acceptable under the right to due process. It has to be remembered that under *Goldberg*, and other decisions that have followed in its wake (such as in relation to prisoner's rights[24]), the recognition of damage to the security, dignity and self-worth of a party subject to an adjudicative process, is a recognition of an impact that is distinct from the desire for a neutral, factfinding expert who is expected to reach accurate decisions. When conceptualised in this way, due process involves giving people judicial procedures that they perceive as fair.

(2) RELEVANT PROCESS VALUES

Studies undertaken in the United States demonstrate that the type of judicial process that people experience influences them independently of the outcome of those procedures. Peoples reactions to judicial procedures are not primarily determined by whether they win or lose their case, or whether they go to jail or go free, or whether they pay a large fine or pay nothing. Studies also show that people's reactions have little to do with the time that it takes to resolve a case or the amount of money that is spent in the effort.

A study by E. Allan Lind suggests that the amount of money won or lost, the duration of the case-disposition process and the cost of the process to the litigant were largely unrelated to judgments of fairness and satisfaction by the litigant. People's reactions to the case are primarily determined by their assessment of the fairness of the case-disposition process. People are affected by the way in which the decisions are made. They are also influenced by judgments about the fairness of the outcome itself.[25] Tom Tyler has also found that the evaluation of fairness of the judicial procedure also influences everyday

---

[24] See, for example *Morrissey v. Brewer* 408 U.S. 471 (1972).
[25] Lind *et al.*, "In the Eye of the Beholder: Tort Litigants' Evaluations of Their Experiences in the Civil Justice System", (1990) 24 *Law & Society Review* 953, pp. 980–984.

behaviour towards the law. If people believe that legal authorities are less legitimate, they are less likely to be law-abiding citizens in their everyday lives.[26] Thus, there have been studies dealing with informal police-citizen interactions,[27] studies dealing with citizen experiences in small claims courts[28] and studies that have focused directly on judicial hearings. In a study undertaken by Jonathon Casper of felony criminal case-disposition,[29] the impact of the case-disposition process was analysed in relation to both satisfaction with the case-disposition process itself and in relation to the attitudes towards law and legal authorities. In this study the defendants received penalties that varied from a suspended sentence to 20 years in prison. Their overall reactions to the case-disposition experiences were not, however, influenced by the severity of the sentence recieved. They were influenced by the fairness of the sentence and by the evaluations of fairness of the case-disposition process.

These findings about the felony case-disposition process are significant because even though substantial deprivations of personal liberty were involved here in relation to people on the margins of society, such as the poor, the minority groups and the unemployed, their reactions were determined by the favourability of the outcomes they recieved, even though they might have been expected to care the least about questions of due process in their situation. A study by Lind and others, which involved law suits between $50,000 and $2 million for negligence claims, found that peoples willingness to accept mediation decisions, instead of going on to have a formal trial was affected by their evaluations of the fairness of the mediation session.[30] Robert J. MacCoun carried out studies for the Rand Corporation that examined the acceptance of arbitration claims in law suits for automobile injuries,[31] and they obtained similar results to those of Lind. It is thus clear, that in civil and criminal cases alike, proceedings are strongly influenced by peoples evaluation of the procedures.

[26] Tyler, "Maintaining Allegience Toward Political Authorities: The Role of Prior Attitudes and the Use of Fair Procedures", (1989) 33 *American Journal of Political Science* 629. Also see, Tyler, "The Role of Perceived Injustice in Defendants Evaluation of Their Coutroom Experience", (1989) 18 *Law & Society Review* 51.
[27] See Tyler and Folger, "Distributional and Procedural Aspects of Satisfaction with Citizen–Police Encounter", (1980) *Basic and Applied Social Psychology* pp. 281–92.
[28] See Tyler, "The Role of Perceived Injustice in Defendants Evaluation of Their Courtroom Experience", (1984) 18 *Law & Society Review* 51.
[29] See Casper, "Procedural Justice in Felony Cases", (1988) 22 *Law & Society Review* 483.
[30] Lind *et al.*, "Outcome and Process Concerns in Organisational Dispute Resolution", *American Bar Foundation* (working paper No. 9109, 1991) *passim.*
[31] MacCoun *et al.*, "Alternative Adjudication: An Evaluation of the New Jersey Automobile Arbitration Program" (Rand Institute for Civil Justice, 1988).

This is important for it shapes peoples behaviour. When people experience a procedure that they judge to be unfair they are less respectful of it and of the law and do not willingly subject themselves to it. They are less likely to accept judicial decisions and less likely to obey the law in the future. If minority groups leave a tribunal thinking that their difficulties with the English language and with the rules of the adversarial procedure have been appreciated by the tribunal of inquiry, they are more likely to adjudge the hearing to be fair, whatever the consequences. If, on the other hand, they leave a hearing with unfavourable views about the legitimacy of legal authorities, this is likely to lead to their cultural and social isolation. In either event, the law is a cultural agent whose instrumental role cannot be ignored. From the above, we can see that people care about procedural justice but they define it in terms of neutrality by drawing attention to lack of bias, honesty, the use of expertise and factual decision making. Of course, all of these aspects influence judgments about a procedures fairness. However, the most important determinants of judgments about procedural fairness concern participation, dignity and trust in the judicial process.

(a) Participation

Where people are allowed to participate in judicial procedures, they have consistently evaluated such procedures to be fairer.[32] Participation means the presentation of evidence and of ones own views so that there is process control. It also means shared decision making so that they feel that they are in a position of decision control. Either forms of participation have enhanced feelings of fair treatment according to studies.[33] Clearly, therefore, a lack of participation for someone who is unable to attend an appeal hearing in London from abroad, will inevitably lead to feelings of gross unfairness. The same feelings are likely to arise where a linguistic or cultural handicap either prevents or precludes participation in the judicial process. This can happen even where an interpreter is present. Witnesses may be needlessly attacked and even abused during cross-examination, with little restraining influence from the tribunal, even though this alienates the witness from the process and hardly makes for easier decision making by the tribunal of inquiry. The fact is that people value the opportunity to present their arguments and state their views

---

[32] See, Lind *et al.*, "Voice, Control, and Procedural Justice: Instrumental and Non–Instrumental Concerns in Fairness Judgements" (1990) 59 *Journal of Personality and Social Psychology* 952.

[33] See, Lind & Tyler, *The Social Psychology of Procedural Justice* (1988).

even when they have known that what they say is having little or no influence on the decision-making authority. Studies show this most plainly in relation to people who have been allowed to present their evidence after a decision has been made.[34]

(b) Dignity

Dignity is another important value that people in their evaluation of the fairness of the adjudicative process rate highly. People care that they are treated with dignity by the legal authorities. They respond well when they are treated with respect and politeness, even if their rights are not fully acknowleged.[35] It is important, therefore, that the legal authorities affirm a persons status as a competent and an equal human being. People regard the procedures as intrinsically unfair if the procedures are not consistent with that affirmation. This means that the entire immigration system from the top down should be reappraised with a view to ensuring that the dignity of the process and its participants is maintained. This means looking not only at the immigration appeals system, to ensure that dignity and courtesy are maintained in relation to witnesses, counsel and the tribunal, but it also means looking at the interviewing process by ECOs and the tests of verification that have sometimes been undertaken, such as medical tests, which impact adversely on human dignity. It must be remembered that official authorities, such as the Immigration Service, have an important role in defining people's views about their value in society.[36]

(c) Trust

Trust is the most important quality in the evaluation of procedural fairness.[37] It is, unfortunately, also the most elusive. People are very interested to know that the authorities they are dealing with are concerned about their welfare and want to treat them fairly. However, in most cases they can only infer whether the authority is or is not motivated to treat them fairly. People regard those authorities which allow them to present evidence as more trustworthy. People also regard authorities who treat them with dignity and respect as being more trustworthy. People, moreover, hold authorities trustworthy where they have sought to explain or account

---

[34] See, Lind et al., supra, n.32.
[35] See, Tyler & Folger, op. cit.
[36] See Lane, "Procedural Goods in a Democracy: How One is Treated v. What One Gets" (1988) 2 Society, Justice, Responsibility pp. 177–192.
[37] See Barber, The Logic and Limits of Trust (1983).

for their decisions. What studies of trustworthiness suggest[38] is that the key issue is not that people have or have not the right to appeal to an authority, but whether the authority involved is attempting to be fair in the implementation of the rules. The simple existence of structures that are associated with fairness alone does not enhance people's perceived fairness.

Conclusion

To conclude, we can say that these studies suggest that the three factors of participation, dignity and trust have more influence on peoples judgments of procedural justice than either the evalution of neutrality or the evaluation of the favourableness of outcome of proceeedings. Due process is a fundamental value in the adjudicative process and the failure to apply due process has clear negative consequences. The failure encourages in people a reluctance to accept decisions, a diminished respect for the judge, mediator or other third party, a diminished respect for the courts and the legal system and a diminished willingness to follow legal rules. These effects are consistent with the ruling of Brennan J. in *Goldberg* that experiencing arbitrary procedures leads to "social malaise"[39] and effects peoples willingness to be integrated into the polity, where basic authorities are voluntarily accepted and core rules willingly followed. But how is this to be done? There are two basic questions that need to be addressed. The first is that of accuracy. Any mediating or adjudicative process must have the ability to make accurate decisions. Studies show that professional decision making can exhibit bias.[40] Accuracy concerns could therefore favour judicial decision making in preference to adminstrative decision making wherever possible. However, how, if at all, can decision making by professionals by improved? Secondly, if people become alienated from authority, being distrustful, feeling vulnerable and lacking security dignity and self-worth, then these consquences are disadvantageous to the polity at large and can presumably be avoided by a concentration on the right values and principles which may be enhanced. Cultural jurisprudence aims, through a promotion of the values of individual autonomy, integrity of the factfinding process, community safety, efficiency and economy, to enhance respect for the authorities, by making the laws and

[38] Tyler & Bies, "Interpersonal Aspects of Procedural Justice" in Carroll, *Applied Social Psychology in Business Settings* (1990).
[39] See *supra*, n.20, p. 265.
[40] See Persoff, "Judicial Deference to Non–Legal Decision–Makers: Imposing Simplistic Solutions on Problems of Cognitive Complexity in Mental Disability Law", (1992) 46 *Southern Methodist University Law Review* 29.

practices of those authorities more culturally sensitive and competent so that people are willing to accept the authorities' decisions. But how is this to be done? The answer lies in the choice of substantive values to which we must now turn.

(3) RELEVANT SUBSTANTIVE VALUES

(a) Cause-and-Result Justification and the New Public Law shift away from Process Justification

Public law concerns are today becoming centred around the role of legislators and administrators. In fact, the most exciting change in legal scholarship generally in recent years has been the movement that has gone beyond the exclusive study of legal doctrine. This has been identified by Professor Edward Rubin in his seminal article in the *Michigan Law Review* entitled "The Concept of Law and the New Public Law Scholarship", where the writer recognises a "new" concept of law that flows from the reality of the modern administrative state and from the fact that today legislatures and administrators are the primary law makers, rather than the judges.[41] The primary, non-judicial law makers are not particularly interested in legal principles and the meticulous reasoning process. Law, for them, is an instrument designed to deal with particular problems. Law is successful if it deals satisfactorily with the problem. Both incrementalism as part of the law making process and reasoning by analogy is inappropriate. Legislation is only "data". Its importance lies in its efficacy rather than its precedential value. This means that the basic evaluative and referent framework of legal analysis is social problems; it is not the body of the law itself. This is a clear rejection of the "old" concept of the law where the "law" was thought of as judge-made, being developed incrementally, on a case-by-case basis. It implies a rejection of the application of prior precedent, reasoned by analogy, where overarching principles are extracted from previously decided cases and applied. The "new" legal scholarship based on this "new" concept of the law addresses recommendations to legislatures and administrators rather than to the judiciary. Professor Rubin argues that this reasoning represents a shift from process justification to cause-and-result justification.[42] This will inevitably involve a search for substantive values. The question is whether cultural sensitivity is one of these values? He argues that when shifting from analogical to

---

[41] (1991) 89 *Michigan Law Review* 792.
[42] *ibid.* p. 820.

instrumental thinking[43] scholars are not searching for solutions which
are intellectually coherent with a pattern of previous decisions, but
for solutions that effectively (achieve) specific goals.[44] This new brand
of scholarship poses a new series of questions, the last one of which
is directly relevant to cultural sensitivity:

> ". . . which rules work best in general? Which work best for particular
> purposes? Under what circumstances is specificity desirable, and under
> what circumstances is it counter productive? What is the best mechanism
> for enforcing various provisions? How important is public participation
> for achieving the purpose and how can such a participation be secured?"[45]

This "New Public Law" scholarship requires legal scholars to be
sensitive to "insights and techniques from social science disciplines".[46] It requires them to study the law's effects and, in part-
nership with social scientists, seek to develop such studies. Clearly,
the "New Public Law" scholarship is relevant to a theory of cultural
jurisprudence. However, the crucial task of the legal scholar is not to
generate data but to use data "to frame recommendations to responsible decision-makers".[47] In normative terms, the "New Public Law"
scholarship is based on the notion that the enhancement of "the
welfare of our society", and the development of "the essential,
deontological norms in which we believe", are "achieveable by
governmental action", and that "the performance of our government
can be improved, that there are techniques of governance that can be
discovered, adopted, and applied".[48] It is suggested that the developments in the "New Public Law" are directly relevant to, and indeed
make absolutely necessary, the development of a theory of cultural
jurisprudence, especially where the rights of minorities are involved.
Cultural jurisprudence looks at the law as a potential cultural agent. It
looks at legal and administrative rules and procedures and at the roles
of legal actors and other players. These other players include not only
lawyers and judges, but many other actors, such as administrators and
professionals. Cultural jurisprudence is accordingly directed not only
at the courts, but also the tribunals and the administrative agencies.
Cultural jurisprudence is vital where the actors operate in a relatively
unconstrained legal field, laying emphasis on the exercise of wide

---

[43] *Supra*, n.41 at p. 812.
[44] *ibid.* p. 819.
[45] *ibid.* p. 815.
[46] *ibid.* p. 827.
[47] *ibid.* p. 796.
[48] *ibid.* p. 836.

discretionary power, which requires cultural training and sensitivity. This is an area that has been largely neglected over the years because of the laws almost exclusive interest in doctrine. Like the "New Legal Scholarship", cultural jurisprudence is also prescriptive, but its prescriptive focus is simply that, within the limits set by the principles of justice, the law should protect and respect the cultural rights and expectations of people. Indeed, in the vast majority of cases where the law impacts upon a diversified citizenry, such an approach is a necessary prerequisite to the attainment of justice. Both the "New Public Law" and the theory of cultural jurisprudence (which may be seen as its off-shoot) are important in defining the relevant substantive values in the adjudicative process. Let us take a more detailed look at some of these substantive values.

(b) Compatibility with Social Science Information

Social science has substantive value, and also public law value in the resolution of public law disputes. Courts, legislators and administrators should learn to utilise social science information. Is a particular view point objectively verifiable? This will have important implications for the search for facts which is the cardinal problem in determining the eligibility of applicants in the immigration process. Chapters Two to Four chronicle the difficulties arising from the accurate ascertainment of facts, ranging from the inability of village women to answer straight questions[49] to unlawful marriage of young children,[50] to the lack of documentary evidence in a rural economy.[51] The reason why the investigative and adjudicative process has failed in these cases, is because it has sought to apply a scientific model in the search for facts. Such a model, however, is throughly inappropriate in the context of village, subsistence based economies.

What the administrative agencies need to do is to develop a social/cultural model for establishing social facts. They need to draw upon social science surveys and studies undertaken by both governmental and non-governmental agencies that provide the social framework for defining social facts. In a series of articles, Professors Monahan and Walker have produced a conceptual bridge that will link social science and its use by legislatures, courts and administrators.[52] Their work,

---

[49] See infra. pp. 66–71.
[50] See infra. pp. 86–87.
[51] See infra. pp. 88–91.
[52] Walker & Monahan, "Social Authority: Obtaining, Evaluating and Establishing Social Science in Law", (1986) 134 U.Pa.I. Rev. 477; Walker & Monahan, "Social Frameworks: A New Use of Social Science in Law", (1987) 73 Va. L. Rev. 559; Walker & Monahan, "Social Facts: Scientific Methodology as Legal Precedent", (1988) 76 Cal. L. Rev. 877; Monahan & Walker, "Social Science Research in Law: A New Paradigm", (1988) 43 Am. Psychol. 465.

undertaken in the United States over the last decade, attempts to "suggest a paradigm in which law-changing research is 'social authority', case-specific research is 'social fact', and a newer hybrid combination of these two is 'social framework'."[53] In this paradigm, the central concept is social authority, where the courts would "treat social science research much as they would legal precedent under the common law."[54] Professors Monahan and Walker recently stipulated a step-by-step procedure to provide guidance for the courts when they have to resolve an empirical question concerning human behaviour. This is worth laying out here. According to their approach, the courts (and administrative tribunals) should undertake the following steps:

(1) determine whether the substantive law governing the case raises an empirical issue to which social science research may be pertinent.

(2) determine whether the empirical issue bears on an assumption underlying the choice of a legal rule that has general applicability, the factual dispute pertaining only to the parties before the court, or a mixture of the two in which general empirical information provides a context for determining a specific fact.

(3) if the empirical issue concerns an assumption underlying the choice of a legal rule of general applicability:

  (a) receive social science studies in briefs submitted by the parties or *amici*.

  (b) if the parties or *amici* do not submit social science studies, request such tudies from the parties or *amici*, or obtain them from the courts own sua ponte investigation of published sources.

  (c) evaluate any available research by determining whether the research has survived the critical review of the scientific community, has used valid reseach methods, is generalisable to the legal issue in question, and is supported by a body of related research.

  (d) if no acceptable research is available, candidly state this conclusion in the opinion. In common law cases, rely upon the empirical assumption that appears to be most plausible. In reviewing state action, rely upon the legally appropriate standard of review in determining where to place responsibility for resolving the empirical issue.

---

[53] Monahan & Walker, "Social Science Research in Law: A New Paradigm", (1988) 43 *Am. Psychol.* 465.
[54] *ibid.* p. 466.

(4) if the empirical issue concerns a factual dispute bearing on only the parties before the court:

    (a) determine the party with the burden of proving the contested fact.

    (b) determine whether the law governing the case makes empirical research an appropriate form of evidence for meeting this burden.

    (c) if empirical research does constitute an appropriate form of evidence, allow the admission of direct and rebuttal expert testimony subject to the applicable federal or state rules of evidence.

    (d) if the party with the burden of proof does not produce relevent expert testimony, weigh this omission in determining whether the burden has been met.

(5) if the empirical issue concerns the provision of a general context within which to determine a fact pertaining only to the parties:

    (a) obtain and evaluate social science research as specified in (iii)(a)–(iii)(c) above.

(b) in cases tried before a jury, communicate the conclusions by means of jury instructions.[55]

This is a very useful system to enable courts and administrative bodies to utilise social science information in a way that would make it commensurate with the use of legal precedent. It would avoid the inaccuracies of the scientific model in ascertaining facts. Indeed, in political asylum cases the use of social science studies in briefs submitted by the parties or *amici* is now regularly used before the immigration tribunals. There are now often detailed reports, prepared by human rights organisations in the United States and United Kingdom, that are made available by the immigration authorities as background information for the determination of "well founded fear" on the part of the applicant seeking to flee from his country of origin.[56] It is regrettable that such a procedure has not been followed in relation to other areas of immigration law, such as marriage cases and family reunification cases. For example, in family application cases even the government minister for immigration has accepted that the factfinders get it wrong,[57] resulting in a relatively high

---

[55] See Monahan & Walker, "Judicial Use of Social Science Research", (1991) 15 *L. & Hum. Beh.* 571.

[56] For a discussion of the law on political asylum see, Jackson, *Immigration: Law and Practice* (London, 1996) pp. 322–388.

[57] See *infra.* p. 62.

success rate on appeals against their decisions, and yet factfinders
have made no attempts to ellicit the help of social science studies in
the ascertainment of accurate facts. Even the Court of Appeal has
spoken out against such a misguided approach by ECOs.[58]

In this area of immigration practice, even the first and second of
Monahan and Walkers rules above are rarely applied. For example,
investigating officers have regularly taken the view that a potential
wife of the sponsor in the United Kingdom could not have been the
mother of older children because the Child Marriage Restraint Act
1929 prohibits the marriage of child girls under 16. They, therefore,
proceed to apply rule (ii) above and promptly dismiss the application
of the potential wife on the basis of the assumption that she could
not have married at an earlier age. Yet, the overwhelming social
evidence suggests that child marriages take place as early as the ages
of 12 or 13.[59] A reference by an investigating officer to this social fact
would bring in the application of rule (i) above and thereby prevent
the choice of a legal rule by the ECO that would inevitably lead to a
refusal of application. Indeed, investigative officers have their own
internal guidelines giving vent to their own particular assumptions
about the situations that they are likely to encounter in family
settlement applications. These guidelines, however, do not, as we
shall see,[60] conform to Monahan and Walkers rule (iii)(c) above
which states that any available research relied upon in the determination of facts should have "survived the critical review of the scientific
community". In fact, there is an internal culture of deep-rooted
doubt and cynicism in the immigration process, which is not just
limited to investigating ECOs but has been known to extend to the
immigration appellate authorities as well. A comprehensive application of a theory of cultural jurisprudence requires us, therefore,
also to address the problem of legal psychology in the adjudicative
process. Legal psychology must be distinguished from psychological
jurisprudence.

(c) Challenging the Laws Behavioural Assumptions

Legal psychology is the scientific study of human behaviour in
relation to the law and it consists of those theories that describe,
explain and predict human behaviour by reference to law.[61] By

---

[58] See *infra*. p. 190.
[59] See *infra*. p. 87.
[60] See *infra*. pp. 76–80.
[61] Faigman, "To Have and To Have Not: Assessing the Value of Social Science to the Law as Science and Policy", (1989) 38 *Emory L.J.* 1005.

contrast, psychological jurisprudence consists of those theories that describe, explain and predict law by reference to human behaviour.[62] Legal psychology, therefore, applies the science of psychology to law. Legal psychology is a science because it applies the scientific method of systematic observation, description and measurement to the study of behaviour that is legally relevant. By contrast, law relies primarily on logic as a foundation of knowledge. The "psychology" in legal psychology comes from the focus on behaviour. This means that judges, witnessess, professionals, administrators, citizens, children and criminals are all studied. The "legal" in legal psychology comes from the application of the study of behaviour and mental processes to laws and legal systems. Legal psychology works within the legal context of substantive and procedural law. The basic function of psycho-legal research is to challenge the specific behavioural assumptions implicit in the law.[63] This means challenging the view in family settlement immigration cases that a particular cultural or ethnic group thinks nothing of substituting a bogus child for a real child[64]; or challenging the view in such circumstances that most documentary proof is forged[65]; or challenging the view that most such applicants are just plain bogus.[66]

In this way legal psychology can be used to examine three questions: (i) what effect[67] do the behavioural assumptions implicit in the law have on the stated goals?; (ii) how do these specific behavioural assumptions contribute[68] to subsequent decision making?; and (iii) how can these assumptions be tested in real world[69]

---

[62] Small, "Advancing Psychological Jurisprudence", (1993) 11 *Behav. Sci. & L.* 3.

[63] Saks, "The Law Does Not Live by Eyewitness Testimony Alone", (1986) 10 *L. & Hum. Behav.* 279.

[64] See *infra.* p. 75.

[65] See *infra.* p. 76.

[66] See *infra.* pp. 76–77.

[67] In the USA both direct and indirect effects have been analysed. Direct effects have been analysed, for example, in relation to the effects of changing civil commitment procedures on the civil commitment of the mentally ill (see Peters *et al.*, "The Effects of Statutory Change of the Civil Commitment of the Mentally Ill", (1987) 11 *L. & Hum. Behav.* 73). An examination of the indirect effects has not been very common (but see Baker *et al.*, "The Impact of Bottle Bill Legisalation on the Incidence of Lacerations in Childhood", (1986) 76 *Am. J. of Pub. Health* 1243.

[68] For example, studies in the USA have shown that marshalling empirical evidence to persuade the Supreme Court that a states programme for administering the death penalty is unconstitutional, is no longer viable: Small, "A Review of Death Penalty Case Law: Future Directions for Program Evaluation", (1991) 5 *Crim. Just. Poly Rev.* 114.

[69] Trial procedures, for example, have been found in the USA to offer settings for testing hypotheses about the accuracy of eyewitness recall and the way this influences the making of group decisions. Recent research has focused on field methods in this regard: Blanck, "The Process of Field Research in the Courtroom: A Descriptive Analysis," (1987) 11 *L. & Hum. Behav.* 337.

settings? We know that the stated goals of the law are to reunite families. We know that the families do get reunited over a number of years. We can measure the effects of the law as being wholly negative, however, because they are directly causative of delay and the resultant anguish in the lives of genuine family members, and indirectly causative of a cultural alienation as a result of the law failing to act as a cultural agent in these circumstances. As regards behavioural assumptions contributing to subsequent decision making, we know that such assumptions are damaging to the legal process and have an overall negative effect on decision making, unless those assumptions can be rationally and scientifically justified. The research in this area has been divided up into formative and summative.[70] Formative research is to do with information that can be fed back to the law-makers for adjusting the laws. Summative research is to do with whether or not the decision makers should adopt or drop particular laws or practices from this. We can say, for example, that the research showing that most young children of families in the Indian sub-continent will not know the names of their elders[71] (because they refer to them only as dignitaries), should be fed back into the legal system to adjust the inaccurate assumptions implicit in the law. On the other hand, we can say from this that the belief that most family members are bogus applicants should be dropped in the light of studies carried out by immigrant welfare organisations.[72] We can, indeed, also say that the difficulties in operating the entry clearance procedure fairly and sensitively to minority populations in family settlement cases, should prompt us to disapply the entry clearance procedure in these cases.[73] Finally, as regards the testing of behavioural assumptions in real world situations, we can say that the psychological theories can be assessed in an environmentally valid setting, in the context of the particular cultural backdrop, to determine their accuracy.

The testing would be undertaken by following a three stage process. First, a behavioural assumption in the law would be discovered. This may be the assumption, for example, that in Bangladesh some 90 per cent of children applicants are bogus because they have been artificially constructed by the sponsoring parent to fit into a bogus family pattern originally declared to the Inland Revenue

---

[70] Weis, "Evaluation Research: Methods of Assessing Program Effectiveness" (Durham, N.C., 1972).
[71] See *infra.* p. 67. Also at pp. 62, 64, 66.
[72] See *infra.* pp. 76–77 and p. 78.
[73] See *infra.* p. 59 and the judgment of Lord Denning and the case of *Phansgskar* therein.

for tax relief purposes.[74] The researcher would determine next, how this assumption relates to the body of law. He would discover that many cases are refused by ECOs, and subsequently also on appeal, on the basis that because the information given to the Inland Revenue does not match up with the account of family members before the immigration authorities, the applicants are bogus. The researcher would determine the applicability of this relevant psychological theory and assess its merits for testing the assumption. He would discover that mistakes had been made because perfectly genuine children had been put down in the wrong order because in Bangladesh with only five per cent of people paying tax, the concept of personal income tax is unknown.[75] The sponsor himself would have been illiterate and would have upon his arrival here, been advised by others as to how to fill in the tax form. Sponsors would be handing in lists of children which were incorrect simply because they do not know that they are incorrect. Consequently in the vast majority of cases for the immigration authorities, applicant children were perfectly genuine. The researcher would determine this by adopting an appropriate methodology for testing the assumption. He would test to see whether, if the existence of a child had been wrongly declared to the Inland Revenue authorities, that child was actually applying for admission to the United Kingdom before the immigration authorities.[76] He would find that in actual fact applications for entry would only be filled in for genuine children. Upon discovery of this information, the researcher would disseminate his findings to the appropriate law-making authorities. It is plain, therefore, that what has been done by the researcher here fits the definition of a "True Scientist". Professor Trubeck describes the True Scientist as follows:

" The True Scientist believes that society obeys natural laws. He searches for the underlying forces that govern the behaviour of groups and individuals. He sees the natural sciences as the model for social science. He believes that 'theory' is a statement of empirically observed regularities. Whether he favours grand or middle-range theory, the True Scientist aspires to produce a body of certifiable knowledge which will hold trur for all time and all places. To be certifiable as scientific, this knowledge must be supported by empirical evidence which meets the evidentiary standards of the social science community."[77]

[74] See infra. p. 78.
[75] See infra. p. 77.
[76] See infra. p. 83.
[77] Trubek, "Back to the Future: The Short Happy Life of the Law and Society Movement", (1990) 18 Fla. St. U. L. Rev. 26.

The standards of the social science community are, after all, what cultural jurisprudence in its finest form seeks to maintain. Cultural jurisprudence sets out empirically to document the nature and extent of the cultural effects of the laws and procedures. Social science would advance the cultural competence of the laws by ensuring that the cultural assumptions in the law are accurately founded, and for those laws that are not founded upon cultural assumptions, then at least making sure that those cultural affects are known. Professor Tanford has suggested that "for a body of empirical research to command a place in jurisprudence, the science must reflect some of the same values as a particular body of law. The more the two value systems converge, the more completely will law accept the science."[78] It is plain from this that cultural jurisprudence is eminently suited to provide the empirical results for law that deal with a culturally diversified citizenry, whether this be the anti-discriminatory laws or the immigration laws. In the chapters that follow in this book, we will see that the science of cultural jurisprudence reflects almost precisely the underlying values of the immigration law and practice that is being applied in this field. To that extent, we will be able to construct a theory of immigration adjudication that is based upon the jurisprudential analysis undertaken in this introduction.

Democratic Pluralism and Cultural Jurisprudence

(1) INTELLECTUAL BASIS

Cultural jurisprudence, when applied to the changed world of religious, cultural and ethnic diversity is the modern-day contemporary heir to the school of jurisprudence known as Legal Realism. The Legal Realist movement that flourished in the earlier part of this century stood in direct contrast to the nineteenth century concept of law that just required the law to be applied mechanically. Pound referred to it as "mechanical jurisprudence".[79] Here law was found in the statute books or in legal precedent and then just mechanically applied. Its consequences were irrelevant. Hence, it came to be seen as "formalistic" or "logical" and therefore, as a self contained and autonomous discipline. The Legal Realist movement looked to

---

[78] Tanford, "The Limits of a Scientific Jurisprudence: The Supreme Court and Psychology", (1898) 66 *Ind. L. Review* 167.
[79] Pound, "Mechanical Jurisprudence", (1908) 8 *Colum. L. Rev.* 605.

beyond law's formalisms and to its deeper workings and practical effects. Holmes challenged this "logic" in the law by saying that "the life of the law has not been logic: it has been experience . . . even the prejudices which judges share with their fellow men, have had a good deal more to do than syllogism in determining the rules by which men should be governed".[80] Pound developed this point of view into a "sociological jurisprudence"[81] forcing the law "to take more account, and more intelligent account, of the social facts upon which law must proceed and to which it is to be applied". Rejecting formalism, he called for "a study of the actual social effects of legal institutions and legal doctrines".[82]

Karl Llewellyn and Jerome Frank, two of the leading exponents of Legal Realism,[83] went on to break this down further. Karl Llewellyn explored the relationship between the descriptive and the normative and argued that "no judgment of what Ought to be done in the future with respect to any part of law can be intelligently made without knowing objectively, as far as possible, what that part of law is now doing".[84] Frank observed that the legal process should be observed from a psycho-analytic viewpoint. He called for "training in the best available methods of psychology".[85] The Legal Realist movement declined in importance by the 1950s, but subsequent contemporary jurisprudential schools of thought have adopted Realist techniques[86] and insights. Thus, for example, there are definite resonances of Realism in feminist legal theory,[87] in social science and law,[88] critical legal studies,[89] the law and society movement,[90] law and economics,[91] and most recently, therapeutic jurisprudence.[92] The latter is the latest attempt to locate law as a therapeutic agent within

---

[80] Holmes, *The Common Law* (Harvard University Press, 1963) p. 5 (written in 1881).
[81] Pound, "The Scope and Purpose of Sociological Jurisprudence", (1912) *Harv. L. Rev.* 489.
[82] *ibid.* pp. 512–513.
[83] White, "From Sociological Jurisprudence to Realism: Jurisprudence and Social Change in the Early Twentieth Century America", (1971) 58 *Va. L. Rev.* 1017.
[84] Llewellyn, "Some Realism about Realism — Responding to Dean Pound", (1931) 44 *Harv. L.Rev.* 1222, pp. 1236–37.
[85] Frank, *Courts on Trial* (Harvard Univesity Press, 1949), p. 247.
[86] Singer, "Legal Realism Now", (1988) 76 *Cal.L.Rev.* 9.
[87] McKinnon, "Toward Feminist Jurisprudence", (1982) 34 *Stan. L.Rev.* 703, p. 705.
[88] Monahan & Walker, *Social Science in Law: Cases and Materials* (New York, 2nd ed., 1990), p. 21.
[89] Unger, *The Critical Legal Studies Movement,* Harvard University Press (1986), p. 1.
[90] Friedman, "The Law and Society Movement", (1986) 38 *Stan. L. Rev.* 763.
[91] Posner, *Economic Analysis of Law* (3rd ed., 1986), p. 16.
[92] Wexler, *Therapeutic Jurisprudence: The Law as a Therapeutic Agent* (Carolina Academic Press, Durham, 1990).

the general field of social science in law,[93] and it has made its most
significant contribution in the context of mental health law.[94]
However, cultural jurisprudence, while drawing upon the legacy of
these past movements, makes the unique contribution of focusing
primarily on pluralist democratic values in a racially and ethnically
diverse society. More than any other previous school of thought,
cultural jurisprudence has a direct relevance to globalised man and
his globalised society. It has both a practical justification in the world
today and a rational and philosophical justification. We will briefly
consider both these justifications.

(2) PRACTICAL BASIS

Let us first consider the practical justification for a theory of cultural
jurisprudence. This is based on the emergence of globalisation.
Globalisation both brings pressures on the preservation of distinct
cultures and makes cultural discrimination unacceptable in an
increasingly fluid and mobile society. The seismic effects of globalisation have been recently described by I.D. Davidson and W. Rees-
Mogg in their book, *The Sovereign Individual*. The authors have
adverted to this as "the most sweeping revolution in history . . .
destroying the nation-state and creating a new form of social
organisation".[95] The rise of the "global city" has meant that especially
since the 1980s cultural tensions have become ever more pressing as
new global patterns of immigration and capital flow, new north-south
relations of markets and the environment, and new geo-political
realignments following the breakup of post-war and post-colonial
states in the former Soviet Bloc, have begun to take form. This
globalisation has led to the recognition of the existence of a global
infrastructure; a global harmonisation or convergence; an increased
sense of borderlessness; a global diffusion of localised phenomenon
and characteristics; and a breathtakingly fast geographical dispersion
of core competences in some leading activities. Since the 1980s a
great many states have become involved in globalising major fields of
traditional state activity, such as markets, law and politics, all of
which have become denationalised and are no longer under the
sovereign control of individual states.

---

[93] Wexler, "Reflections on the Scope of Therapeutic Jurisprudence", (1995) 1 Psychol.
Pub. Poly & L. 220, p. 228.
[94] Winick, *Therapeutic Jurisprudence Applied: Essays on Mental Health Law* (Carolina
Academic Press, Durham, 1996).
[95] (McMillan Press, 1997) *(forthcoming)*. The quotation by the authors is from *The
Times*, April 8, 1997.

Immigration has contributed in a major way to these practical changes and is a key basis for asserting a theory of cultural jurisprudence. There is a global migration crisis. Over 35 million people from the developing countries have taken up residence in the industrialised economies since 1960, and about 1.5 million continue to join them each year.[96] There are major migratory movements within developing countries caused by poverty, drought, and ethnic and civil wars, including redeployment of populations in Central and Eastern Europe. There are nearly 15 million people internally displaced in developing countries. In the world at large, however, 100 million people (about two per cent of the worlds population) live outside their countries of birth as refugees, asylum seekers, legal immigrants and unauthorised or illegal immigrants.[97] About one quarter of these are in North America and another one quarter live in the industrialised countries of Western Europe and Asia. In fact, Ernest Gellner has identified a number of important questions that now face liberal society, one of which is, How will advanced nations cope with massive migrations?[98] This worldwide process of migration is seriously challenging the traditional concept of the nation. This is because the traditional notion of an ethnically and culturally integrated and homogenised nation is no longer accurate or feasible given these worldwide movements which interact with other global forces. The concept of the nation state, therefore, as traditionally understood, is obsolete.

However, the mismatch between the nation state and the "global village" only arises because of the misunderstanding that arises over the organisation of the global political system (which continues to be based on notions of national sovereignty) and the organisation of the global economy. Professor David Jackson, the Vice-President of the Immigration Appeals Tribunal, astutely recognises in his recent book that strict immigration controls are justified because they "are seen by some as a general protection of culture",[99] but this will in the future not make sense, if there is no one culture to protect, but a series of inter-connected and inter-dependent cultures. The worlds economy creates major incentives for people to migrate from low

---

[96] G. de Lusignan, "Global migration and European Integration", (1994) 2 *Ind. J. of Global L.S.* 179.
[97] Passel & Fix, "US Immigration in a Global Context: Past, Present and Future", (1994) 2 Ind. J. of Global L.S. 5, p. 6.
[98] See Young, "After the Tears We Seek New Heroes", *The Guardian*, November 7, 1995 (quoted in Juss, "Somersett's Case, The Constitution and Common Law Rights: A Re-Appraisal", (1996) 1 *Int. J. of Discrimination & the L.* 335, p. 350).
[99] Jackson, *op. cit.*, p. 3.

wage regions to higher wage regions, from oppressive political systems to more liberal political systems. Governments, however, want to control the migration of people across their borders. Yet, political control over international migration is becoming more and more impossible. One only has to look at the dramatic reduction in the costs of international movement, the rapid growth of global airline travel, the spread of international communications media, and the internationalisation of commerce, to learn that preventing migration from other countries is both practically and politically unwise. Internationally mobile labour is as essential to the global economic system as is the international circulation of capital. In the United States, new immigration is helping to forge network linkages to dynamic global players making it possible to consolidate a pan-regional, Western Atlantic hemisphere system.[1] It is clear from this that globalisation means not only denationalisation of political decision making, but also the realisation that global decison-making is designed to serve the "public interest" of the world community, rather than the narrow "national interest".

It is in this way that the obsolete nation state can reinvent itself. It can be more culturally sensitive. The State has to become an integrated community of citizens where there is accommodation for a culturally and ethnically diverse citizenry.[2] This is so as a matter of practical necessity. This State recognises not only individual relations between the state but also the relations of the individual to the global world outside. It is a state that recognises transnational systems of political organisation where space-time differences have collapsed and the nation state is deterritorialised. In this way, the State can contribute to the formation of new communities, new alliances and new multicultural exchanges. In the "global village" the modern state can ill afford not to educate foreign students, foster joint research programmes, train other countries scientists, security personnel and health practitioners. They can ill afford not to welcome foreign diplomats and administrators of international organisations, or to respect the human rights of tourists, visitors, business persons, missionaries, adopted children and family members of citizens already settled in the state.[3] To do so is quite simply impracticable in the "global village". The motif of the modern state should become

[1] Conway, "Are There New Complexities in Global Migration Systems of Consequence for the United States 'Nation-State'?" *Ind. J. of Global L.S.* (Vol. 2, 1995) 31, p. 36.
[2] Delbruck, "Global Migration–Immigration–Multiethnicity: Challenges to the Concept of the Nation–State, Ind. J. of Global L.S. (Vol. 2, 1995) 45, p. 57.
[3] See Conway, *op. cit.* p. 41.

"equal citizenship" and not ethnic belonging, which can form no part of a meaningful "civic culture" in the new world.

(3) RATIONAL AND PHILOSOPHICAL BASIS

Let us next consider the rational and philosophical justification for a theory of cultural jurisprudence. Having recognised above that states cannot just hang onto a single idea of a monolithic unchanging culture, we must now consider how they can protect other diverse cultures. Cultural jurisprudence is rooted in the emerging area of "minority rights law" that speaks to the development of national minorities in nearly all Western European democracies in the latter half of this century. This area of the law is centred around the preservation of culture, traditions, religion or language; and of course immigration control impacts on all these values in a big way. It is recognised that minority rights will not endear themselves to everybody. However, there is a body of customary international law on this area which cannot be ignored. It is true that the concept of "minorities" sits uneasily with the theoretical paradigm of the state. The State, whether based on the individual social-contract theory of contemporary Western democracies or on the outdated precepts of class based Marxism, is regarded as a collection of shifting coalitions, whether founded on individual self interest or on the self interest of economic classes. This is despite the fact that ethnic, cultural, or linguistic ties are much more influential in the dynamics of the constitution of the state than considerations of class or individual interest. There is, in fact, already in existence, a cultural jurisprudence that is at work here. Indeed, such concerns are not marginal to the tragic, conflictive issues of our time which have involved ethnicity, racism, group hatred, or rights of self determination, separation or segregation. However, minority rights law has failed to acquire a venerated position in international or domestic law because the existence of minorities contradicts the philosophical basis of democratic and Marxist societies. Much of the contemporary world has been organised on the theory of the nation state as developed in the nineteenth century, comprising largely heterogenous states. The recognition of minority rights is now seen to encourage fragmentation or separation and stands to undermine national unity.

In this work, a discussion of the development of the philosophical and legal rights of minorities cannot do justice to the huge detail and complexity of this body of law. Therefore the discussion that ensues is intended only to describe the basic tenets of minority rights law in so far as that is relevant to the development of a theory of cultural

jurisprudence. A brief sketch is here provided. The first matter is that
of definition. No definition of a "minority" has been widely accepted
by international lawyers. However, the best and most commonly
cited definition of a "minority" comes from F. Francesco Capotorti
who, as Special Rapporteur to the UN Sub-Commission on Prevention of Discrimination and Protection of Minorities, produced in
1978 the leading study on discrimination against minorities. He
defines a minority as:

> ". . . a group numerically inferior to the rest of the population of a State,
> in a non-dominant position, whose members — being nationals of the
> State — possess ethnic, religious or linguistic characteristics differing
> from those of the rest of the population and show, if only implicitly, a
> sense of solidarity, *directed towards preserving their culture, traditions, religion or
> language*."[4] (Authors emphasis.)

The Indian sub-continental group discussed in this work is certainly
a minority in all these senses here described. Indeed, they constitute a
national minority as they comprise nearly four per cent of the
national population. It is clear from this definition that a minority
may be constituted whenever there is a desire in a group that is in a
non-dominant position within a State, to preserve its culture,
traditions, religion or language. Historically, the most important of
these rights has been that of religious expression although religion
clearly does not stand alone and may be related to other rights of
minorities to varying degrees.

The international protection of minorities began with the concern
for religious freedom and is traceable at least to the Treaty of
Westphalia in 1648, whereby the parties to an agreement undertook
to respect the rights of certain religious minorities within their
jurisdiction.[5] In the words of Theodor Meron, "Freedom of religion
is indeed the oldest of the internationally recognised human freedoms and therefore the one with which the international community
has had the longest experience."[6] and Paul Sieghart has pointed out
that the movement for "freedom of belief" in fact, "precedes every
other in the history of the struggle for human rights and fundamental

---

[4] See Capotorti, *Study on the Rights of Persons Belonging to Ethnic, Religious and Linguistic
Minorities* (UN Doc. E/CN/4 Sub. 2/384/Rev., Vol. 1, UN Sales Number E.78.xiv.1,
1979) pp. 16–26. Also see Capotorti, *Study on the Rights of Persons Belonging to Ethnic,
Religious and Linguistic Minorities* (New York, 1991).
[5] For an excellent survey of the early treatment of minorities, see Muldoon, "The
Development of Group Rights" in Sigler, *Minority Rights: A Comparative Analysis* (New
York, 1983), p. 31.
[6] Meron, *Human Rights in International Law* (Oxford, 1985), p. 176.

freedoms".[7] The Congress of Vienna that followed the Napoleonic Wars in 1815 also, to some extent, chose to protect the rights of national minorities. The Treaty of Berlin in 1876 provided protection for the "traditional rights and liberties" of the religious community of Mount Athos in Greece.[8]

The most comprehensive attempt, however, to protect through international legal means the rights of ethnic and religious minorities, was through the so-called Minority Treaties adopted at the end of the First World War, which finally found expression in the League of Nations. In the treaties and unilateral declarations that followed the First World War (imposing obligations on the defeated states of Austria, Hungary, Bulgaria and Turkey; or providing for rights of "self determination" to states within the Ottoman Empire, such as Czechoslovakia, Greece, Poland, Romania and Yugoslavia) the emphasis was not on the particular nature of the group, but on the fact that such a group existed, that it had a well individualised indentity and was entitled to have such intentity protected without being forcibly assimilated. The protected groups were often a combination of ethnic, cultural and religious groups. The League of Nations Treaties are important in giving expression to what have been regarded as traditional minority rights dealing with religion, language and cultural activities. The Great Powers, however, were not bound by minority rights protection.[9]

Unlike its predecessor, however, the United Nations Charter 1948 contains no provision protecting minority rights. The UN Charter assumes that minority rights can be satisfied if individual rights, particularly those of equality and non-discrimination, are respected; and that there is a reference to a principle of self determination which can be used to resolve the problem of colonialism.[10] Notwithstanding this, however, the United Nations became actively involved in minority issues during the 1950s. In 1960, the United Nations Educational, Scientific and Cultural Organisation (UNESCO) adopted the Convention Against Discrimination in Education, which

---

[7] Sieghart, *The International Law of Human Rights* (New York, 1983), p. 324.

[8] For an account of these early developments see, del Russo, *International Protection of Human Rights* (Washington, 1971) and see, Neff, An Evolving International Legal Law of Religious Freedom: Problems and Prospects, (1977) 7 *Cal. Western Int. L. J.*, pp. 543–582.

[9] For an account see, Thornberry, *International Law and the Rights of Minorities* (Oxford, 1991). See also, Hannum, "New Developments in Indigenous Rights" (1988) 28 *Va. J. Intl. L.* 649.

[10] For the basic text, see Brownlei, *Basic Documents in International Law* (2nd ed., Oxford, 1972), p. 1. On human rights in the UN Charter see, Lauterpacht, *International Law and Human Rights* (London, 1950).

recognised the right of members of national minorities to engage in their own educational activities, including the maintenance of schools and the use or teaching of their own language, subject to the educational policy of each state.[11]

The implementation of the UN Declaration of Human Rights 1948 was gradually undertaken through the adoption of binding international agreements, such as the International Covenant on Civil and Political Rights (ICCPR) in 1966. Article 27 of this Covenant states that:

> ". . . in those states in which ethnic, religious or linguistic minorities exist, persons belonging to such minorities shall not be denied the right, in community with the other members of their group, to enjoy their own culture, to profess and practice their own religion, or to use their own language."[12]

This provision addresses only minimal, traditional minority rights of culture, religion and language, and the rights are granted to "persons belonging to such minorities" rather than to minority groups themselves. In the context of immigration rights that are being discussed in the work, this is of little consequence, although it is an indication of the individualistic orientation of the ICCPR. A violation of Article 27 was claimed by Canada in the well-known case of *Sandra Lovelace*,[13] in which an Indian woman who lost her status and rights as an Indian after having married a non-Indian. The Committee emphasised the relevance of Article 27 to the issues of cultural and community rights and the loss of identity.[14]

In 1969 the International Convention on the Elimination of all Forms of Racial Discrimination came into force.[15] It has not been ratified by Great Britain on grounds of national security, even though it remains one of the most widely ratified instruments in the field of human rights. In a broad sense, it is presently the most important treaty regarding discrimination. Discrimination is defined as:

> ". . . any distinction, exclusion, restriction or preference based on race, colour, descent, or national or ethnic origin which has the purpose or

---

[11] *Adopted* December 14, 1960, 429 U.N.T.S. p. 93.
[12] See, *International Covenant on Economic, Social and Cultural Rights, International Covenant on Civil and Political Rights and Optional Protocol to the International Covenant on Civil and Political Rights*, G.A. Res. 2200, 21 UN GAOR Supp. (No. 16), p. 56.
[13] See, Human Rights Committee, Fifth Report (GAOR 36th session Supp. No. 40 (A/36/40) Annex XVIII).
[14] See, *Selected Decisions Under the Optional Protocol* (Vol. 1, UN Sales Numberø E.84.xix.2, 1985), p. 74.
[15] *Open for Signature*, March 7, 1966, 660 U.N.T.S. 195, *Entered into Force*, January 4, 1969.

effect of nullifying or impairing the recognition, enjoyment or exercise, *on an equal footing*, of human rights and fundamental freedoms in the political, economic, social, cultural or any other field of public life."

These provisions apply to situations where the ethnicity and religious orientation of a person overlap. Thus, for Jews, Arabs, Sikh, Kurds, Armenians and others, ethnicity and religion cannot be separated. This can be seen also in the definition of "racial discrimination". Article 1 prohibits any distinction "based on race, colour, descent, or *national or ethnic origins*" which affects the exercise of human rights. Under Article 2 of the Convention, state parties are required to take "special and concrete measures to ensure the adequte development and protection of certain racial groups or individuals belonging to them, for the purpose of guaranteeing them the full and equal enjoyment of human rights and fundamental freedoms."

Clearly, the development of a theory of cultural jurisprudence would be a small but necessary step in the fight against such specified discriminatory practices. There has been a movement towards the adjustment of minority rights law to the needs of modern society whereby the principle of equality is intended to imply full equality between men and women. Thus, in 1979 the Convention on the Elimination of All Forms of Discrimination Against Women was signed to take notice of the fact that:

> "[t]he most comprehensive challenges mounted by states to the international norms guaranteeing womens rights, and their application, have been couched as defenses of religious liberty."[16]

However, the principles in this Convention are relevant not only within religion but outside it, so that, for example, the immigration practices of a state that disproportionately impinge upon womens rights, are in violation of this Convention.

Further work in minority rights has been carried out following the leading study on discrimination by Francesco Capotorti in 1978, for the UN Sub-Commission on Prevention of Discrimination and Protection of Minorities. The Sub-Commission subsequently suggested that a Declaration on the Rights of Minorities be prepared. A draft Declaration was accordingly submitted to the UN Commission

---

[16] On the Convention generally see, Meron, *Human Rights Law Making in the United Nations* (Oxford, 1986) pp. 53–82. An extensive bibliography of womens rights is provided by Sullivan in "Gender Equality and Religious Freedom: Toward a Framework for Conflict Resolution", (1992) 24 *NYU . J. Intl Law & Politics* pp. 795–856.

on Human Rights by Yugoslavia in 1979.[17] This revised Yugoslav
draft is today the basic working draft, as put forward in 1981, and the
Commission has been considering this draft Declaration in an "open
ended" working group since 1979 whilst meeting during the Commission's annual sessions.[18] Although, the draft is by no means a
radical document it does represent the first attempt by the international community in over 60 years to detail the norms relating to
the protection of minorities. Thus, the preamble recognises that the
effective protection of minority rights will "contribute to the political
and social stability of states in which they live" and that this will in
turn, "contribute to the strengthening of friendship and co-operation
among peoples and states".[19]

In the meantime, however, specific rights of minority law have
been given more attention. For example, in 1981 the Declaration on
the Elimination of All Forms of Intolerance and Discrimination
Based on Religion or Belief was proclaimed by the General Assembly
of the UN.[20] This is the most important international instrument on
religious rights and the prohibition of intolerance or discrimination
based on religion or belief today. It is of particular significance to
immigration rights because Article 1 of the Declaration uses the term
"everyone" thereby implying that it will give protection to nationals
and aliens, whether permanent or non-permanent residents. It is also
of relevance to immigration rights because paragraph 1 proclaims
three fundamental freedoms: thought, conscience and religion,
including "whatever belief" of one's choice, to the extent that the
right to marry someone of ones faith and of one's community is a
matter of conscience for someone living in Britain who wishes to
bring in his cousin as his wife, for example. A Declaration is not a
Treaty of course, and is, therefore, not binding. Nevertheless, it
carries with it the weight of a UN solemn statement. It gives
expression to the prevailing trends in the international community.
To the extent that it states rules of customary international law, it
does have certain limited legal effects and it does imply an expectation of obedience by members of the international community.

---

[17] UN Doc. E/CN.4/L1367/Rev. 1(1979).
[18] UN Doc. E/CN.4/Sub.2/L.734 (1981).
[19] See, *Report of the Working Group on the Rights of Persons Belonging to National, Ethnic,
Religious and Linguistic Minorities* (UN Doc. E/CN.4/1991/53, Vol. 20, 1991) in the
Preamble.
[20] For the text see, *Human Rights, A Compilation of International Instruments* (Vol.1, part 1,
1993) (Sales Number E.93.xiv.1), p. 122. An analysis of this Declaration is undertaken
by Lerner, in *Group Rights and Discrimination in International Law* (Dordrecht, 1991),
pp. 75–96. Also see, Sullivan, Advancing the Freedom of Religion or Belief Through
the UN Declaration on the Elimination of Religious Intolerance and Discrimination",
(1988) 82 *A.J.I.L.* pp. 487–520.

However, the most recent and progressive inter-governmental articulation of minority rights was adopted in June 1990 during the Copenhagen Meeting of the Conference on the Human Dimension of the Conference on Security and Co-operation in Europe (CSCE).[21] This has now been superseded by the Organisation for Security and Co-operation in Europe (OSCE). The CSCE opened in 1973 and concluded in August 1975 with the signing of the Helsinki Accord by 35 participating states. Thereafter the CSCE process continued throughout the late 1970s and 1980s and there were "concluding documents" of various follow-up meetings.[22] In the human rights context the most important of these agreements were held over "the human dimension of the CSCE". The meetings were concluded in Vienna and Paris in 1989, in Copenhagen in 1990, in Moscow in 1991 and in Geneva in 1992. In 1995 the CSCE was officially designated the "OSCE". The OSCE has been institutionalised with, *inter alia*, a parliamentary assembly, a council of ministers for foreign affairs, a committee of senior officials. The standards that this body establishes are solemn undertakings but are not in a treaty form and are not formally binding. The membership extends to 53 states and is therefore wider than the European Union and the Council of Europe.

The Copenhagen Meeting in 1990 was the most significant in contributing to the minority rights of language, education and political participation. The repression of minorities often involves the systematic denial of linguistic rights and paragraph 32 of the Copenhagen Principles state that persons belonging to a minority should be able to "freely express, preserve and develop their . . . linguistic . . . identity". This is clearly relevent to the development of principles of cultural jurisprudence. Education is likewise a fundamental activity for the preservation of a minority culture. Majority societies have traditionally attempted to assimilate minority cultures through the imposition of their own language. The right, therefore, to maintain minority educational institutions is essential for minority self preservation. However, in the context of this work the principle at stake is not so much the use of language *per se*, but rather the ability of a minority to preserve its cultural distinctiveness, including its language, in a manner that is compatible with its relationship with

---

[21] See, the Document of CSCE at (1990) 11 *Hum. Rts. L. J.*, p. 232. For a general account see, Steiner & Alston, *International Human Rights in Context* (Oxford, 1996), pp. 577–580.
[22] See, for example, "Concluding Document of the Madrid Session of the Conference on Security and Co-operation in Europe", November 11, 1980–September 9, 1983, reprinted in *I.L.M.* (Vol. 22), p. 1398.

the majority society in which it lives. The participation of minorities
in public affairs, however, as stipulated in paragraph 35 of the
Copenhagen Principles, is the most far-reaching principle that was
enunciated in 1990. The principle is, however, weakly formulated,
and requires only minimal effort by states to establish "appropriate
local or autonomous administrations" for effective participation in
political life. The Copenhagen Principles have paved the way most
recently to a proposed European Convention for the Protection of
Minorities. A draft of this has been prepared by a non-governmental
consultative body of the Council of Europe, the European Commission for Democracy through Law. The draft is the result of a
realisation that "an adequate solution to the problem of minorities in
Europe is an essential factor for democracy, justice, stability and
peace".[23] The draft concerns itself with ethnic, religious, and linguistic minorities, which are defined as:

> ". . . a group which is smaller in number than the rest of the population
> of the State, whose members, who are nationals of that State, have
> ethnical, religious or linguistic features different from those of the rest of
> the population, and are guided by the will to safeguard their culture,
> traditions, religion,or language."[24]

Under this draft European Convention a European Committee for
the Protection of Minorities would also be created. States would be
obliged to submit periodic reports to the Committee. Upon a two-
thirds vote, the Committee could make "any necessary recommendations"[25] to a State party.

In the meantime, the UN has also been active during this period
in the promotion of similar rights as the CSCE, although not to the
same degree. In 1992, the UN General Assembly adopted the
Declaration on the Rights of Persons Belonging to National or
Ethnic, Religious and Linguistic Minorities.[26] This document is
inspired by Article 27 of the ICCPR. It is not group orientated,
although it promotes religious, ethnic and cultural rights. Article 1
requires states to "protect" the identity of minorities and to "encourage" conditions for the promotion of their identity. Article 4 states

[23] See, "Proposal for a European Convention for the Protection of Minorities", in
(1991) 12 *Hum. Rts. L.J.* 270 (the preamble).
[24] *ibid.* at Article 2.
[25] *ibid.* at Article 24.
[26] For the text see, *Human Rights: A Compilation of International Instruments* (Vol. 1, 1993)
(Sales Number E.93.xiv.1), p. 140. A commentary on this Declaration is provided by
Lerner, "The 1992 UN Declaration on Minorities", *Israel Yearbook on Hum. Rts.* (Tel
Aviv, 1993).

that people should be able to express their characteristics and develop their culture, language, religion, traditions and customs, except where these specifically infringe national law, legal provisions or internationally accepted norms.

To conclude this discussion on minority rights, we can say that there is an emerging consensus of a minimum content of international minority rights which State institutions and jurisprudential systems of thought should be taking into account. Unfortunately, there has been little concerted action in the protection of these rights in either of these guises. There has been a marked absence of a jurisprudential discourse on these rights at a national level and little attempt to set up an intellectually coherent framework for an analysis of such rights. These rights have yet to come of age. Much of the blame for this lies at an international level. The substantive development of minority rights since 1945 has indeed been minimal. However, there are positive legal obligations arising under Article 27 of the ICCPR and there is a clear prohibition of racial discrimination in the Convention on the Elimination of All Forms of Racial Discrimination, which cannot go unnoticed in any treatment of minority groups by national systems of law. It is arguable that there is still no universal consensus as to the intellectual, rational or philosophical basis of minority rights. However, the fundamental principles of non-discrimination and equality before the law have now acquired the status of customary international law that is binding on all states. The recognition of the rights of minority groups as a valid principle in law has become almost universally accepted among the family of nations. Specific principles of minority rights law, such as the right to religious expression and freedom of conscience, have become the normative principles for most of the nations of the world[27] and a denial of such rights is viewed almost everywhere as morally and legally unacceptable. Minority rights, like all other human rights, are based on the sanctity or intrinsic worth ascribed to the human person. This is especially so where one human being is different from another. In the words of a former Chief Justice of the United States Supreme Court, Charles Evans Hughes, "when we lose the right to be different, we lose the privilege to be free".[28]

---

[27] Juss, "Kokkinakis and Freedom of Conscience Rights in Europe", (1996) 2 *Jnl. of Civil Lib.* 246, pp. 246–251.
[28] Address at Faneuil Hall, Boston, Mass., on the 150th Anniversary of the Battle of Bunker Hill, June 17, 1925: Hughes Papers, Library of Congress.

Chapter One

The Entry Clearance System

> *"Any system of control necessarily involves restrictions; and to have an appeal system is one way of ensuring that the restrictions are fairly applied. To be fairly applied does not mean to be ineffectively applied."*

> *Report of the Committee on Immigration Appeals* (at para. 59)

The Law

When the first Commonwealth Immigrants Act was passed in 1962 to curb the rising tide of immigrants from the New Commonwealth that followed the Second World War in the 1950s and 1960s, the right of Commonwealth wives and children to join their husbands in the United Kingdom was preserved intact. Section 2(2)(b) of that Act set down that:

> "The power to refuse admission or admit subject to conditions shall not be exercised . . . in the case of any person who satisfied an immigration officer that he or she . . . *is the wife or child* under sixteen years of age *of a Commonwealth citizen* who is resident in the UK . . ." (Author's emphasis.)

Four years later, with still ever-increasing concern over immigrants, this time from the East African territories, the second Commonwealth Immigration Act of 1968 was passed, but this also left unaffected the rights of wives and children to join their husbands in exactly the same way as the Act of 1962.[1] However, with increased curbs came the concern over due-process rights for immigrants

---

[1] Commonwealth Immigrants Act 1968, s.22(2)(b)

refused entry, so that the following year the Immigration Appeals Act 1969 was passed providing a right of appeal to an independent administrative tribunal.[2] Remarkably, however, an Act to confer rights of appeal also brought with it a procedural obstacle for dependent relatives. The same right now read "after the words 'satisfies an immigration officer' there shall be inserted the words 'that she holds a current entry certificate granted for the purpose of this paragraph', and this also applied to a child of under 16 who sought entry."[3]

The Immigration Act 1971, the legal basis for immigration control today, diminished this right yet again by taking it out of its enshrinement in primary legislation and placing it in the immigration rules,[4] a species of quasi-legislation which could be altered and amended at will by the Minister in charge without proper scrutiny from the legislature.[5] Section 1(5) of the 1971 Act signified a move of that right away from the statutory entitlement into a more informal regulation:

> "The rules shall be so framed that Commonwealth citizens settled in the United Kingdom *at the coming into force of this Act*, and their wives and children are not, by virtue of anything in the rules, any less free to come and go from the United Kingdom than if this Act had not been passed." (Author's emphasis.)

What this means is that any Commonwealth citizen that settles in the United Kingdom after "the coming into force of this Act", that is January 1, 1973, no longer has the *legal* right to have his wife and children join him here. Indeed, the Immigration Act 1988 now specifically removes altogether such a right in section 1, which is plainly headed "Termination of saving in respect of Commonwealth citizens settled here before 1973" and simply reads: "Section 1(5) of the Immigration Act 1971 . . . is hereby repealed". Dummett and Nicol have recently referred to this as the removal of "the only statutory right to family unity in British law. It is now the case, as a result of that Act, that *no* British Citizen has a right to be joined in the United Kingdom by a spouse of either sex."[6]

---

[2] Immigration Appeals Act 1969, ss.1 and 8.
[3] *ibid.*, s.20(1) and (2).
[4] *Statement of Immigration Rules for Control of Entry* (1973) (Commonwealth Citizens) H.C. Vol. 79.
[5] Juss, "Rule-making and the Immigration Rules — A Retreat from Law?" (1992) 13 No. 2 Autumn *Statute Law Review*, pp. 150–164.
[6] Dummett and Nicol, *op. cit.* at p. 253–254.

Entry Certification: Politics, Policy and Reality

Since 1962 a voluntary entry clearance procedure had been available at posts overseas for intending immigrants. However this was only an optional facility. They could apply for this form of a stamp to be endorsed in their passport in New Delhi, Islamabad or Dacca, and enter without further difficulty through the port of entry in the United Kingdom. The Immigration Appeals Act 1969, in making entry certification compulsory, described it as "a certificate which . . . is to be taken as evidence of eligibility for admission into the United Kingdom".[7] The Immigration Appeals Act 1969 was itself presaged by the *Report of the Committee on Immigration Appeals*[8] set up in August 1967 by the Government under Sir Roy Wilson, Q.C., to consider what rights, if any, applicants should have in appealing an immigration decision against them. The concern of the "Wilson Committee", as it was popularly known, was one of "basic principle", in its own words, that "however well administered the present control may be, it is fundamentally wrong and inconsistent with the rule of law that power to take decisions affecting a man's whole future should be vested in officer's of the executive, from whose findings there is no appeal."[9] The Wilson Committee reported in 1969. It set its face against making entry certification mandatory. This was not, however, because it found the proposed procedure unhelpful, but rather because there was a fundamental point of principle involved here. It held:

> "When such a certificate is granted, the Commonwealth citizen who has properly obtained it has normally a virtual guarantee of admission. When it is refused, the Commonwealth citizen not only saves the cost of his fare but is relieved of the strain of waiting in a kind of no man's land for his fate to be decided at the port."

There was, however, the paradox of applying this requirement to Commonwealth citizens when "even the great majority of aliens were now free from the visa requirement."[10] In its view, it would be wrong to encumber the statutory rights of wives and children through the onerous imposition of compulsory certification upon them. The tenor of the Wilson Committee's recommendations was thus in favour of less restrictions, rather than more.

---

[7] Section 24(2).
[8] *Report of the Committee on Immigration Appeals*, Cmnd. 3387 (August 1967).
[9] *ibid.*, p. 280.
[10] *ibid.*, para. 70.

Nevertheless, in May 1969, the Labour Government announced its
intention to introduce compulsory certification. The political machi-
nations of this saga are most interesting. Mr James Callaghan, the
then Home Secretary, explained that the change was necessary
because many

> "dependants of Commonwealth citizens whose credentials for settlement
> in this country need detailed investigation, sometimes spread over several
> days. We have decided that it would be more humane and lead to
> improved efficiency if those with claims to settle here have their cases
> scrutinised and decided before they set out on their journey. The effect
> will be that Commonwealth dependants who satisfy the requirements will
> be issued before they leave their own country with an entry certificate by
> the British representative overseas. They will be admitted here only if
> they have such a certificate".[11]

He emphasised that the proposal was not meant to "reduce the
number of Commonwealth immigrants, nor are any rights of entry
taken away. The change is in substance *an administrative one.*"[12]
Information disseminated by the Government through British immigration agencies overseas similarly explained the new situation. Press
releases by British Information Services in Pakistan referred to the
unhappy situation of people detained at London Airport which
averaged 20 a day, rising perhaps to 40 over a weekend which the
new measures were designed to deal with. "The British Government
has," it claimed, "acted in the interests of the genuine immigrant."[13]
  In reality, this was not how the Labour Government fully viewed
the situation. When it was first discussed at a Cabinet Committee
meeting on October 7, 1968 Callaghan was himself against making
entry certificates compulsory as was everyone else. Only David
Ennals and Richard Crossman were in favour. Crossman vividly
explains in his Diaries that as far as he was concerned his main reason
was simply that the Labour Government should do it before the
Conservatives beat them to it:

> ". . . we had a paper signed by officials strongly opposing it. Callaghan
> started with a thoroughly reasoned statement of the arguments for not
> doing it, David Ennals made an extremely powerful case for doing it and

[11] *H.C. Official Report* (5th series), May 1, 1969 at cols 1631, 1633.
[12] *ibid.*
[13] See *Select Committee on Race Relations and Immigration* (1968–70), Control of Commonwealth Immigration (appendices and the Minutes of Evidence) May 27, 1970); 17
XXVIII at p. 83.

then everybody round the table, looking at their departmental briefs, said that if the Home Office didn't want certificates their Department didn't want them either. I then said, 'I am sure I am not the only one in the room this morning who is by no means certain that we shouldn't have them. I notice that this is one of the things Heath is demanding with Hogg's support. Should we turn them down flat: . . . surely if the Tories want compulsory entry certificates and with the issue of race looming largely over the election, we should be careful before turning this down.' Nobody gave an inch and finally I said, 'Are you quite sure that between now and the election we shan't have to introduce quotas? If you are going to refuse compulsory entry certificates and then concede on quotas you will get the worst of both worlds. I propose that this should be referred to the Parliamentary Committee.'"[14]

It was only then that everyone came around instantly. By April 1969 everyone was in favour of compulsory entry certificates and Crossman went on to recount on April 24, how six months ago last October he had been

"the only member of the Committee who had seen its advantages and who had pointed out that the Tories were demanding the same thing. I had said that we would have to do this some time and for God's sake we should do it quickly".

Crossman's detailed description of the affair is even more illuminating in demonstrating the importance of individual personalities in the formulation of policy. As he explains, at the Immigration Committee meeting of April 24, 1969,

". . . nobody except Judith, who was against the change, saw the difference between the official attitude last October and the attitude now. All the Ministers were briefed by the Officials to accept the change, including David Ennals, who I had thought might possibly join Judith. At the end of the meeting I asked Jim Callaghan what had made the difference and I learnt that when the chief immigration man at the Home Office had been shifted there had been a change of policy and something which Callaghan had not been able to get past his Department before had got past them now. To be fair, there was also the fact that this amendment could be tacked on to an Immigrant Appeals Bill, and of course with a system of appeal the requirement is far more justifiable. But it is one of those cases where one sees that when the officials are all against a policy it is difficult to get it through and when they switch the change can take place".[15]

[14] Crossman, *The Diaries of a Cabinet Minister* (London, Vols. 2–3, 1997), Vol. 3, pp. 214–215.
[15] *ibid.*, p. 454.

This was not, however, how voluntary and representative organisations outside Parliament saw the new change. The National Council for Civil Liberties regarded it as an attempt "to sabotage the operation"[16] of the 1969 Act on immigration appeal rights. The Joint Council for the Welfare of Immigrants (JCWI), a national independent organisation offering advice and representation on British immigration and nationality law issues today, and in existence since 1967, opposed the change because of the difficulties already existing for many applicants in presenting their cases at posts overseas. On the other hand, the Government continued to maintain the position that "there will be no question of an extremely long. examination because "it is not the intention of the amendment — nor could it be by virtue of the rights involved — to lead to a reduction in the manner of dependants coming in."[17]

The Government's view was soon disproven. The system began to operate like a quota on the number of family members admitted each year. Queues soon developed. The waiting period for first interview in the main settlement queue reached its meridian between 1974 and 1980 in the sub-continent:

Bangladesh	38 months	(1974)
Pakistan	23 3/4 months	(1980)
India	16 months	(New Delhi 1975/6, Bombay 1976)

By the end of the third quarter of 1981 the waiting times in all three countries were still very high:

(End of Sept 1981)	Those interviewed had waited	Those applying expected to wait
Bangladesh	22 months	18 months
Pakistan	20 1/4 months	12 months
India — New Delhi	12 months	15 months
Bombay	10 3/4 months	12 months[18]

[16] See *Memorandum of the National Council for Civil Liberties (NCCL) to the Select Committee on Race Relations and Immigration, op. cit.*, n.13 at p. 839.
[17] Quoted in the memorandum submitted by the JCWI to the *First Report from the Select Committee on Race Relations and Immigration* (1997–78 H.C. 303–I), p. 191.
[18] *Control of Immigration Statistics*, Cmnd. 8199 (1980), Table 5. Reproduced in JCWI Memorandum to the *Fifth Report from the Home Affairs Committee*, "Immigration from the Indian sub-continent", (1981–82) H.C. 90–I, p. 58.

In the 1990s, queues of this length are still very much in existence. They are not a thing of the past, nor do they show any signs of abating, as we shall see.[19]

Applying for Entry Certificate

These difficulties were bound to arise. The new procedure meant that an application was made for entry certificate, not by the more well-informed and better-placed sponsor in the United Kingdom, but by an invariably illiterate applicant in the Indian sub-continent unacquainted with the demands of British bureaucracy. The applicant had to make a personal visit to an overseas post merely to file an application. A further visit had to be made for the first interview and applicants were known to have travelled 280 miles one way to New Delhi for this purpose.[20] Documentary requirements that applicants had to meet were formidable and frequently unrealistic in the context of the societies concerned. It was not always made clear to an applicant that failure to produce listed documents was not fatal to the application so that genuine applicants often resorted to agents and scribes and presented false documents only to then be rejected. Those documents that were credible were given insufficient weight. Interviews which applicants underwent were essentially a search for discrepancies in the answers to questions asked. Many questions could not be unequivocally answered in the context of village extended households or were based on unrealistic expectations about what children knew about family relationships and circumstances and applicants could also be subjected to medical examinations which caused such a scandal in the 1970s.

In the 1980s the majority of applicants for entry clearance came from Bangladesh as this was the last group of New Commonwealth migrants to come to Britain. The pattern of migration from the West Indies and the Indian sub-continent showed that men came for work in the 1950s and 1960s and then sent for their families after quite long periods, frequently 10 to 15 years. Since the West Indians came first, followed by Indians, Pakistanis and finally, the Bangladeshis, the migration of families followed the same pattern, with the result that before the Immigration Appeals Act 1969 required entry certificates for dependents, most West Indian families had already arrived.[21]

---

[19] See *infra*, pp. 49–50.
[20] See *Amar Kaur v. Secretary of State for the Home Department* TH/990/71, d. 11.8.71 (unreported) at p. 2.
[21] Juss, *Immigration, Nationality and Citizenship, op. cit.*, at p. 39.

The number of Indian families entering the United Kingdom began to decline sharply in the mid-1970s and the Pakistani figures declined in the late 1970s. However, many of the male immigrants from Bangladesh came here in around 1963, with a small surge in 1972. Dependent migrants in the Indian sub-continent came generally from a few geographically well-defined areas. In India, they came mainly from the Jullunder district in the Punjab and from the Gujarat; in Pakistan, from the Mirpur district of Azad Kashmir; and in Bangladesh, from the Sylhet district. All of these areas were generally poor and exhibited broadly similar characteristics. It is suggested that important lessons can be learnt from this because in the 1990s there are yet new demands on entry certificates from entirely new regions, which are described by the Home Affairs Committee in its 1990 Report and which look set to cause new problems.

The Home Affairs Committee Report in 1990

The Home Affairs Committee is appointed to examine the expenditure, administration and policy of the Home Office. In 1990 it defined five identifiable aspects to British immigration policy. First, the control exercised through entry clearance procedures. These, as we have seen, comprise the obtaining of a visa or an entry certificate or a letter of consent[22] before departure for the United Kingdom to ensure entry upon arrival. The Committee found that the imposition of visa requirements on ever more countries in recent years, now put "greater emphasis on this aspect"[23] of immigration control. Secondly, as emphasised by the Committee, there was the work carried out by the Immigration Service at ports of entry under which immigration officers were empowered to grant limited or indefinite leave to immigrants to enter, subject to conditions if necessary, or refuse them leave altogether.[24] Thirdly, the Committee highlighted the after-entry controls in which both the Immigration and Nationality Department (IND) and the Immigration Service played a large part:

---

[22] These are issued at British Embassies, High Commissions or Consulates abroad before travel to the U.K. The people who have to apply before travel are the visa nationals (and are listed in the immigration rules), the people who are coming to permanently settle here and people who are coming to work. Other people may apply voluntarily to reduce problems upon arrival.

[23] See the Home Affairs Committee Report on *Administrative Delays in the Immigration and Nationality Department* (1989–90, H.C. 319) p. v., para. 5.

[24] *Loc. cit.*

variations of leave to stay in the United Kingdom were dealt with by the IND, while the Immigration Service carried out both the enforcement powers under the Immigration Act 1971 as well as the deportation procedures under the Immigration Act 1988. Fourthly, the Committee drew attention to the exercise of detention powers pending expulsion, as being an important aspect of control of illegal entrants, deportees and others who may be awaiting removal from the United Kingdom. Finally, the Committee wished to point out that there was an appeals system, critical to the provision of due process, for those adversely affected by the exercise of these powers.

Clearly the first of these five aspects is the most important in terms of its potential worldwide effect. The Home Affairs Committee, when sitting, has wide powers to send for persons, papers and records and to appoint specialist advisers to supply them with information. It heard evidence from Mr Montgomery, the Head of the Foreign and Commonwealth Office (FCO), Migration and Visa Department, that demand for entry clearance throughout the world is growing, and that this is "a reflection of the vastly greater volume of people wanting to travel today, either wanting to travel or wanting to travel and settle."[25] Particular mention was made of pressure on posts in Eastern Europe, caused by recent political changes there, and the FCO, predicting growths in applications of up to 150 per cent in 1990, told the Committee that it had increased staffing levels at some posts to meet the demand. The FCO said that these rising demands have "been taken fully into account in our forward projections on the supply of staff".[26]

This did not satisfy the Home Affairs Committee which was unhappy with the way these aspects of British immigration policy were being administered. It had already expressed concern in 1986 in a most thorough review of entry clearance procedures over the variations in waiting times between various posts throughout the world. In 1990 it found that it was still not easy to estimate the average waiting time between first interview and a decision at a post, because it depended on whether a case needed referring to London, and some posts referred cases more frequently than others which caused longer delays.[27] There was a waiting time of four months for a second time applicant interviewed in Karachi in 1989, while one in Islamabad had to wait 23 months! In Bangkok, the average waiting time for those seeking entry clearance for settlement, according to

---

[25] *ibid.*, p. xi, para. 30.
[26] *Loc. cit.*
[27] *ibid.*, p. x, para. 25.

the Committee, was eight weeks, in Manila 16 weeks and in Kingston, Jamaica 20 weeks! "Nevertheless, the delays in the sub-continent" it said, remained the worst.[28] Yet ironically, as we have seen the system of entry clearance certification was introduced in 1969 precisely to cater for, and expedite, the applications of entrants from the Indian sub-continent.

The Committee was also dissatisfied over the question of staffing. It found that although the number of arrivals at United Kingdom ports was expected to have risen between 1984–85 and 1989–90 by 39 per cent and applications for refugee status by asylum seekers had risen even more markedly,[29] there were serious problems of under-staffing and poor training of personnel resulting in low morale. Even more seriously, at the IND at Lunar House in Croydon the Committee found there to be an "enforced freeze on recruitment since September 1989", so that:

> "At the beginning of March 1990 the gap between budgeted posts and staff in post had grown to 121.5 — the largest gap since at least before 1987. This is a self-inflicted wound: the result of *a deliberate policy rather than recruitment difficulties*. The trades unions at the IND told us that the cessation of recruitment had led to 'a poorer service to the public . . . an identifiable fall in staff morale' and was 'not cost-effective in the long term'."[30] (Author's emphasis.)

A voluntary immigrant representative organisation gave evidence that "new staff are not always adequately trained before they take on their duties . . . Staff morale is low, and staff turnover high, because the volume of casework produces little job satisfaction".[31] The Civil and Public Services Association (CPSA), a trade union representing clerical and typing grade staff within the IND, said that "morale . . . is extremely low due to constant understaffing and poor training."[32] The position was, again ironically, even worse in the Indian sub-continent where delays induced by falling staffing levels were known to have persisted for many years. The Committee therefore urged the IND "to resume recruitment at once to ensure that the number of staff in post matched budgeted posts by the end of 1990."[33] This meant more expenditure on which the Home Office did not have a

---

[28] *ibid.*, p. xii, para. 34.
[29] *ibid.*, p. xvii, para. 45.
[30] *ibid.*, p. xix, para. 53.
[31] *ibid.*, p. xix, para. 54.
[32] *Loc. cit.*
[33] *ibid.*, p. xix, para. 55.

good record because although "significant real terms increases are planned for the next three financial years", these increases "seem less noted when they are measured against indicators of demand for the services of the IND".[34] In this setting the Home Affairs Committee was forced to conclude that,

> "We would not wish the IND to be the Cinderella of any future internal Home Office review of expenditure priorities, nor should the IND's budget be used to compensate for deficiencies elsewhere in the Home Office".[35]

The evidence therefore indicates that there is clearly a policy of short-termism in respect of immigration affairs and it is bound also to affect the system of administrative appeals in immigration law, where most appeals first go to an Immigration Adjudicator and thereafter to the three-member Immigration Appeals Tribunal. The Home Affairs Committee emphasised the importance of the immigration appeals procedure as helping to "provide a vital safeguard against alleged tightening of immigration control or unfair decisions by those enforcing the immigration rules".[36] Indeed, the number of appeals considered by Adjudicators "increased from 11,605 in 1987 to 22,136 in 1989".[37] Yet the Committee was quick to note that, "As with other aspects of immigration control work, the backlog of immigration appeals has grown steadily in recent years" so that by "the end of 1989 over 21,000 cases were outstanding, almost as many cases as were considered by the adjudicators in that year".[38] Once again, the Committee was perturbed by this and held that "The current delays are clearly quite unacceptable,"[39] and here again the situation was particularly serious in relation to appeals from those in the Indian sub-continent with the result that the Committee considered the possibility of conducting entry clearance appeals in the sub-continent, but found both the FCO and the Lord Chancellor's Department opposed to this proposal.

It is submitted that this disagreement suggests there to be a fundamental issue relating to aims and purposes here. Is the immigration service there to prevent abuse or is it there to provide a service to potential immigrants and their relatives settled here? In

[34] *ibid.*, p. xvii, para. 45.
[35] *ibid.*, p. xviii, para. 50.
[36] *ibid.*, p. xiii, para. 35.
[37] *ibid.*, p. xiii, para. 37.
[38] *ibid.*, p. xiii, para. 36.
[39] *ibid.*, p. xv, para. 38.

1990 the Tory-dominated Home Affairs Committee went further in addressing this question in favour of the latter principle than any other Committee before it. The Committee's Report entitled, *Administrative Delays in the Immigration and Nationality Department*, opened with the principled and uncompromising remark that "The effectiveness and fairness with which the IND performs its work affects both the maintenance of good race relations within the United Kingdom and Britain's standing in the world."[40] In its conclusions it showed a clear sympathy for the views of representative and voluntary organisations such as United Kingdom Immigrants Advisory Service (UKIAS), a registered charity funded by the Home Office and providing representation and advice in half of all appeals, and the JCWI, a voluntary body, that what was basically needed was a change of culture in immigration work that concentrated more on providing a service. Thus the JCWI told the Committee that administrative delay in the IND arose from

"... a pervasive attitude to immigration matters which *stresses the negative, control element*: that the role of immigration staff is to prevent abuse rather than to provide a service."[41] (Author's emphasis.)

UKIAS told the Committee that administrative delays within the IND were connected to the control of immigration which were

"... placing serious obstacles in the *path of those seeking to exercise their legitimate immigration rights* under the law and the rules. The result was that people were having to wait unreasonably long times (periods of years in some cases) to have their cases dealt with by the system, so much so that the underlying pattern of immigration into the United Kingdom was actually being distorted by delay."[42] (Author's emphasis.)

Mr Langdon, the Head of the IND, however told it that:

"We should not flinch from the difficult decisions that need to be taken in immigration control work, but neither do I think we should glory in them. I think that we should aim to operate a clean professionally run service. I do not think that we can forget that the service that we are operating is a *regulatory* one. *It is the immigration control business*."[43] (Author's emphasis.)

---

[40] *ibid.*, p. 5, para. 1.
[41] *ibid.*, p. 21, para. 61.
[42] *ibid.*, *loc. cit.*
[43] *ibid.*, p. 21, para. 62.

Clearly, there is an ambivalence of approach here to the question of purpose. This must first be resolved if the practice in this area is to be reformed. It is, however, significant that the Home Affairs Committee's own response was to recognise the viewpoint of the representative organisations on this occasion:

> "A poor quality of service within the IND cannot be attributable solely to concern with immigration control, since it is apparent in the nationality work of the Department, which does not directly affect immigration control. Nevertheless, poor service gives rise to *understandable suspicion that bureaucratic delay is an instrument of control*."[44] (Author's emphasis.)

The Committee had no hesitation in concluding that, "considerable improvements can be made to the quality of service offered to the public by the IND without affecting the statutory obligations of the IND with regard to immigration control".[45] However, no practice can ever be reformed satisfactorily unless its underlying policy basis is first altered. It may well be said that Government policy over the years has not at all been in line with what the Committee proposed in 1990.

Government Policy

Evidence submitted at the end of 1981 by the Home Office to the *Fifth Report from the Home Affairs Committee on Immigration from the Indian sub-continent* explained the Government's immigration policy to be as follows:

> "The basis of the Government's policy is the belief that firm immigration control is essential to achieve good community relations. To that end the Government's policy has three broad objectives. First, it is the Government's *aim to restrict primary immigration* — that is the admission for settlement of heads of household in their own right — as tightly as is consistent with humanity and the country's need for scarce skills. Second, the Government is firmly committed to continuing the special voucher scheme for United Kingdom Passport holders, and to accepting for settlement the wives and children of men settled here. Third, the Government is determined to take firm action to enforce the immigration control against those who overstay and against illegal entrants."[46] (Author's emphasis.)

---

[44] *ibid.*, p. xxi, paras. 61 and 62.
[45] *ibid.*, p. xxi, para. 62.
[46] *Fifth Report, op. cit.*, Vol. II, p. 1, para. 2.

As a Commission of Racial Equality (CRE) report observes, "Governments have never denied that the procedures used have placed difficult obstacles in the way of genuine applicants. They have consistently argued, however, that the procedures have been as fair as they could be in all the circumstances given the need to prevent 'evasion and abuse' of the control".[47] Thus in 1979 the Government's response before the Select Committee on Race Relations and Immigration was to say that,

"The prevention and detection of attempted evasion and abuse of the control, where it is shown to exist, is one of the main features of the Government's immigration policy . . . It is a regrettable though *inevitable consequence* of the need to prevent abuse that *some genuine applicants suffer inconvenience*, for example those who have to travel long distances for entry clearance interviews in their country of origin".[48] (Author's emphasis.)

The most striking effect of the pursuance of this policy is that there has been a decline in the level of total immigration into the United Kingdom from the New Commonwealth since 1978.[49] Between 1976 and 1979 the total acceptances for settlement form the Indian sub-continent were between 24,000 and 27,000 annually, comprising one-third of all settlement. This fell to 22,300 in 1980, comprising 32 per cent of all settlement.[50] The emphasis on admitting dependants but curtailing further primary immigration is reflected, once again, in the percentages of total arrivals for settlement. For much of the 1980s, 90 per cent of all settlers from Bangladesh and Pakistan were women and children; for India the figure was 60 per cent of all settlers.[51]

However, in line with the general declining trend for all categories, applications for settlement by wives and children have also dropped markedly. From a figure of 24,000 to 26,000 per annum for the years 1977–1979 inclusive, there was a drop to under 19,000 in 1980, while in the twelve months ending September 1981, only 14,200 applied. This fall affected all types of applicants. In Pakistan new applications fell from 13,000 in 1977 and 1978 to as low as 5,000 in 1982. Similarly, in India applications fell from 6,000 between 1977 to 1979

[47] See *Immigration Control Procedures: Report of a Formal Investigation*, by the Commission for Racial Equality, February 1985, p. 7, para. 2.4.1.
[48] *First Report from the Select Committee on Race Relations and Immigration* (1997–78, H.C. 303–I).
[49] *Supra*, Vol II, p. 141, Q.479.
[50] *ibid.*, Vol. I, p. v., para. 1.
[51] *ibid.*, p. 4, para. 15. Also see *Control of Immigration Statistics*, Cmnd. 1899 (1980), Table 12.

to 3,000 in 1982.[52] However in Bangladesh, applications rose from 5,000 in 1977 to 8,000 in 1979 and although they then fell to 6,000 in 1982, this figure was still above the level of applications in 1977.[53] These figures suggested that other than in Bangladesh, most wives and children from the Indian sub-continent had by the 1980s joined their husbands here.

In the number of applications that were actually granted by the authorities, a similar pattern was seen with the special position of Bangladesh being preserved once more. The total number of applications fell from 20,500 in 1977 to under 16,000 in the 12 months ending September 30, 1981. The fall occurred only in India and Pakistan. In Bangladesh, the applications granted rose from 3,400 in 1977 to 6,300 in 1982. Overall, the rate of refusal was 30 per cent of all applications made.[54]

The queues also naturally fell in the last decade. The number of people awaiting decisions on their applications for entry clearance for immediate settlement fell from 28,000 at the end of 1978 to just over 17,000 at the end of September 1981. However, the change varied from one country to another. In India it altered little between the end of 1978 to September 30, 1981; in Pakistan it fell from 12,000 to about 3,000 for the same period; and in Bangladesh it fell from just over 13,000 to just over 11,000 in the same time. In both Bangladesh and Pakistan the waiting period for non-priority applicants before their first interview had remained just under two years since the end of 1978. In India, the waiting time in New Delhi actually doubled from about six months in 1977 to one year. This is confounding and once again ironical because, given that the pool of dependants is finite and (as the figures show) declining, the aim, so far as possible, should have been to increase the rate of processing, or at any rate to maintain its existing levels. Instead, it had been cut by half due to scarce resources. These disparities in waiting times in the 1990s have continued as demonstrated, and are indeed no less dramatic.

It is important to note that the basis of entry for these wives and children, who presently constitute Britain's major immigration commitment, is their statutory entitlement to settlement as the families of men settled here on January 1, 1973 when the Immigration Act 1971 came into force. In the 1990s this statutory entitlement will finally come to an end, making this area of practice ripe for a penetrating

---

[52] *ibid.*, Vol I, p. xlix, Annex 2.
[53] *ibid.*, Vol. II, p. 4, para. 18.
[54] *Loc. cit.*

and critical evaluative analysis. So will the number of wives in other categories come to an end. The only commitment that will remain will be that of wives and children of men who have been allowed to settle here after four years of approved employment.[55] However, if the issue of work permits peters out, so too will the number of wives and children under this head, although in the 1990s this is now more unlikely than it was in the 1980's.[56]

The reductions, as this section reveals, have not all been achieved as a consequence of the numbers applying but also as a result of a Government policy that accepts that "genuine applicants suffer inconvenience" caused by the manner of the administration of immigration control.

The Surveys and Studies

Empirical work on the administration of the entry clearance system had in fact already been undertaken in the 1980s. In 1982 UKIAS sent out a research team on village visits to Bangladesh for five months. Its findings were published in its *Split Families* Report.[57] Originally, the team investigated 100 unsuccessful cases of dependants. In 45 of these cases a thorough anthropological research through field investigations, supplemented by academic research, was carried out. The team visited the village home of applicants and discussions were carried out with administrative authorities.[58] The

---

[55] The rules were revised thoroughly in 1994 and all administrative decisions taken on or before October 1, 1994 are now subject to the later rules of H.C. 395. But the previous rules, H.C. 251, will remain relevant at the appellate level for many years yet. Thus para. 122 of the previous immigration rules states that if an extension to remain is given to a work permit holder, "A corresponding extention should be granted to the applicant's spouse and children . . .": see *Statement of Changes in Immigration Rules* (March 23, 1990, H.C. 251), para. 122. See also H.C. 395, paras. 122–127 for the later rules.

[56] The previous immigration rules allow "the holder of a current work permit, incuding a permit for training and work experience" to be admitted and "permitting him to take or change employment" with the permission of the Department of Employment: see *Statement of Changes in Immigrations Rules, op. cit.*, para. 35 and see paras. 204, 215, 225 and 233 of H.C. 395 for the later rules. In recent years this provision has been very useful to employers who have wanted to apply for work permits for workers to fill in specialist posts for which equally qualified resident labour was not available.

[57] *Split Families*, An Examination of the Immigration Control System Relating to Dependants, in Bangladesh (UKIAS Research Project 1982).

[58] These included the passport issuing authorities, the Civil Surgeon, the District Commissioner of Sylhet, various bank managers, postmasters, etc.

cases had certain common features. For example, they were mostly applications of the entire family, that is, wife and children; they were all refused by the ECO on the ground of "discrepancies" in the answers to questions asked; appeals to adjudicators were subsequently dismissed; and leave to appeal to the Tribunal was invariably refused in all cases. At the end, the team was able to draw a number of clear conclusions. It found that refusals were based on discrepancies regarding birth, age, schooling, names of distant relatives and close "affinal" relations, concept of time and distance, and so forth. In many cases the only basis for refusal was a difference between the claimed age and the British High Commission Medical Officer's assessment of the age of the applicant. The team found that many of the so-called discrepancies arose from misunderstandings of certain socio-cultural customs, norms and beliefs prevalent in that society. Out of 35 unsuccessful cases originally investigated in depth, it was felt that the wife and any children below the age of two were genuinely related.[59] In a number of cases the team was "satisfied beyond reasonable doubt", and "sometimes beyond a shadow of doubt", that the applicants were related to the sponsor in the United Kingdom.[60]

An even more ambitious project was a four year survey published by the CRE in February 1984.[61] This included similar empirical work and concluded that families are deliberately prevented from uniting, and since this is the most detailed of all surveys it will be extensively referred to in this work as and when necessary.

The most important official study of entry clearance procedures at this time was the *Fifth Report from the Home Affairs Committee on Immigration from the Indian sub-continent* published in 1982. This Report reached similar conclusions to the studies above and even commended the *Split Families* report to ECOs "to improve further their ability to appreciate the difficulties of applicants" since "to

[59] *Supra*, n.57, pp. iv, v and vi.
[60] *Supra*, n.46, Vol. II, Mr. Choudhary pp. 114–115. This finding has parallels with a Runnymede Trust investigation of 58 cases undertaken in 1977. (See memorandum of the Runnymede Trust to the *First Report*, *op. cit.*, Vol. I, pp. 175–187). It found that generally speaking, the standard of proof required of applicants was "beyond any doubt". (at p. 181).
[61] *Immigration Control Procedures*: Report of a Formal Investigation (CRE, London, 1985). Reforms at the Immigration and Nationality Department, (based in Croydon), recently seem to have been instituted, in part at least, as an attempt "to preempt criticisms which are expected" following the publication of this Report: See New Society, July 26, 1984, p. 30.

conduct interviews fairly requires some knowledge, of Bangladeshi Society".[62] The mandate of the Committee was to examine "what" trends can be observed in immigration as a whole" and the "working of the entry clearance system" with an "attempt to judge how effective it was and whether its operation could be improved"[63] and once again, it was concerned "primarily with the position in Bangladesh".[64]

All these reports highlighted similar concerns and similar trends and they led to considerable awareness about the arbitrary aspects of modern immigration control, especially in its implementation of the entry clearance system. The matter was critical to family reunification, which the Government was committed to preserving, and its findings were therefore all the more important for that purpose. No similarly thorough and detailed surveys have been undertaken since of this, or any other substantive sphere of immigration control. As a result extensive reference is made in this study to the penetrating insights afforded by these three reports which are remarkably consistent in their findings and the concerns highlighted in them. Although these concerns are not all unrelated, they can be broken down into the following: (i) that the delays inherent in the system are unacceptable; (ii) that the system is inaccurate; (iii) that it is, in fact, deliberately unfair in its operation; and (iv) that it takes no account of the socio-cultural norms and conditions of the societies in which it operates. These are grave charges against a system that was avowedly created "in the interests of the genuine immigrant".[65] In the next chapter accordingly, the problem is first described in its context; it is then assessed from the viewpoint of those independent investigations that have helped in the 1980s to highlight it; and finally, its relevance is evaluated from the perspective of the author's own findings in the decided appeal cases. Such a methodology involving detailed analyses at each stage is vital. No understanding of immigration official decision making is possible without some comprehension of what these problems are, how they arise and how they eventually impact on the appeals system. Accordingly, we must first examine these issues.

---

[62] See *Fifth Report, op. cit.*, Vol. I at p. xviii–xix, para. 48.
[63] *ibid.*, at Vol. I, p. vi, para. 4.
[64] *ibid.*, p. vii, para. 9.
[65] *Supra*, p. 43 at n.13.

Chapter Two

Delays, Inaccuracies and the Extended Family Pattern

Decency, security and liberty alike demand that government officials shall be subjected to the same rules of conduct that are commands to the citizen. In a government of laws, existence of the government will be imperilled if it fails to observe the law scrupulously. If the Government becomes a law-breaker, it breeds contempt for law."

> Mr Justice Louis D. Brandeis (dissenting) in
> *Olmstead v. United States*, 277 U.S. 438 (1928).

Delays

Practitioners in this field experience many delays. These are caused by protracted methods of verification at posts overseas. However, if reduction of immigrant numbers is one objective of immigration law, then it could be argued that institutionalised delay is an obvious method of achieving it. It can be applied at any number of places from the time that an application is lodged to the time that an appeal against its refusal is heard. A decade after the system of compulsory entry certification was introduced by the Immigration Appeals Act 1969 delays were so commonplace that they were considered to be "the greatest source of grievance within the Asian Community" and "souring race relations by prolonging the separation of families and denying educational opportunity to children whose working lives are to be in Britain".[1] More important than the delays were the reasons

---

[1] Memorandum by JCWI to the *First Report from the Select Committee on Race Relations and Immigration* (1977–78 H.C. 303–I), Vol. I, pp. 192–193.

for the delays, for the general belief amongst immigrants and immigrant groups was that they were the result of a deliberate policy, rather than necessity. Two decades after the system was introduced the JCWI in 1981 complained that "Its ostensible causes are the time-consuming methods of 'verification' used. But even if these are taken as given, delays are a function of the unwillingness to make available adequate staff resources".[2] Three decades later in 1990 the Home Affairs Committee, in looking at administrative delays, itself accepted the delays to be dictated by a deliberate Home Office policy. There have been three aspects to delay that require mentioning.

First, delay in obtaining an interview date is only the first delay that many applicants will endure. In Bangladesh at least 40 per cent of all applications are either deferred for further local inquiries or referred to the Home Office in London for the Sponsor to be interviewed there. Some nine months may pass before the applicant is re-interviewed again at the post overseas.

Secondly, "patrial" wives and children have been prevented from early entry by the imposition of a queue which unlawfully requires them to submit to delays, particularly in Bangladesh. A child applicant whose father is a British citizen is himself a British citizen by descent and a woman who married a British citizen before December 31, 1982 (when the British Nationality Act came into force) is a patrial having the right of abode in the United Kingdom.[3] A substantial proportion of applicants from Bangladesh fall into this category.

Thirdly, section 1(1) of the Immigration Act 1971 expressly states that, "All those who are in this Act expressed to have the right of abode in the United Kingdom shall be free to live in, and to come and go into and from, the United Kingdom without let or hindrance . . .". In this respect, delay of any manner infringes this rule. When two wives of patrial men who were settled in Britain from India and Bangladesh decided to travel to England rather than submit their applications at posts overseas, Lord Denning M.R. said:

> "If they had been able to do so, each of those ladies would have applied there. They would not have undertaken the long and expensive trip to England. As things are, however, a wife who applies in Bombay or Dacca for a certificate of patriality has to join a long queue of those who require leave to enter. By the time she is granted an interview, 14 months or more will have passed."[4]

---

[2] Memorandum by JCWI to the *Fifth Report from the Home Affairs Committee on Race Relations and Immigration* (1981–82 H.C. 90–I), Vol. II, p. 58, para. 3.
[3] See *British Nationality Act 1981*, s.3(9).
[4] *R v. Secretary of State for the Home Department, ex parte Phansopkar* [1975] 3 All E.R. 497 at 507.

Lord Scarman objected to how "the delay may impose great hardship and stress on private and family life" and quoting from Magna Carta, that "Justice delayed is justice denied" went on to ask:

> "What principle or authority in English law requires the court to read into the rule a let or hindrance on the exercise of the right which the rule does not specify? I know of none. The Act, after all, does describe the right as freedom. If the Secretary of State wishes to compel these applicants to stand in that long queue waiting in India and Bangladesh, he should say so in an appropriate immigration rule so that all who claim the right may know."[5]

As everyone knows, however, no immigration rule has ever specified the matter of delays for the benefit of intending applicants that followed in the wake of making entry certification compulsory. Yet even in the 1990s this remained a matter of principal concern for the Home Affairs Committee as we saw earlier when it considered the administration of immigration control.

Inaccuracy of the System

Inaccuracy is often a by-product of delays when the delay is caused by methods of verification, and the regular practitioner in this field will be aware of this. Delays are followed by a high refusal rate, which is a second source of complaint of the operation of the entry clearance system. In 1981 one-third of all applicants for immediate settlement were refused. Three-quarters of these appealed and less than a quarter were then successful.[6] It was the combination of delays and high refusals that prompted the Home Affairs Committee to then undertake its review:

> If these delays, which do still exist however rapidly they might be falling, were the only or major cause of concern over immigration from the Sub-Continent there would have been little justification for our having undertaken a major inquiry . . . Concern still exists over whether the way in which applicants are required to prove their relationship to their sponsor is, given the *local circumstances* . . . unfair. Some argue that entry clearance officers (ECOs) refuse applicants on the grounds of *trivial discrepancies* regardless of the weight of any other evidence that the applicant is related to the sponsor as claimed."[7] (Author's emphasis.)

---

[5] *ibid.*, p. 512, E and F.
[6] See *Fifth Report, op. cit.*, Vol. I, p. v, para. 2.
[7] *Loc. cit.* In fact, this was one of the two reasons for the Home Affairs Committee's investigations. The other reason was the concern over second generation immigrants marrying in the sub–continent, referred to as the "second-generation effect".

The system is therefore inaccurate as it fails to take into account "local circumstances" and attaches undue importance to "trivial discrepancies". These allegations require further examination if they are to be justified.

(1) THE DISCREPANCY SYSTEM

The "discrepancy system" means that even if an applicant has satisfied the legal standard of proof his application will be dismissed if there are discrepancies in the answers that he has given to questions asked. The "system" operates by questioning each applicant separately (with special arrangements being made for children) as to every detail of family life and history, partly in accordance with a printed questionnaire. If the answers of the interviewees do not then correspond, a discrepancy arises which can form the basis of an ECOs decision to refuse. It is justified on the basis that if the parties are truly related there should not be any discrepancies in what they say.

There is some justification for this approach in regard to applicants from the Third World. In Sylhet, Bangladesh, the immigration authorities had encountered genuine difficulties. There was little documentation in the country which meant that illiterate villagers often had recourse to scribes and touts in an attempt to produce documentary evidence at the interview. Sometimes bogus applicants masqueraded as sons of the wife and sponsor because of the pressure amongst families to migrate. There were many cases of Sylheti men who declared false dependent children to the Income Tax authorities in the United Kingdom in order to increase their tax allowances and when they had to prove their claim they too would have recourse to falsified documents.[8] These are, however, problems that can arise from any country where there is pressure to migrate, particularly in the Third World. It is, however, the job of governments and their bureaucracies to respond to these problems and this is a point well worth making in representations before the Tribunal. Government authorities must not themselves become prey to the problems. They must still make sure that the genuine applicant is always — without exception — admitted, but the bogus one is not. If they fail to see this, they may be accused of taking the easy way out of these problems. In 1982 a JCWI Executive member explained the matter thus to the Home Affairs Committee:

---

[8] See Memorandum by UKIAS to the Home Affairs Committee, Race Relations and Immigration Sub-Committee (1983–84, H.C. 223), p. 17, paras. 16 and 17.

"One of the most saddening aspects of dealing with this sort of problem is that although you can often arrive at a decision where you are quite certain that the relationship is as claimed, perhaps because, as in my experience, I have walked round a village and asked everybody about the particular family, nevertheless the adjudicator still feels unhappy because he has not resolved the discrepancy in the evidence which he regards as important. He has evidence that the family is related as claimed but does not understand why the wife has said that the husband's cousin has x children and things like that, and therefore the appeal is dismissed and one is left with the position where one knows quite well that it is quite genuine".[9]

The criticism is, however, rejected by the former Minister for Immigration, Mr Raison:

". . . there is not something called the discrepancy system; it is more of a factual system. What essentially the system is doing is looking at facts. It is trying to find out whether certain facts stated are accurate or inaccurate. Whether this system is a perfect system, whether the collection of facts is perfect or not, obviously sometimes one gets it wrong. I can think of cases where we have been wrong. What I would say is that by and large it is operated thoroughly and there is, of course, behind it an appeals system . . . and there is a relatively high success rate at appeal . . . and I would not accept the overall system is an inadequate system".[10]

The view of the JCWI is, however, that the system is flawed, because "if you interview members of a family for hours about their domestic circumstances and family history you will always come across differences which can be elevated into a reason for refusal".[11] Young children still continue to be interviewed. There is a strong probability that their evidence will be riddled with discrepancies.[12] It seems that children as young as five years have been interviewed.[13] In 1977, the Central Policy Review Staff recommended that "children under the age of 14 should no longer be interviewed in full but they should be asked to attend with an adult relative in case an obvious discrepancy in their age emerges". Children aged 10 to 14 are, however, still interviewed, although no longer alone.[14]

---

[9] See the *Fifth Report*, *op. cit.*, Vol. II, p. 78, Q.258.
[10] *ibid.*, pp. 144–143, Q.489.
[11] *Supra*, n.1, Vol. II, p. 63, para. 28. JCWI stated that the discrepancy system for this reason acts as a sort of lucky dip.
[12] See, *e.g.*, the cases of *Roushan Begum* and *Maqsood Begum*, *infra*. nn.15 and 16.
[13] *Supra*, n.2, Vol. II, p. 62, para. 26.
[14] See also *Immigration Control Procedures: Report of a Formal Investigation* where the CRE following their discussions with ECOs in Bangladesh recorded that, "one ECO mentioned interviewing a child of 'nine or ten' and others told us that they would not interview a child under the age of about ten, and would interview those between about ten and 13–14 years of age in the company of an adult" (CRE, London, February 1985), p. 35, para. 4.9.4.

The writer's own research has pointed to some of these difficulties in the decided cases. In *Roushon Begum v. Entry Clearance Officer Dacca* a 15-year-old boy was asked the names of elderly relatives which he did not know. The Tribunal said, "The explanatory statement shows the various discrepancies on family matters between the principal appellant (*i.e.* the wife) and the appellant Mohd Zakaria"[15] being the youngest of four children who sought entry. In *Maqsood Begum v. Visa Officer Islamabad* the Tribunal again found discrepancies between what the wife and a 12-year-old child from Pakistan (who sought entry as her son), had to say. It said: "Khalid (*i.e.* the child) knew very little of the events surrounding the alleged deaths of his brother Maqsood and his sister Shaheen".[16] Again, this was one of the reasons which led to the refusal. Similarly, the CRE research team in Bangladesh found that ECOs were obsessed with discrepancies. In all the applications that it investigated at posts, it found that "it was normal practice to check any files which may be related to the application, for example, the file on the sponsor and any other relative who may previously have applied for entry clearance".[17] The applicant's file or dossier would then be checked against any related or "link" file. These findings correspond to what the JCWI found in its survey. Thus in one application of a woman and her three claimed sons, the ECO noted: "Unable to find any more links but have enough to refuse." In another an ECO wrote:

> "We would be in trouble without the related papers as the only thing we
> would have to go on otherwise would be her leaving out (M) at first
> interview and discrepancies on twins or not twins. However, related
> papers are strong enough evidence to tie this lot. Refuse them all, (Second
> Secretary) agrees."[18]

The CRE team also found ample evidence to show that applications were dismissed on the basis of "trivial discrepancies". Indeed, in some cases it is questionable whether the term "discrepancy" is an appropriate description. They explained that:

> ". . . a Second Secretary in Dhaka said that, in the 'broad mass' of cases, it
> was a matter of whether applicants agreed on how they lived their lives,
> what they had done and what they were doing; if they could not agree on
> that, it was sufficient to refuse without going too much further. Another

---

[15] TH/23944/78 (1824) d. 22.7.80 (unreported) at p. 2.
[16] TH/25569/78 (1840) d. 28.8.80 (unreported), 2.
[17] *Immigration Control Procedures, supra*, n.14, p. 37, paras. 4.14.1 and 4.14.2.
[18] *ibid.*, p. 39, paras. 4.14.5 and 4.14.6.

senior officer said that the applicant would be expected to describe the house and its surroundings. In Islamabad we were told that it was expected that genuine relatives would know their family tree and living accommodation and inability to answer questions about them would throw doubt on the claimed relationship".[19]

A recently appointed ECO told the team that "when he first started he asked what he now regarded as irrelevant questions, such as the colour of the sari worn by a woman at the wedding". However, the CRE Report states that despite the acceptance by this ECO of the "irrelevance" of such a question, "a letter seen by CRE staff at the post about an interview to be conducted with a sponsor in the UK asked for him to be asked about the colour of the sari his claimed wife wore at the wedding along with other details of the wedding". In Islamabad, one ECO referred to such questions as where the water was obtained and "what material the house was built of".[20] The decided cases that the writer himself investigated bear this out. In one case from Pakistan, the Tribunal allowed an appeal because, "some of the differences are of no real import — whether the buffaloes provided milk or not — and did not take the matter any further". It continued:

"There remain the differences in the accounts of the wedding of Razzia [*i.e.* the daughter]. We doubt whether any bride's father would have precisely the same recollection of the details of his daughter's wedding as the bride's mother after an interval of 3 years".[21]

In *Visa Officer Islamabad v. Alam Bi* questions were asked by the ECO of the number of children that the wife's brother had and "all the interviewees told the ECO that Ishmail (wife's brother) had only one son, Nadim, aged 16/17 years. The sponsor told the adjudicator that Irshad had two children".[22] The evidential value of such a question is doubtful however, even if it could be accurately answered, as is the question "as to who, if anybody, met the sponsor at the airport on his arrival in Pakistan shortly before the interviews with the ECO," since here again any number of people could have gone to meet the sponsor apart from his immediate family. In *Visa Officer Islamabad v. Sabran Bi* the ECO listed a number of "major discrepancies" in the

---

[19] *ibid.*, p. 35, para. 4.9.8.
[20] *ibid.*, p. 35, paras. 4.9.10 and 4.9.11.
[21] *Sarwar Begum v. Visa Officer Islamabad* TH/9141/76 (1266) d. 12.7.78 (unreported), at p. 3–4.
[22] TH/20164/77 (1373) d. 3.10.78 (unreported), at 3–4.

explanatory statement consisting of "the number of return visits to Pakistan made by the sponsor; the length of time the family had had their buffalo, the location of Chaman's school, the names of Chaman's barber and tailor, and the details of their journey to the Embassy for interview".[23] As the Tribunal stated, however, "human memory is fallible and whether or not the sponsor had made 3 or 4 visits to Pakistan could easily fall into the area of memory fallibility" and "buffaloes have offspring and the mother buffalo is sold and the calves kept".[24] It accepted that "a legitimate error could arise here".[25] But in *Santai Bibi v. Entry Clearance Officer Dacca* the adjudicator refused an appeal because of the discrepancy as to whether the appellant's wife's brother was a spiritual leader or a married man without drawing attention to the fact that it is possible to be both.[26] In *Entry Clearance Officer Dacca v. Fultera Begum* the adjudicator considered the discrepancies to be "of a glaring nature":

> "(i) Fultera Begum (the wife) said that the sponsor's brother Jamil Ali had 1 son and 1 daughter, but the sponsor said that he had 2 sons and 1 daughter. (v) Fultera Begum said that her one brother was named Shomed Ali, but the sponsor said that he was named Abdul Shomed".[27]

If the sponsor is in England and the wife abroad there are bound to be some differences in the answers they give especially when they have not lived together for many months or even years. Also, one party is bound in this situation to know more about his or her relative than the other, and the difference between "Shomed Ali" and "Abdul Shomed" is very often a matter of how a person is addressed and by whom. Sometimes, however, even these details are omitted from an explanatory statement or Tribunal decision. In *Begum Bi v. Entry Clearance Officer Islamabad* the reference is only to discrepancies "regarding the education and mosque attendance of the eldest boys" with no further details so it is impossible to evaluate their importance.[28] In *Shivinder Kaur v. Secretary of State for the Home Department* there were discrepancies as to living accommodation, where the sponsor's brothers in India lived, and where the one buffalo owned by the family was kept.[29] There were also differences in the accounts

---

[23] TH/2363/76 (1467) d. 6.3.79 (unreported).
[24] *ibid.*, at 2.
[25] *ibid.*, at 3.
[26] TH/42341/79 (1866) d. 23.9.80 (unreported), at 3.
[27] TH/64779/80 (2221) d. 4.12.81 (unreported), at 2–3.
[28] TH/25572/72 (419) d. 12.2.75 (unreported), at 2.
[29] TH/5807/75 (895) d. 14.2.77 (unreported), at 2.

of the schools which the minor appellants had attended and the
length of time for which they had been educated — all matters about
which a sponsor in the United Kingdom more concerned with the
re-union of his family than trivial details, may well be only
peripherally concerned. In *Choudhary v. Entry Clearance Officer Dacca*
the wife was accompanied by the sponsor's brother, Tofori Ali, to the
interview in Dacca, apparently in order to lend moral support. At the
interview it was found that there were "startling discrepancies", one
of which was that "they were even unable to agree on Tofori Ali's
proper name".[30] How this helps a decision maker determine the
relation of a wife to her husband is not, in the circumstances, made
clear. These cases are not unique.[31] Many interviewees, as the CRE
report states, were at a loss to understand "why the ECO wanted the
information he was asking for".[32]

(2) "LOCAL CONDITIONS"

To understand why many of these questions — leaving aside their
relevance and probative value for the moment — cannot be answered
to the full satisfaction of the interviewer, one needs to look at the
local conditions. This is an aspect of immigration cases that a
practitioner can simply not ignore. Indeed, it will become apparent to
him how ill-suited the English adversarial system of a hearing is to a
quest for the truth in immigration cases. The Home Affairs Committee acknowledged this peculiarity itself when in 1982 it said:

"It should be borne in mind that these people come from a subsistence-
based village society in one of the poorest countries in the world. Illiterate

---

[30] TH/77768/81 (2532) d. 12.1.83 (unreported), at 1–2.
[31] Other cases which the writer investigated are *Maytab Bibi v. Entry Clearance Officer,
Rawalpindi* TH/2656/72 (334) d. 29.7.74 (unreported); *Asmat Bibi v. Visa Officer
Islamabad* TH/39005/78 (1988) d. 24.3.81 (unreported); *Manzoor Begum v. Entry
Clearsance Officer, Islamabad* TH/2976/74 (569) d. 5.1.76 (unreported). The Memorandum submitted by the JCWI to the *Home Affairs Committee, Race Relations and
Immigration Sub–Committee* (1983–84 H.C.223), also mentions extreme examples. It
states that "the assumption of fraud which guides the approach of ECOs can have
ludicrous results. One client was accompanied by a distant relative, there to give moral
support, who had no connection with the application. During the interview the ECO
asked him his occupation and he replied that he worked in a chemist's shop. When he
was unable correctly to identify the use of a nasal spray the ECO concluded, 'I was not
satisfied that this gentleman was who or what he claimed to be' (p. 3, para. 6)."
[32] *Immigration Control Procedures, supra,* p. 35, para. 4.9.9, and p. 38, para. 4.12.5. Some
of the difficulties inherent in this form of questioning were also referred to in the
immigration debate in Parliament on March 5, 1984 by Mr. Lamond (Oldham Central
and Royton) when he said: "An interviewing officer might ask about the colour of the
sari worn by a woman at her wedding. Weddings may last four of five days, and
naturally she might wear several saris in that time." See *H.C. Official Report* (5th
series), Vol. 55 (March 5, 1984), at col. 675.

villagers are *inaccurate on dates, personal questions* on often complicated family structures are bound to *produce differing answers*, there are so many different forms of education in Bangladeshi village society that differing accounts may be given by a child and his mother. *Forms of address make it improbable that a village child will know his elder relatives by name. Women are often overawed by interviews, however carefully conducted*, since they are unlikely to have ever left their village, still less spoken to a white man. For them to be out of their village home at all during the day is very unusual in Bangladesh. *Clearly to conduct interviews fairly requires some knowledge of Bangladeshi society* . . ."[33] (Author's emphasis.)

The JCWI in its evidence to the Committee said that "the answers to sets of questions will always vary, no matter what the truth". Experience teaches that members of families are actually unable to give consistent answers to such questions as "what form at school was x at when he left? Who met the father at the airport when he last arrived home? When did y die? What did y die of? Indeed, one will find when interviewing village people that the same person will give different answers to the same question at different times, even when one knows that the relationship is genuine".[34] There are many reasons for this the Committee observed, but basically they can be reduced to:

". . . [a] lack of understanding of the importance of answering questions carefully and with thought rather than simply trying to get them over with. Another is that illiterate village people do not remember dates and details better than literate ones, but worse, as they have no access to any written record which can fix details in the mind. Any question related to dates and ages is made problematic by the fact that many people cannot reckon and as people in the sub-continent do not celebrate birthdays ages are always given in a very appropriate manner. Someone who is 'about 25' may be 20 or may be 30. No importance is attached to exact ages."[35]

Some 95 per cent of all applicants in Bangladesh come from the Sylhet District, situated about 150 miles from Dacca. Over 80 per cent of the inhabitants of Sylhet are totally illiterate, many women are unable even to count accurately.[36] The interviewing of women raises the acutest difficulty. Village women live a very cocooned life. Such a

[33] *Fifth Report, op. cit.*, Vol. I, p. xix, para. 49.
[34] See the evidence of Sarah Leigh to the *Fifth Report, op. cit.*, Vol. II, p. 78, Q.258.
[35] *Supra*, n.2, Vol. II, p. 62, para. 23. An almost exact point is made in the UKIAS *Split Families* Report, pp. 49–56.
[36] *Split Families* Report. An examinationof the Immigration Control System Relating to Dependants in Bangladesh (UKIAS Research Project 1982), p. 38.

woman would never leave her house and compound except to visit a woman in a neighbouring house. Once a year she may go to visit her father's house under the escort of an older woman or male relative. They are rarely seen out in public and when they do appear they are wearing a burqua (a black garment covering the head with a mesh over the face and almost reaching the floor). They do not go to the bazaar to shop, all such shopping being done by a male member of the family. In fact, most women will never before have seen a conveyance such as a train or plane in which they travelled to Dacca, never before seen a white man, and never before have been unveiled in the company of any strange man. Not unnaturally, they are easily non-plussed and fatigued when questioned. JCWI pointed out:

> "It is an odd fact that a woman who normally works 14 hours a day on food processing and other household tasks (according to a recent study) will be totally exhausted after half an hour of being asked such questions as 'How long after that was your next child born?' and will give random or careless answers just to get the questioning to stop. They have no skills in reckoning. One woman, asked by a visitor to the village, 'How old are you?' replied, 'About 40'. Asked 'How long ago were you married?' she replied 'Over 40 years ago'."[37]

It seems that "One of the subjects taught in village development programmes is 'basic reckoning'. Such women cannot give a history of their family which makes sense, so unless they are carefully coached before they go to the interview they are bound to commit 'discrepancies'."[38] The UKIAS *Split Families* research project found that men also laboured under the same disabilities even though they were not subject to the same social restrictions as women were. It found that the overwhelming factor "which is closely connected with illiteracy and the mode of life, seems to be the fact that accuracy in such matters (as), *e.g.* time, distance, date, are not at all as significant in the minds of such illiterate people who seldom need to use such faculties with accuracy in the course of their life." Reference is made in the Report to a dissertation submitted by Professor M. Habibullah at the All Pakistan Sociology Seminar in June 1963 who observed that "the same question which seems to be quite reasonable to an educated person or to an alert urban dweller appears to be understandable to the rural respondent. This renders him callous in his conduct". He explains:

---

[37] *Supra*, n.2, *op. cit.*, Vol. II, p. 62, para. 24.
[38] *Supra*, n.2, *op. cit.*, Vol. II, p. 62, para. 25.

". . . in our Sabilpur study a respondent was asked about the age of his wife. He promptly said that the age of his wife was 35. Later, on being asked about the age of his first child out of that wife, he said with the same promptness that his first child's age was 30 years".[39]

The difficulties in understanding what types of evidence an applicant should tender is even more acute, even where he or she understands or learns the art of answering questions accurately. Thus the UKIAS research team found that throughout "our village investigations it was manifestly clear to us that hardly any of the applicants could appreciate which types of evidence is relevant to their claim and what is its probative value".[40] This is of crucial importance in practical terms because "not only the burden of proof is on the applicants, but the burden of adducing and producing the evidence also lies on the applicants".[41] For the applicants, however, this is "inscrutable legal jargon". Most of them do "not have the faintest idea of what is proof, what the burden is, and where it is".[42] This again has far-reaching implications for practitioners in the conduct of a hearing. They cannot do much about it save to keep the matter fully in the attention of the Tribunal who in its inquisitional approach is known to have been sympathetic. These matters are reflected in the cases only too vividly. In *Entry Clearance Officer Islamabad v. Begum and Tahira*[43] both the adjudicator and the IAT allowed the appeals of the applicants even though, in the words of the adjudicator, there had been much "unnecessary lying" by the sponsor and "numerous discrepancies", adding:

"I do not believe that the sponsor or his wife were even necessarily trying to be truthful on these matters. However, this does not shake my central conviction that the substantial relationship is that which is claimed."[44]

In *Firuza Khatun v. Entry Clearance Officer Dacca* again, the applicants' appeals were allowed, the Tribunal concurring with the adjudicator that "many of the discrepancies related to ages and timing matters which in the context of the appellant's community do not have a

[39] *Split Families* Report, *op. cit.*, p. 50. Professor Habibullah's findings are cited by Afsamuddin in *Sociology and Social Research* (Pakistan Sociological Association, 1963) p. 45.
[40] *Supra*, n.2, *op. cit.*, Vol. II, p. 63, para. 26.
[41] *ibid.*, at para. 27.
[42] *Supra*, n.39 at 19.
[43] TH/1391/73 (295) d. 7.5.74 (unreported), at 2. Reference may also be made to *Kaur Jit v. Entry Clearance Officer New Delhi* TH/6305/75 (698) d. 12.5.76 (unreported).
[44] *ibid.*

great significance on their consciousness".[45] In *Swaran Kaur v.
Entry Clearance Officer Delhi*, concerning an Indian applicant, the Tribunal
allowed the appeal saying of the sponsor that "although as a witness
he certainly left very much to be desired — we gained the impression
that this was due to his mental limitations and not necessarily to a
desire to be misleading", even though earlier the adjudicator spoke of
the same witness as "a disaster in his own cause".[46] Similarly, in
Amina Bibi v. Visa Officer Islamabad[47] the Tribunal allowed the appeal
when both the sponsor and his alleged wife differed on the question
of when their son died, the sponsor claiming it was three years and
10 months ago and the wife, that it was five years ago. In *Hasena
Khatun v. Entry Clearance Office Dacca* the adjudicator allowed the
appeal despite "serious discrepancies, some of which are really
substantial", on grounds that "when simple country women who
have led a sheltered life have to leave their homes and attend the
British High Commission, it may be a frightening ordeal for them".[48]
When in *Visa Officer Islamabad v. Sarwar Jan*[49] the argument was put by
the Visa Officer that one cannot accept confusion of simple people as
an explanation of all discrepancies and that a line must be drawn
somewhere the adjudicator replied:

> "With this statement I am in complete agreement but I feel that I must
> draw that line so as to enable me to accept *such confusion as the explanation of
> discrepancies relating to dates and timing*, particularly in the context of the
> Indian sub-continent. It is the *common experience* of all concerned in
> immigration appeals that *even the more intelligent people from rural communities
> have little concept of time and dates* and still less have any memory for
> them."[50] (Author's emphasis.)

In *Entry Clearance Officer v. Fultera Begum* the Tribunal went very
much further stating that many discrepancies "stem from illiteracy,
ignorance, nervousness or unintended confusion. Discrepancies are
not necessarily indicative of a false claim."[51] These cases demonstrate
how the immigration appellate authorities have often succeeded in

---

[45] TH/58495/80 (2192) d. 27.10.81 (unreported), at 3.
[46] TH/3617/75 (736) d. 29.6.76 (unreported), at 2.
[47] TH/17090/77 (1229) d. 3.5.76 (unreported).
[48] TH/4288/74 (688) d. 6.4.76 (unreported), at 2.
[49] TH/32146/78 (1721) d. 22.2.80 (unreported), at 2.
[50] *ibid.*, at. 2.
[51] TH/64779/80 (2221) d. 4.12.81 (unreported), at 3. Crucially, the Tribunal in this
case added that a "consistency in family trees given by a sponsor and an applicant for
entry clearance could indicate rehearsal by the parties of inaccurate details to be put
forward".

tackling many of the problems that have eluded them on other occasions. One question that needs inquiring into, however, is how far the Tribunal's far-sighted and perspicacious approach in *Fultera Begum* can be taken. Unfortunately, the decided cases often show that there are serious limitations to this approach which may take those representing by surprise if they are not careful.

(3) "ILLITERACY, IGNORANCE, NERVOUSNESS OR UNINTENDED CONSEQUENCES"

The Tribunal's approach in *Fultera Begum* had been echoed in earlier cases such as *Amena Khatun v. Entry Clearance Officer Dacca*[52] where the adjudicator said:

> "I have little doubt that for many applicants the interview by the ECO is a *deeply worrying event, particularly for women who have had no prior dealings with British officials.* Even people who have lived in this country for many years seem to find the giving of evidence at an appeal hearing a *terrifying experience.*"[53] (Author's emphasis.)

It is well known that wives applying in the Indian sub-continent are under the most extreme pressure because a wife invariably sees herself as the principal architect of her family's fortunes as far as the success or failure of the appeal is concerned. The effect is that:

> "the monetary loss of composure, and a simultaneous determination to answer questions without hesitation, can produce the most inaccurate, sometimes absurd, answers to matters fully within her knowledge which could be correctly stated with a few moments of deliberation when she is completely at ease."[54]

An interviewing officer in all immigration cases is required to make sure that an interviewee "is not fatigued, nervous or unwell" and is able to understand the interpreter.[55] In its sample of a hundred cases the UKIAS research team did not find a single case where an interviewee replied in the negative to such an inquiry:

> "Many experienced and observant adjudicators must have been mystified by this. The main reason for this, we believe, is the apprehension in the

---

[52] TH/31081/78 (1698) d. 13.11.79 (unreported), at 3.
[53] *ibid.*, at 3.
[54] *Split Families* Report, *op. cit.*, pp. 50–51.
[55] *ibid.*, p. 10.

mind of the applicant that, if he/she claims to be unwell or unable to understand the interpreter, *the entire interview, might be postponed for a long period, thus causing further delay* and, more importantly, making the entire journey and the expenses involved absolutely futile for which the wife often apprehends that she would be likely to be reprimanded by the husband."[56] (Author's emphasis.)

Yet, the reality is more often than not different from this and interviewees are often exhausted as the research team proceeded to explain:

"During our village investigation of cases, *the claimed wife often stated that she was feeling very unwell on the day of the interview, and also in many cases that she was unable to follow the interpreter's questions fully.* When asked to explain why she did not mention that to the ECO, in many cases the explanation was as given above. The train journey from Sylhet to Dacca alone takes 13 hours, added to that, of course, the cumbersome boat, bus journey, including miles of walking to reach Sylhet town from the village. [Most wives were also] carrying an infant and other children of very young age through the long journey."[57] (Author's emphasis.)

Nevertheless, the immigration appellate authorities have sometimes taken a very unsympathetic approach to the difficulties before them. In *Sarwar Jan v. Entry Clearance Officer Dacca*[58] the adjudicators said the Bangladeshi applicant claimed "that she was so confused and upset as to be virtually out of her mind. I cannot think that a journey however exhausting, could have brought her to such a state", he said, as he dismissed her appeal on the discrepancies.

In *Shaiba Khatun v. Entry Clearance Officer Dacca*[59] the adjudicator explained that the claimed wife had been inconsistent "in relating the birth of their children to specific major events of their life, such as, for example, the departure of the sponsor for the United Kingdom in 1955 or 1956". Her representative at the Tribunal hearing blamed "the illiteracy and stupidity of the first applicant" for the inconsistencies.[60] The appeal was heard by the IAT in 1976 and the wife was being questioned about events 20 years previously! By the time the case reached the Tribunal she had given birth to yet another boy (and had three previous children) and had, remarkably, been interviewed

---

[56] *ibid.*, p. 11. The same conclusions are reached by the CRE in their Report, *op. cit.*, p. 36, para. 4.9.14.
[57] *Loc. cit.*
[58] TH/22706/77 (1757) d. 25.3.80 (unreported), at 3.
[59] TH/1527/75 (792) d. 3.9.76 (unreported).
[60] *ibid.*, at 2.

six times by ECOs. Her appeal was still dismissed by the IAT on the ground of discrepancies. In *Monwara Begum v. Entry Clearance Officer Dacca* the sponsor giving evidence before the IAT said that his wife told him that "she did not understand what she was being asked and she said anything that came into her mouth. No one was allowed to accompany her and they kept asking her questions."[61] In fact in *Anwar Begum v. Entry Clearance Officer Islamabad* the Tribunal itself accepted that of 10 different cases at Islamabad "In each case the Home Office statement recorded that the entry clearance officer had made sure that there was no misunderstanding, but in eight cases this was not so".[62]

It is clear from this analysis therefore, that if the system is to operate fairly and accurately it must do so in the context of the needs and aspirations of the applicants' respective local communities, for "trivial discrepancies" can be justified on any grounds. A member of Parliament once expressed his disapproval of this system of questioning by asking the same kind of questions to his own children who were now grown up: "How many uncles and aunts do you have?" he had asked them. They were not able to give him an accurate answer.[63]

The Extended Family, Fraud, the "Sylhet Tax Pattern" and Marriage

(1) THE EXTENDED FAMILY

Practitioners and the Tribunal will also have to fully acquaint themselves with the cultural backdrop to the extended family system as the pre-eminent social institution. It is prone to being interpreted simplistically by outsiders, but in reality it is a deeply complex social phenomenon.

The extended family system, as is widely known, exists throughout the Indian sub-continent. Under this regime the obligation to help and support a relative does not just end with helping those in the nuclear family. As C Harris explains:

> "To the British, 'dependants' means nuclear family members, but to migrants from solitary local communities made up of clusters of extended

[61] TH/1127/73 (585) d. 28.1.76 (unreported), at 4.
[62] TH/1367/75 (948) d. 2.6.77 (unreported), at 3.
[63] Mr Lamond M.P. (Oldham Central and Royton) in *H.C. Official Report* (5th series) Vol. 55 (March 5, 1984) at cols. 675–696.

families, patterns of dependency and economic obligation are infinitely more complex . . .".[64]

For such migrants, status in society will not just come from improving one's material position but by expressing a desire to help anyone in distress or need or doing important social work like building village mosques, schools and other institutions. It is this obligation to the wider community which also furnishes the reason for a man wishing to bring a relative who fell outside the immediate nuclear family into the United Kingdom. The UKIAS *Split Families* Report also referred to, "an assiduous endeavour among these immigrants to achieve a social recognition in his land of origin: a desire to elevate his social status from a humble, unknown, poor, illiterate peasant to a respectable and influential member of the community."[65]

The system can, however, be easily misunderstood as providing a vehicle for purveying bogus family applicants and this is where lawyers and the adjudicating authorities have a role to play. The *Split Families* report referred to "community sanctions"[66] which prevent a person from either not carrying out his full obligations towards the immediate members of his family or from abusing or exploiting the social customs with regard to third parties. The UKIAS research team similarly found that a man who tried to bring a woman here who was not his own wife would be disgraced and ostracised from the community. It would be a "repugnant venture" as it would entail "falsely and publicly claiming a woman as wife".[67] Where women are still expected to be in *purdah* when appearing before others and where they are subjected to social restrictions, this would be intolerable. The same applies to bringing in a child in preference to one's real child. They explain that the suggestion that "most Sylhetis have tried to call to the United Kingdom a totally fictitious family for financial and other gains is in glaring contradiction to their actual mode and aspirations in life", for such a person's "social status will be greatly disparaged".[68]

---

[64] C.C. Harris, *The Family* (ed. by Prof. W. William, Studies in Sociology, Swansea, 1969), p. 141.
[65] *Split Families* Report, *op. cit.*, p. 40.
[66] *ibid.*, p. 39.
[67] *ibid.*, p. 40.
[68] *Loc. cit.* This firm conclusion was reached by the UKIAS research team after it had discussed this subject "with a whole variety of people ranging from the sponsors in the cases . . . appellants, the Union Council Chairman, to leading members of the Bangladesh Association in the U.K. All of them fully endorsed the above observations concerning the public policy and community sanctions that ensue when they are grossly violated", see *Split Families*, *op. cit.*, p. 39, footnote 2.

However, the CRE report states that its team found that both in Pakistan and Bangladesh a guidance had been issued to ECOs in Islamabad and Dacca (which was probably secret) strongly intimating that most applicants are bogus! A paper on documentation in Pakistan and Azad Kashmir available to ECOs in Islamabad stated that:

> ". . . the close family ties prevalent in Pakistan lead to a position where it is regarded as *legitimate* to make false statements, *particularly to foreign officials*, if so doing will assist a fellow member of the extended family group".[69] (Author's emphasis.)

The status of such a species of quasi-legislation is not entirely clear, but it is clearly an internal circular not necessarily in the public domain. The guidance warned ECOs that the substitution of one person for another is a well-established practice in Asia and that documents are not to be taken on trust because of the ease with which they can be obtained.[70] The guidance further stated that fraud and misrepresentation made with the intention of bringing in even unrelated bogus applicants is quite consistent with Sylheti culture. The paper contained a detail manual which is worth quoting:

> "It is necessary to have an appreciation of just how important UK immigration is to a Sylheti family, and how much time and effort they are willing to expend to obtain entry of family members. There is increasing evidence that the first application to this office is the beginning of the operation as they see [it], and they are *quite happy to spend several years over an application*, hoping for subsequent success via a well presented appeal or a partial confession. It is often maintained that if a man has consistently tried to bring the same family members to the UK for many years, then there is an overwhelming inference that they are his own. This ignores the fact, as discussed above, that he *sees no distinction between members of his extended family*, and in the case of an unrelated bogus applicant he will have made an irrevocable commitment, perhaps even accepted money or land, and *will not be able to back out*. The UKIAS set great store by family letters written after dismissal of appeal, arguing that having exhausted all possible [procedures] they will have given up hope of bringing their families to the UK. Again this is simply not true. Almost half of the applications received in 1982 have been from those who have previously been refused and lost appeal and there are a number of cases on file where applicants have been admitted bogus up to 10 years after application."[71] (Author's emphasis.)

---

[69] Immigration Control Procedures, *op. cit.* p. 20, para. 4.4.2.
[70] *ibid.*
[71] *ibid.*

No statistical or empirical data is given in support of these allegations. There are the strongest objections in principle to officialdom
interpreting the social system of a people in this slanted and
prejudicial way. It clearly does not help to facilitate the entry of
genuine applicants. In fact, some would disagree with the accuracy of
this manual as is illustrated in a parliamentary immigration debate in
June 1984 by Mr Lamond M.P. when he said: "I have constituents
whose cases have been going on since 1970 — 14 years ago. I have
seen constituents whose wives and children have died while waiting
for the Home Office to relent".[72]

(2) Fraud

However, the CRE also found that the overwhelming proportion of
applicants in Dacca are considered by officials to be bogus. It found
that the figure has been put as high as 99 per cent by one senior
officer and another ECO believed that there was deception or deceit
in 95 per cent of the cases. When pressed to substantiate this neither
were able to do so.[73] Documentary evidence, even when it is
available, is similarly disparaged on the grounds that if "the document is entirely genuine in all respects, there can be no guarantee
that the person presenting it is equally genuine".[74] If lawyers have a
role to play in this complex area of civil adjudication by Tribunals
then such evidence must be taken at its face value on a balance of
probabilities like all such evidence in civil cases. It does not do to
apply the rule in the one case but not in the other as it is capriciously
done here.

(3) The "Sylhet Tax Pattern"

In this respect, the outstanding example of fraud in Bangladesh until
the 1980s was what had been termed by officials the "Sylhet Tax
Pattern". This description took its name from a dossier prepared by
the British High Commission in Dacca in October 1976 which was
of that name and which was sent to all ECOs.[75] It alleged that "ninety
per cent of all sponsors seeking entry for dependants attempt to take in
bogus children" and that "most applications . . . have been artificially

[72] Supra, n.63, cols 676–677.
[73] Supra, n.70, p. 21, para. 4.4.7.
[74] ibid., p. 30, para. 4.7.3.
[75] Split Families Report, op. cit., p. 40–41.

constructed to fit a bogus family pattern originally declared to the Inland Revenue for tax relief purposes."[76] (Author's emphasis.)

The dossier alleged that Bangladeshi men who emigrated to the United Kingdom in the 1950s and 1960s claimed tax relief from the Inland Revenue for dependants in Bangladesh which did not exist. This was done by married as well as by single men. Married men, it suggested, gave the date of their marriage some years earlier than it had actually occurred and they claimed to have children in that period when, in reality, they had none, but single men also invented wives and children. In both cases the Inland Revenue was unable to verify the claims. It accepted them on the basis of affidavits and evidence of remittances to Bangladesh sent by men in support of their alleged dependants. It further alleged that this practice started before there was any control on the admission of dependants to the United Kingdom and before Bengalis became a distinct community in England as opposed to being just migratory workers. In time, however, husbands began to return to Sylhet and to have children for whom they claimed tax relief. Single men also, when they went back to Sylhet, got married and had children. In both cases the tax claims then had to be adjusted in order to accommodate the real family members.

A dependant who wished to join a sponsor in the United Kingdom had to prove his or her identity to the ECO. In this event, the existing tax fraud either had to be explained or somehow circumvented. There were three ways of doing this as set out in the dossier. First, the original fictitious wife and children could be said now to be dead by the sponsor. Secondly, it could be said that they existed but were not applying to come to the United Kingdom — another family member was; for example, another wife or child. Thirdly, someone else (not necessarily related) could impersonate those family members who had been originally invented for tax purposes and thus, in the process, gain entry into the United Kingdom.

There is little doubt that such a pattern of tax fraud was widely prevalent in Sylhet. A member of the JCWI Executive Committee, explained it to the Home Affairs Committee as follows:

"In Bangladesh the concept of personal income tax is unknown. Only 5 per cent of people pay tax, so most people know nothing about it. When

---

[76] *Immigration Control Procedures, op. cit.*, p. 21, para. 4.4.5. For its part the *Split Families* Report reached similar conclusions. It declared: "This so-called 'Sylhet Tax Pattern' . . . reached certain categorical conclusions concerning the socio-religious customs and other syndromes about the 'usual practice of the Sylhetis'. Much of it (like the age of marriage of Sylheti immigrants) is 'a perfect antithesis to reliable social research conducted by eminent authorities' . . ." (p. 41).

they first came here and received tax return forms they did not understand what it was about and how to deal with it, and the few educated people who were already here gave advice on how to make false claims for dependants, . . . That was the root of these tax claims . . . The sponsors had to give an explanation as to why the man should do it and his explanation was that for his journey to this country his family had to sell plots of land and borrow money. The whole idea of the sacrifice by the family was that once he came here he would earn money and send money back to maintain his whole family . . . It was the joint family system which justified it; it meant that he had dependants in Bangladesh."[77]

In his view, the figure for false tax claims was not 90 per cent as the British High Commission dossier suggested, but "40–50 per cent or an average of 60 per cent".[78] Mr Alf Dubs M.P., a member of the Home Affairs Committee, went on to show how badly these men were advised because many of them invented fictitious family members even though they were not at the tax threshold. Thus these men were not defrauding the Inland Revenue at all because their incomes were so low, yet they had gone through the whole rigmarole of making false statements.[79] Another JCWI Executive Committee member said that the solution to the problems of genuine dependants who were wrongly rejected because of a pre-existing wrongful disclosure of information was "to make sponsors understand that once they had put forward accounts of their families to the Inland Revenue they do not have to stick to them". However, sponsors had been reluctant to do this (again this is something that practitioners in this area should bring to light before Tribunals) and not always because they had been deceitful, but because:

". . . there are cases where perfectly genuine children have been put down in the wrong order, or perhaps the eldest child has been left out and has never been claimed for. [In many cases] the sponsor cannot read the list of children. It has been written out for him but he cannot read it himself. *I have known cases of sponsors handing in lists of children which are incorrect simply because they do not know they are incorrect.* Once they have given up an account of their families they think that nobody will believe what they say if they change it, even if they explain how it has arisen . . .".[80] (Author's emphasis.)

---

[77] Evidence of Mr Hassan, Executive Committee member of JCWI, to the *Fifth Report*, *op. cit.*, Vol. II, p. 80, Q.273.
[78] *Loc.cit.*, whereupon Mr Lyon replied that 50% is a huge figure (p. 80, Q.274).
[79] *ibid.*, p. 81, Q.281.
[80] Evidence by Sarah Leigh, Executive Committee member of JCWI, to the *Fifth Report, op. cit.*, p. 81, Q.283.

In 1977, the British High Commission revised its dossier and, realising that it had overstated its case, substituted "many" for "most" and "a very high proportion" for "ninety per cent" in its statement. Following this, the practice began of attaching this dossier to explanatory statements submitted by ECOs to adjudicators hearing appeals in cases where there was believed to be tax fraud.[81] Adjudicators placed much reliance on this statement in such cases as *Khanam*[82], *Choudhary*[83] and *Phull Begum v. Entry Clearance Officer Dacca*[84] which we shall consider duly. Following protests from representative organisations the practice of attaching the dossier to explanatory statements was discontinued.

Nevertheless, the "findings" of the British High Commission are still deeply ingrained in the minds of immigration officials and the appellate authorities.[85] Several of the case files that the CRE research team examined in Dacca showed the importance attached to the "Sylhet Tax Pattern" by ECOs in the assessment of cases.[86] In most of the cases the "tax" children were non-applicants, and the indications that the tax pattern was relevant were either that the wife looked to the ECO to be younger than claimed, or the marriage was claimed to be a second marriage and there was no evidence provided of the first. In only a small number of cases were any of the applicants found to be bogus.[87]

One of the cases where the applicant seemed to the ECO to be younger than her claimed age was where an ECO wrote in his interview notes: "I am not going to accept this arrant nonsense any more — she is clearly a lot younger than 37 and cannot be the mother of the non-applicant children."[88]

Medical age estimation took place of the wife and the doctor concluded that her age was about 30. The ECO noted in his summary of case:

". . . this is clear STP [*i.e.* Sylhet Tax Pattern] — She is never 36/37 . . . 30 at the very most and more likely 26/27 . . . no remittance receipts or

---

[81] *Immigration Control Procedures, op. cit.*, p. 21, para. 4.4.5.
[82] TH/60512/80 (2381) d. 15.7.82 (unreported).
[83] *Supra*, n.30.
[84] TH/14255/75 (861) d. 8.12.76 (unreported), discussed, at p. 83 *infra*.
[85] *Immigration Control Procedures, op. cit.*, p. 21, para. 4.4.5. Support also comes for this view from the *Split Families* Report which records the case of *Enamyl Haque v. Entry Clearance Officer Dacca* where the applicant claimed to have married at the age of 18. The ECO, however, rejected the application, "In view of the prevailing strict Muslim tradition which decreed that Bengali males wait until they are well established in their life before taking a single bride . . ." which made the marriage date "highly improbable".
[86] *Immigration Control Procedures, op. cit.*, p. 21, para. 4.5.1.
[87] *ibid.*, p. 21, para. 4.4.6.
[88] *Loc. cit.*

letters before application was made. Clear to me they never married in 1956. So there must be a marriage certificate somewhere . . .".[89]

A further interview took place where the principal appellant was given a "last chance to tell the truth" and the application was then refused. There was, however, on the file, no evidence suggesting that the ECO believed the applicants and sponsor to be bogus. The file only showed that the ECO expressed doubt about the principal appellant's claimed age and date of marriage and about the existence of the non-applicant children. The adjudicator on appeal upheld the refusal declaring that "it may be that the appellants are related to the sponsor as claimed" but the ECOs finding was not unreasonable.[90]

In another case where a marriage was claimed to be a second marriage the ECO had doubts and automatically assumed this to be a tax fraud case. His notes contain the following:

"On the surface quite straightforward STP . . . Sponsor married first wife at 18 — she was 15 — and produced 3 children by 1964 — he went to UK in 1963 — so the picture of the tax family had to be maintained. Abdur Rahin has been named in the sponsorship form of 28.9.76 but is not applying yet — he will some time later (when they have found someone to suit the family tree and learn his lines). And that should be the main problem — *both applicants here are the 2nd wife's family*".[91] (Author's emphasis.)

Although the ECO accepted that both applicants were related as claimed he did not issue entry clearances. According to his note he "asked them to let me know when they can produce originals — probably issue when seen, if they are OK".[92] This case shows not only how eager ECOs are to jump to the conclusion that a tax fraud has been perpetrated but also provides the clearest example of cases where applications are refused even though the parties are found to be related as claimed.

In another case the ECO wrote:

"Sponsor agreed to age estimate on principal applicant and [child] then said that he did not have enough money. I was tempted to refuse *but it would be painfully thin*. Therefore defer *for possible tax checks. I may have to issue here*, but draw the line at including a bogus boy. Sponsor may decide in the interview to tell truth".[93] (Author's emphasis.)

---

[89] *Loc. cit.*
[90] *ibid.*, p. 22, para. 4.5.6 and 4.5.7.
[91] *Loc. cit.*
[92] *ibid.*, pp. 21–21, para. 4.5.2.
[93] *ibid.*, p. 23, para. 4.5.15.

The excessive preoccupation by ECOs with tax fraud situations is explained by the JCWI in its memorandum to the Home Affairs Committee as follows:

> It appears that a great deal of emphasis at BHC Dacca is placed on the procuring of confessions to fraudulent tax claims. A JCWI Executive member was told by an interpreter that records are kept of the number of confessions elicited by each interpreter, and interpreters who did not bully families into confessing bogus children were not kept in employment. However that may be (and it is possible that this practice was restricted to the Second Secretary who has since left the post) it is clear that much emphasis is placed on 'cracking families'."[94]

However, it needs to be said that defrauding the Inland Revenue does not affect the rights of genuine and entitled entrants. Even the Inland Revenue has given assurance that it will not prosecute those men who had made fraudulent claims. The question then is why immigration officials should attach so much importance to it. This question was put by Mr Dubs to Mr Raison, the Immigration Minister, in 1982 when he pointed out that fraud has "no direct relationship to immigration". Mr Raison agreed but added that "where there is a pattern of lies . . . it makes it harder to get at the truth. . ."[95] The decided cases that the writer himself examined showed this to be very true since it is apparent that an inordinate degree of importance has been placed in the detection of "a pattern of lies" by the sponsor.

In the case of *Choudhary* the sponsor had been making false claims to tax allowances in respect of a first "wife" and four children. This false family pattern was handed in as a list to the immigration authorities in Dacca when he tried to bring his real wife and three children. His application was refused by the authorities because the facts as to family matters did not later tally. He then confessed to having invented the first set of family members. The Secretary of State instructed the ECO to maintain his refusal "in view of the lies which had been told".[96] On appeal to the adjudicator there was more compelling evidence because two further witnesses testified to knowing that the sponsor had "invented" his first wife and children. The sponsor himself in addition testified that the discrepancies which had arisen in the various accounts of family matters "had been due to the

[94] Memorandum by JCWI to the Fifth Report, *op. cit.*, Vol. II, p. 61, para. 19.
[95] *ibid.*, Vol. II, p. 144, Q.494.
[96] *Supra*, n.30 at 3 (unreported).

necessity to maintain the deception which he had practised upon the Inland Revenue". One of the witnesses said he was his cousin and he knew the sponsor's wife and children and the other said he was a family friend and had attended the sponsor's wedding and knew the children. The adjudicator having rejected the appeal, it was argued before the Tribunal that the fact that lies had been told was not necessarily fatal to the appeal. However, the Tribunal also dismissed the appeal on the grounds that "a web of deceit had been woven in this case".[97] A case such as this is so wrong that it arguably should have been challenged on judicial review. Yet this can only be done if there is a general awareness amongst practitioners about the sort of difficulties involved which has by no means always been the case.

In another case, *Phull Begum*,[98] the Chief Adjudicator refused to accept any further evidence as authentic, once the commission of fraud by the sponsor was proved. The transcript states:

> "The Chief Adjudicator was not satisfied by the explanation of the discrepancies. He also, by reference to the *prevalence of frauds on the Inland Revenue* discounted the fact that the right thumb impression of the first appellant [*i.e.* the wife] on her application form of 1973 was the same as that on the affidavit to the Inland Revenue of 1964 — this consistency had been argued to indicate a true relationship. Not being satisfied as to the claimed relationship he dismissed the appeal."[99] (Author's emphasis.)

This case indicates that once a fraud has been committed an applicant stands little chance of success. However, most "Sylhet Tax Pattern" cases did not lead to the making of false entry clearance applications. The British High Commission in Dacca accepted that only 15 per cent of children admitted to be bogus were applicants because all the others were non-applicants.[1] This is a long cry from maintaining that 90 per cent of all sponsors attempt to take in bogus children and "most applicants" are bogus.[2] Although the dossier itself was modified the idea still persisted so that in 1982 the Home Affairs Committee stated that "In 1980 the High Commission in Dacca received letters admitting relationships were not as claimed in 412 cases (271 wives and 1103 children) and that "most of these were a consequence of the Sylhet Tax Pattern".[3] The immediate impression

---

[97] *Loc.cit.* In fact, it was accepted that the sponsor in this case had repaid most of the money that had been defrauded.

[98] *Supra*, n.84.

[99] ibid., at 7.

[1] *Immigration Control Procedures, op. cit.,* p. 21, para. 4.4.6.

[2] ibid., at p. 21, para. 4.4.7.

[3] *Fifth Report, op. cit.,* Vol. I, p. xviii, para. 46.

given by this is that in 1981, for instance, sponsors who were settled in the United Kingdom tried to bring in 415 bogus wives and 1946 bogus children. Similarly, it is said that in the first half of 1982, 340 confessions involving 1060 children were made. The CRE team observes, however, that the post in Dacca "were unable to estimate in what proportion of applications such confessions were made and we were told that they had only recently begun to distinguish between applicants and non-applicants in their records of confessions."[4]

The information provided by the FCO regarding confessions in the last quarter of 1981 was given in more sedate terms. The FCO found that in this period 547 children were admitted to be bogus but entry clearance was sought for only 37 children (*i.e.* 6.7 per cent). The remainder were stated to be non-applicants invented for tax purposes. Furthermore, 98 cases (*i.e.* 54.7 per cent) involved bogus wives invented for tax purposes. However, of these, 46 per cent were wholly genuine having been masqueraded as an earlier wife instead of applying in her true identity. What about the remaining 8.7 per cent? The information given suggests that despite any tax fraud, of those that actually applied to go to the United Kingdom to settle, these must all have been genuine for it is stated that: "In each of these cases entry certificates were issued on their amended application with their true name or age."[5] No attempt would therefore appear to have been made to bring a woman as a wife who was not, in fact, the wife of a sponsor in the United Kingdom. In the first half of 1982 only 15 per cent of children admitted to be false over this period had been applicants for entry clearances, the remaining 84 per cent were children listed by sponsors as theirs but not applying for entry clearances.[6] Fortunately, cases involving the "Sylhet Tax Pattern" have now been exhausted and are no longer a cause of concern. As we have seen their effect was actually to increase pressure on sponsors to make applications for non-existent children. They caused enormous hardship. But they are still a fascinating example of a practice in the phenomenon of migration which once again could have been much better dealt with by officialdom than it, in the event, was.

[4] *Immigration Control Procedures, op. cit.*, p. 21, para. 4.4.6.
[5] See the Letter to the Clerk to the sub-committee from the Foreign and Common-wealth Office, *Fifth Report, op. cit.*, Vol. II, p. 225. The Home Affairs Committee used these very figures to demonstrate that "there certainly is some fraud", pp. 33–34, *supra*, p. 59, n.2.
[6] *Immigration Control Procedures, op. cit.*, p. 21, para. 4.4.6.

(4) MARRIAGE

(a) Bangladeshi Men

The same British High Commission dossier of October 1976 which raised the hue and cry about the "Sylhet Tax Pattern" also included information on Bangladeshi marriages. It said:

". . . The combined experience of ECOs gained from case histories and from *interviewing many thousands of Sylhetis* in addition to much research into local custom shows that Sylheti males who emigrated to the UK often do not return to marry until they have saved sufficient funds to support a wife and children."[7] (Author's emphasis.)

It seems that the authorities firstly believed that most Sylheti men who arrived in the United Kingdom in the 1960s were unmarried since in Sylhet men only marry in their late twenties when they have saved up enough money to support a family. Secondly, they believed that if there are older children in a family and the mother looks even a few years younger than her stated age, it is highly probably that the children are bogus.[8]

Both theories as to marriage and age are untrue. Sociological studies show that Sylheti males marry at ages almost identical with their United Kingdom counterparts: that is, 25 years. As in the United Kingdom, some males in Sylhet marry young and some do not. Significantly, however, in Sylhet almost every male does marry. Only 0.15 per cent of the rural male population has never been married by the time they reach the age of between 45–49 years.[9]

Once again, it is evident from the decided cases that ECOs have been greatly influenced by the "findings" of the British High Commission in Dacca. They were therefore refusing applications simply on the basis of the assumptions above so that in *Bibi Khatun*, the ECO remarked:

"Surveys conducted by the Governments of Pakistan and Bangladesh have shown that over 90 per cent of the Sylheti males do not marry until they

---

[7] Quoted in the UKIAS *Split Families* Report, *op. cit.*, p. 41.
[8] Memorandum by the JCWI to the Fifth Report, *op. cit.*, Vol. II, p. 60, para. 18. Reference may here also be made to the research by Armindo Miranda and his team which concluded that "due to obvious administrative reasons" problems of law enforcement meant that many marriages went unregistered. Even after the Muslim Family Laws Ordinance promulgated in 1961 making registration of all marriages compulsory "confusion and ineffectiveness continued to prevail in this field." See A. Miranda, *Nuptiality in Bangladesh* (DERAP Publication, Norway, 1980), p. 4.
[9] See *Fifth Report, Loc.cit.*

are in their late twenties and thirties and then to a girl about ten years younger than themselves."[10]

On the basis of this assertion the ECO felt justified in making a refusal. He said:

"In this case in 1950 the sponsor would have been only 7 years old and would have been marrying a girl of only 13. This seemed to Mr Bell to be out of the question."[11]

No source or reference is given, however, of the survey to which the ECO attached so much weight. Similarly in, *Enamyl Haque* the ECO said of a sponsor who claimed to have married at 16:

"In view of the prevailing strict Muslim tradition which decreed that Bengali males wait until they are well established in their life before taking a single bride . . . I find the marriage date of 1957 highly improbable".[12]

So here again the application was rejected out of hand because the ECO did not believe the sponsor to be married to the applicant as claimed.

The question is, however, why should officials feel compelled to proceed in this manner when considering an application by a wife to join her husband in the United Kingdom? Cases which the writer has examined bring this issue into sharper focus. In *Soydun Nessa v. Entry Clearance Officer Dacca*[13] the principal appellant sought entry as a wife with her six children. The two eldest children Ala Uddin, and Siraj Uddin were aged 20 years and 15 years respectively. The sponsor had been a United Kingdom citizen for the last 10 years. In 1961, 20 years before the date of the appeal hearing before the Tribunal, he swore an affidavit specifying the members of his family. There were no discrepancies here. He also put in evidence receipts of remittances of money sent by him as long ago as December 1966. There was also a sponsorship declaration dated March 6, 1974. The ECO, however, refused the application of the principal appellant and her six children. The transcript reads:

"The ECO found no significant inconsistencies in the accounts of family details given him by the principal appellant, Ala Uddin and Siraj Uddin.

---

[10] Quoted in the *Split Families* Report, p. 41 with the reference given as TH/41154/79 at p. 8 of the explanatory statement.
[11] *ibid.*
[12] *ibid.*, p. 42.
[13] TH/64047/80 (2214) d. 7.12.81 (unreported).

THE EXTENDED FAMILY, FRAUD AND MARRIAGE 87His suspicions of the genuineness of the claims were however aroused by two matters. Firstly, the early age of the sponsor when he married. If all that had been put before him was true, *he would have been only 21 whereas in the respondent's experience Bangladeshi Muslim males rarely married before their late twenties or early thirties.*[14] (Author's emphasis.)

Here the ECO's decision is reached not only in disregard of existing evidence on the one hand, but on the basis of no evidence on the other. The decision of the ECO in *Mubibur Nessa v. Entry Clearance Officer Dacca* was also reached in the same way. Here the principal appellant and her four children sought to join the sponsor in the United Kingdom. Again, there were no discrepancies in the evidence and no reason to suppose that this was a tax fraud case. Nevertheless, the ECO refused the application because, as the transcript states: "The sponsor was born in 1936 and claimed to be married in 1955 when he was not yet 19 years old. The ECO felt that it was unlikely that he had been married at such a young age."[15]

The adjudicator accepted on appeal the findings of the ECO. When the case went up to the Tribunal, two UKIAS counsellors who had recently been to Bangladesh and investigated this case tendered in evidence a report of their investigations. The Tribunal found it to be a "compelling report" as it "set out in great detail the results of the two unexpected visits which they paid to the home of the appellants and which left them in no doubt that the claimed relationships were genuine".[16]

To sum up, in the first of these cases, *Soydun Nessa*[17] the appeal of the applicants was dismissed all the way up to the Tribunal. In the second case, the Tribunal only allowed the appeal because somebody else had undertaken independent field research into the matter. In both these cases and those investigated by the UKIAS research team in 1981, the ECOs disregarded positive evidence to reach their decisions. These two cases highlight that even as late as 1981 ECOs in Dacca were still applying the dossier of October 1976.

(b) Bangladeshi Women

Similar assumptions were applied to Bangladeshi women. ECOs believed that women who appear to be about 13 years of age at marriage cannot be the mothers of older children, born to them, for

---

[14] *ibid.*, at 2.
[15] TH/55235/79 (2158) d. 5.10.81 (unreported) at 2.
[16] *ibid.*
[17] *Supra*, n.13.

example, when they were 14 years old. Statistical information shows, however, that the average age of marriage for women born between 1941 and 1945 was 11 years. In the 1960s it went up to 13 years. This was still well below the legally prescribed age for marriages which under the Child Marriage Restraint Act 1929 was stipulated at 16 for women. In fact, almost all marriages of girls has been under that age until recently. As marriage registration was unknown before 1961 marriage contracts falsely stated the wife to be over 16.[18] JCWI have stated that:

> "if ECOs based their general assumptions on the facts, they would come to the conclusion that women married at a much earlier age than their documentation shows, that almost every adult male will have a spouse, and that consequently most women are genuine applicants (since it is hard to imagine why anyone would bring in someone else's wife instead of his own)."[19]

Conclusions

This chapter suggests that mandatory entry certification is indefensible if it is used as a quota for cases involving family reunification. The position described in this chapter is all the more intolerable when one remembers that most applicants are, by law, not subject to any restriction, being wives and children of Commonwealth men settled in the United Kingdom before 1981, and therefore able to come and go without let or hindrance. Instead, what this chapter shows is that the entry clearance system, in its present form, is an elaborate network of specially constituted administrative trappings — such as the so-called "discrepancy system", the "Sylhet Tax Pattern" and official "theories" about when people marry — which are all designed to help officials reach a decision on matters other than the merits of the evidence before them. The chapter shows that this makes it impossible to apply proof on the balance of probabilities. This is a practice which would not be acceptable in any other sphere of civil litigation since it is so far removed from any application of the basic principles of law. In the next chapter, we see further and yet more serious evidence of this.

---

[18] These findings are supported by the research of Armindo Miranda, *op. cit.*, pp. 4–28.
[19] Other researches are mentioned in the *Split Families* Report *op. cit.*, pp. 42–45, as well as in the Memorandum by JCWI to the *Fifth Report, op. cit. FS, Vol. II, p. 61, para. 18, which drew the same conclusions.*

Chapter Three

Documentary and Medical Eviden

". . . the Secretary of State owed duties of candour and helpfulness not only to individuals but also to the statutory appellate tribunal whose function it was to do justice . . ."

Mr Justice Sedley in *R. v. Secretary of State for the Home Department. ex p. Abdi. The Times*, March 10, 1994

In this chapter we examine a particularly complex and problematic area concerning the evidential value of private and public documents in the immigration process. Then we consider the use of medical evidence in this area. We have seen that until recently documentation throughout the Indian sub-continent has been relatively sparse. In some rural areas it is still so. As the UKIAS *Split Families* report states, in these areas "all through the life time of a person one may not need to fill in a single form for claiming or recording anything about his existence in the society".[1] Even the fact of one's marriage need not be recorded in any form under traditional Moslem law. Under these circumstances to meet the requirement of proof on a balance of probabilities can be an insuperable difficulty even though the requirement relates to the most mundane matters, like one's marriage or the birth of one's children. This difficulty is compounded by the fact that what documents *are* available are not given adequate credence by the authorities. The official explanation for this is that in the absence of a proper and comprehensive system of documentation[2] applicants have recourse to scribes and spivs who

---

[1] *Split Families* Report: An Examination of the Immigration Control System Relating to Dependants in Bangladesh (UKIAS Research Project 1982), at p. 26.
[2] In Bangladesh it is fair to say that the position is now considerably better than previously, but nevertheless difficulties are still bound to occur.

forge documents for them. Here again, however, official manoeuvres at the grass roots go beyond simple attitudes of perspicacity and due caution.

Thus a guidance issued to ECOs in Islamabad and Dacca actually instructs them on the probative value to be attached to documents. This guidance, "Documentation in Pakistan and Azad Kashmir", was prepared in the mid-seventies. Some of it is out of date, but the CRE team, upon investigation, were told that its conclusions were still regarded by ECOs to be valid. The guidance concludes by saying:

> "The system of registration of births, deaths and marriages depends for its efficient operation upon junior officials who are badly paid and, in remoter areas, sometimes only semi-literate. The inducement to increase their income by taking bribes is great. Corruption is widespread at all levels, despite the efforts of the Central Government, and shows no signs of decreasing."[3]

It continues: "as long as there is a demand, forged and falsified documents, including passports, will continue to be available to those who need them". It then explains that there is a further problem in the consideration of documents because not all are forgeries. Many documents, it warns, are perfectly valid but have been acquired through misrepresentation:

> "Thus, a document which is verified at source may still be completely misleading. Even when the document is *entirely genuine in all respects*, there can be no guarantee that the person presenting it is actually genuine: substitution of one person for another is a well-established practice in Asia."[4] (Author's emphasis.)

This is a sweeping claim, however. Granting that substitution is feasible, but is it equally feasible to suggest that a genuine son can be substituted for a bogus one using the genuine son's documents, for example, a birth certificate? Or a genuine wife for a bogus one? The guidance prescribes its solution:

> "From the above, it can be seen that all documents of Pakistani origin must be treated with reserve. Relationships and identification can only be established with any degree of accuracy by personal interview and *exhaustive cross-checking*."[5] (Author's emphasis.)

---

[3] *Supra*, n.1.
[4] ibid.
[5] ibid.

As for the evidential value of a genuine document, ECOs are directed that "there are . . . few instances where documents, even after authentication by responsible authorities can be treated as anything more than supporting evidence".[6]

It will be observed that the precise wording and content of this guidance is no different, in terms of its purport and methodology, to the British High Commission guidance on fraud and the "Sylhet Tax Pattern". Like that guidance this one is open to the same objections. As with false statements the contention is not to refute the allegation that fraud exists (because it does), but to question the wisdom, and indeed the necessity, of briefing officials in such wide, sweeping and unmitigated terms. There are aspects of these guidances which have nothing to do with the difficulties facing immigration officials. For it is a case of definite overkill to suggest that documentary proof cannot count as "anything more than supporting evidence".

At a more fundamental level the guidance is open to question simply because its particular statement misrepresents the problem. As the UKIAS ask, what part of the world is free from fabrication and forgery? "Penal codes of the free countries of the world invariably provide for the offences of forgery and fabrication of documents . . . Such evidence cannot justify a generalised treatment of relevant documents as forged without due consideration and examination of the documents."[7]

But such has been the effect of this blanket rule that in India, it seems, the immigration authorities do not even accept a Memoranda of Marriages issued by the Registrar of Marriages under the Hindu Marriages Act of 1955 as constituting proof of marriage. They require, in addition, further proof that the marriage has actually taken place under Hindu law. The rejection of statutory instruments enacted under Hindu law is an indefensible practice, bearing in mind that, as far as marriages are concerned, section 8 of the Hindu Marriages Act 1955 stipulates that the registration of a marriage facilitates proof of the factum of marriage should a dispute arise.[8] As in all the other cases that we have discussed ECOs in this case have also far exceeded the remit of their brief. Thus locally prepared general guidance for ECOs in Dacca adds that "The only documents which can generally be relied upon to contain true details are

[6] *Immigration Control Procedures: Report of a Formal Investigation* (CRE, London, February 1985), pp. 25–30.
[7] Memorandum by UKIAS to the *Fifth Report from the Home Affairs Committee on Race Relations and Immigration* (1981-82 H.C. 90–I), Vol. II, p. 91–92.
[8] *ibid.*, p. 95.

genuinely issued land deeds".[9] However, it is not unusual for even land deeds to have been disparaged not only by ECOs but by the appellate authorities as well.[10]

These assertions and the value of documentary evidence in immigration law, need now to be illustrated.

Some Examples of Documentary Proof

In Pakistan and Bangladesh particularly one or more of the following documents are known to have been tendered by applicants at the interview: (1) passport; (2) *Nikanama* (marriage licence); (3) identity cards; (4) birth/death certificates; (5) registered title deeds of immovable property; (6) divorce deeds; (7) electoral lists; (8) domicile certificates; (9) bank deposit books; (10) bank payment of foreign remittances of money vouchers; (11) insurance policies; (12) post authority payment of British postal money orders; (13) counterfoils of postal orders; (14) private correspondence; (15) photographs; (16) school leaving certificates issued by headmasters of schools; (17) certificates issued by Class I gazetted officers and members of legislative assemblies; (18) affidavits sworn before authorised persons; (19) army pension books; (20) seaman discharge books.[11]

Documents (1) to (8) are statutory documents. They are issued subject to a prescribed procedure. Copies of documents (2) to (8) are obtainable by any member of the public. They are verifiable at source from records kept by statutory functionaries who keep permanent records of the documents. Despite this, however, these documents are not acceptable on their own by British Embassy officials. Documents (9) to (20) are private documents which are issued by various individuals but which can also be easily verified, like character references from employers and photographs. Like statutory documents they are not accorded much credence *per se*.[12] The result, as the ensuing analysis shows, is that the assessment of evidence is, quite often, partial and improper leading to the drawing of defective conclusions. The role ascribed to some of the documents mentioned above may now be considered.

(1) PASSPORTS

Although passports in Bangladesh are issued subject to a police investigation to ensure that the applicant is suitable for travel abroad

---

[9] *Supra*, n.6, p. 30, para 4.7.4.
[10] See *infra*, at pp. 101–102.
[11] These documents are also mentioned in the Memorandum by UKIAS to the *Fifth Report*, *op. cit.*, Vol. II, at p. 95.
[12] *ibid.*, pp. 92 and 95.

and satisfies other details as to age and address,[13] there is still room
for recorded inaccuracies here. This can arise from the making of
false representations to the passport or the alteration of other details.
Moreover, officials themselves can make mistakes. Often the passport
issuing officer will rely on his own visual assessment of age even if
this is different from the stated age of the applicant. If there are
doubts he will refer the applicant to the Government Civil Surgeon
for a medical age assessment which (as will be seen subsequently) is
sometimes wrong.[14] The date of birth which appears in the passport
may not therefore correspond with the date appearing in other
documents, for example the school certificate or the birth certificate,
or with the date given by the applicant or his/her parents.

This is not to say, however, that all passports are unreliable as
proof of identity. Indeed, the kind of cases where their evidential
importance has been disparaged are not normally the kind of cases
discussed above, for example, in *Quiamat Bibi v. Visa Officer
Islamabad*[15] the issue arose as to whether the sponsor had actually
married the principal applicant when he sought to bring her here as
his wife. Various forms of documentary evidence, for instance a
marriage certificate, a sponsorship declaration and remittance slips of
money were tendered in evidence. In addition, the sponsor's passport
was produced showing that he left the United Kingdom on March 4,
1972 and returned in October 1972, thus indicating that he was in
Pakistan at the time of the alleged wedding. Although the passport, in
conjunction with the other documents produced, constituted cogent
proof of marriage on a balance of probabilities, it was not so regarded
either by the immigration authorities in Pakistan or by the appellate
authorities in the United Kingdom. Yet the passport endorsement in
these circumstances would have been the best evidence available.

(2) *NIKANAMA* (MARRIAGE LICENCE) AND BIRTH/DEATH CERTIFICATES

A marriage certificate is also a statutory document which is verifiable
at source by any member of the public. Again, however, their
evidential value is invariably underplayed. Indeed, in *Visa Officer*

---

[13] Passports are issued under the Bangladesh Passport Order 1973 and in accordance
with statutory rules made in 1974. A passport is essential for the issue of an entry
clearance certificate and this requirement was stipulated in the immigration rules: see,
for example, *Statement of Changes in Immigration Rules* (February 9, 1983) H.C. 169, at
para. 3. (See also n.55, p. 56.)
[14] See *infra.*, at pp. 114–121.
[15] TH/10600/75 (875) d. 30.12.76 (unreported).

Islamabad v. Mrs Bibi the marriage certificate was found by the Visa Officer to be genuine. Nevertheless, he proceeded to find that the sponsor and the applicant were not husband and wife, the Tribunal explaining:

> "A Nikanama was produced by the applicant which was referred to the appropriate Nikah register and authenticated by him. In spite of this, in view of the basic discrepancies in the information before him, the Visa Officer was not satisfied that the applicant was related to Iqbal Shah as she claimed and refused her application".[16]

In *Visa Officer Islamabad v. Nazir Begum*, similarly, a marriage certificate was produced the authenticity of which was not challenged by the Visa Officer, yet the application was refused because of the discrepancies in the evidence of the applicants.[17] Indeed, such is the suspicion of the authorities at posts abroad that the CRE team recounts that one Second Secretary in Dacca told them that birth, marriage and death certificates carried no weight with them at all.[18] The writer also found that in *Entry Clearance Officer v. Fultera Begum* an ECO sealed the applicant's fate on this very basis, contending:

> "A marriage certificate in the prescribed form had now been presented but I observed that such documents were not proof in themselves of a claimed marriage and recalled the facility with which they could be obtained, with the relevant details inserted, to suit any occasion."[19]

A far as evidence in respect of births is concerned, in *Soydun Nessa v. Entry Clearance Officer* (a case already considered), birth certificates for four out of the six children were available. The children were aged 20 years, 15 years and two sets of twins aged six years and five years. In respect of both the older children there were no birth certificates available — a situation not unusual in itself in view of the sparsity of available documentation until recently. The ECO refused all the applications, including those for which birth certificates were available, because the eldest child "looked to the ECO to be much younger than the age he claimed to be".[20] In fact, the ECO

---

[16] TH/11123/77 (1219) d. 18.5.78 (unreported).
[17] TH/338500/78 (1655) d. 19.10.79 (unreported) at 3.
[18] *Immigration Control Procedures, op. cit.*, p. 31, para 4.7.9. Indeed, in *Mubibur Nessa* TH/55235/79 (2156) d. 5.10.81 (unreported) a marriage certificate obtained from the marriage register was disregarded even though it was made at the time of the marriage as required.
[19] TH/64779/80 (2221) d. 4.12.81 (unreported) at 1.
[20] TH/64047/80 (2214) d. 7.12.81 (unreported), at 2.

interviewed the "suspect" child thoroughly but found "no significant inconsistencies in the accounts of family details". Despite this, cogent evidence was rejected once again, and a decision reached on the basis of no evidence. In *Rajia Khatun v. Entry Clearance Officer Dacca* a late registration birth certificate was rejected in the same way.[21]

(3) REMITTANCES OF MONEY, BANK TRANSFERS, ETC

Remittances of money have often been rejected by ECOs and the immigration appellate authorities without a statement of cogent reasons for their rejection, thus indicating that this kind of documentary proof is not rated very highly. This is a mistaken view because in the majority of cases an applicant will be able to prove that she was sent money by the sponsor over a period of time as a dependent relative. ECOs do not attach much importance to this, themselves, on the grounds that the evidence of remittances neither proves the claimed relationship nor clearly identifies the applicants as wife and/ or children.[22] Upon consideration of the cases, an ECO or a Tribunal should give all remittances a very proper consideration since remittances often extend over more than a decade because of the waiting period in the queues, and in many cases the sum total remitted annually is far in excess of any tax relief that a person would hope to gain by making false remittances. Accordingly, the issue should be approached on the basis that there is a presumption in these circumstances that the alleged relationship exists as claimed. However, in *Soydon Nessa*, a case decided in 1981, the remittances to the claimed wife went back 15 years and for the eldest child at least five years.[23] From the transcript of the case it is not clear how the ECO or the appellate authorities proceeded to evaluate importance of such evidence and yet both proceeded to dismiss the application. In *Tula Bibi v. Entry Clearance Officer Dacca*, decided in 1982, there were 38 remittances of money going back 14 years[24] but here also the application was dismissed on the ground that the relationship had not been established on the balance of probabilities. In *Visa Officer Islamabad v. Alam Bi*[25] there was "evidence of dependency over a long period in the shape of remittance slips" and two family photographs, but the Tribunal held that this had to be balanced against the

---

[21] TH/93066/82 (2662) d. 8.4.83 (unreported).
[22] *Split Families* Report at p. 19.
[23] *Supra*, n.20 at 2.
[24] TH/48214/70 (2310) d. 18.3.83 (unreported), at pp. 2–3.
[25] TH/28164/77 (1373) d. 3.10.78 (unreported).

discrepancy which the ECO found, concerning what can only be described as trifling matters, such as how many radios the family had and who met the sponsor at the airport on his arrival in Pakistan shortly before the interviews with the EC0. The greatest evidential value of remittances, however, lies in their combination with various other documentary proofs. A simple straight-forward example here is *Sundi Bibi v. Entry Clearance Officer Dacca* where remittance slips were joined with correspondence between the parties. As the Tribunal explained, it was "impressed by the correspondence between the sponsor and the alleged Sundi Bibi and the remittances",[26] but still found it necessary to uphold the ECOs refusal on discrepancies. In *Suriya Begum v. Visa Officer Islamabad* there was even stronger evidence in favour of the claimed relationship in the form of remittance slips and a letter from the Inland Revenue accompanied by an affidavit sworn by the first applicant in 1962 — 19 years ago! Despite this, both the ECO and the Tribunal dismissed the appeal.[27]

Linked with this is the question of bank transfer certificates, which are similarly disregarded but ought not to be if one stops to consider their evidential value. Thus in *Hazera Begum v. Entry Clearance Officer Dacca* some 18 documents were produced, including money order certificates and bank transfer certificates, dating from 1963 to 1974, totalling about £500. The ECO rejected the application on the basis of discrepancies at the interview, even though these related to the circumstances of the first wife's death, whether she died at night or during daytime, "and how often they visited her grave". However the Tribunal accepted that there were no discrepancies to the family tree, and with regard to those discrepancies that did occur, it heard argument that these "were due to the lack of any records in Bangladesh and the simple mentality of the appellants rather than any deceit".[28] Yet here again, the appeal was dismissed without further discussion about the evidential value of the documents, even when these were set against trivial discrepancies.

(4) AFFIDAVITS

Affidavits are the most widely found document in family cases,[29] but naturally their probative value is limited. In conjunction with other

---

[26] TH/2508/78 (1700) d. 11.12.79 (unreported), at 2.

[27] TH/29361/78 (1858) d. 13.10.80 (unreported), at 2.

[28] TH/8436/75 (859) d. 15.12.76 (unreported) at p. 2–3. Another example worth noting is *Shaiba Khatun v. Entry Clearance Officer, Dacca* TH//1527/75 (792) d. 3.9.76 (unreported) where there were three bank transfers and yet the appeal was dismissed.

[29] An affidavit is a unilateral private document comprising a deponent's declaration of certain facts under oath before a magistrate. The magistrate does not attest to the genuineness or truth of the document.

documents, however, they can help displace the burden of proof on a balance of probabilities. The UKIAS, *Split Families* Report states that "in some cases in a circulous way it may provide vital evidence". The example it gives is that,

". . . if the affidavit was made by the claimed wife just after the sponsor first arrived in the UK and if the document had put on her thumbprint, one may then compare the thumbprint forensically with the recent thumbprint of the same claimed wife, generally found in a recent affidavit or in the application form for Entry Clearance (Form IM2), and if they are found to be of the same person, then any suggestions that the sponsor has been claiming tax relief for a fictitious wife and children . . . from the beginning and may have only married recently following the so-called Sylhet Tax Pattern, would clearly appear to be erroneous, for the original affidavit would thus substantiate the claim that the sponsor was a married man when he first entered the UK, and more pertinently, it would also establish that the person now seeking entry is that wife — the vital question of the identity of the applicant."[30]

There is clear evidence, however, that even in these circumstances documents have been deemed unimportant. Thus in *Phull Begum v. Entry Clearance Officer Dacca* the Chief Adjudicator "discounted the fact that the right thumb impression of the first appellant (*i.e.* the claimed wife) on her application form of 1973 was the same as that on the affidavit to the Inland Revenue of 1964 — this consistency had been argued to indicate a true relationship".[31] The Tribunal concurred in this. The evidence before it consisted *inter alia* of a further seven affidavits all sworn by persons living in the United Kingdom and all purporting to come from the same area in Bangladesh as the sponsor. They testified to knowing the claimed wife and children.

In others cases, such as *Suriya Begum v. Visa Officer Islamabad*[32] and *Fatima Bibi v. Entry Clearance Officer Islamabad*[33] affidavits, although presented in combination with other documents (such as evidence of remittances), have been accorded no importance.

(5) PHOTOGRAPHS

There cannot be evidence as axiomatic in its probity as photographs which are subsequently accurately identified by the applicants and/or

[30] *Split Families* Report, *op. cit.*, at p. 14–15.
[31] TH/14255/75 (861) d. 8.12.76 (unreported), at 2.
[32] TH/29361/78 (1858) d. 13.10.80 (unreported).
[33] TH/1504/73 (440) d. 6.3.75 (unreported) at 5. In this case there were a number of photographs, receipts for payments to Fatima Bibi and two affidavits as to identity.

witnesses at the interview or hearing. Photographs are mostly introduced at the appeals level. Their function in the immigration process will, for the most part, have to be deduced from their handling by the adjudicator and the IAT. However, in *Begum Bi v. Entry Clearance Officer Islamabad* photographs were made available at the interview with the ECO. The ECO was thorough in interviewing the principal applicant:

> "I produced to her the above mentioned photograph and asked her to name the persons shown. She did so successfully. I asked her when the group photograph was taken, and she said that it had been taken two years prior to the date of the interview, after refusal of entry clearances. I asked her if she was certain that it had been taken after the refusal, and she said that she was, as the sponsor, on the advice of his lawyer had written to her requesting that she obtain it. I produced to her the individual photograph of herself and the other appellants and asked her when these were taken. She said these were taken six months before the group photograph."[34]

The ECO refused the application as did the adjudicator and the Tribunal on appeal. It was accepted that there were no discrepancies as to the family tree and the Tribunal whilst accepting that the sponsor was married to someone called Begum Bi found that the evidence of photographs failed to "resolve the question of identity."[35] In *Shafait Bi v. Entry Clearance Officer Islamabad* a photograph was produced before the Tribunal of the sponsor and his claimed wife. A number of witnesses appeared at the hearing who could easily have identified the lady in the photograph, particularly a man who claimed that the principal applicant was the daughter of his cousin and that he came from the same village as the sponsor. This opportunity does not appear to have been taken by the Tribunal and the appeal was dismissed in the face of an impressive array of documentary evidence consisting of a letter from the income tax authorities, evidence of remittances, an affidavit sworn by the appellant in 1972, two marriage certificates and the photograph itself.[36] In *Visa Officer v. Alam Bi* the Tribunal reversed the adjudicator's finding in favour of the applicants because the evidence of dependency over a long period in the shape of remittance slips and the two family photographs could not obviate the existence of discrepancies at the interview.[37] Once again, there-fore, documentary evidence, regardless of its import, had been

---

[34] TH/2557/72 (419) d. 12.2.75 (unreported), at 3.
[35] *ibid.* at 5.
[36] TH/2900/73 (627) d. 15.3.76 (unreported), at 2.
[37] TH/20164/77 (1373) d. 13.10.78 (unreported) at 4.

ignored because of existing discrepancies. In *Visa Officer Islamabad v. Nazir Begum* also the adjudicator allowed the appeal because the marriage certificate had not been challenged, remarking that:

"A photograph has been produced of a family group consisting of the appellant, some of her stepchildren and her stepparents, which has recently been attested, and I accept that a *likeness exists* between the appellant as shown thereon and the photograph attached to the declaration (Annex F) dated 1977."[38] (Author's emphasis.)

The Tribunal, however, again reversed this determination on the grounds that if the parties were truly related as claimed the discrepancies ought not to have arisen.

(6) PRIVATE CORRESPONDENCE

According to the *Split Families* Report the evidential value of private and personal correspondence can be "of a unique nature", because:

". . . when letters between the sponsor and the claimed wife, written many years before the application are available with a clear post mark on the air letter, the probative value of such correspondence are of a unique nature. The question of identity may still remain but they at least suggest that the sponsor has been married long ago and has children. The nature of the contents is important. A close study of such letters often portrays a clear picture of a husband writing to his wife. When a number of these letters are read collectively, in a genuine case they would clearly convey a noticeable consistency of facts relating to various matters of family affairs. . ."[39]

As the Report all too readily acknowledges, however, the immigration authorities do not pay much heed to such correspondence. In *Shaiba Khatun v. Entry Clearance Officer Dacca*[40] seven letters were produced in evidence before the Tribunal in addition to other documentary evidence. The appeal was dismissed without any evaluation of such evidence. In *Sundi Bibi v. Entry Clearance Officer Dacca*[41] there was apparently a long list of correspondence between the

---

[38] TH/33850/78 (1655) d. 19.10.79 (unreported), at 3.
[39] *Split Families* Report, *op. cit.*, p. 18.
[40] TH/1527/75 (792) d. 3.9.76 (unreported), at 3.
[41] TH/2508/78 (1700) d. 11.12.79 (unreported) at 2. Similarly in *Quiamat Bibi* (TH/10600/75 (875) d. 30.12.76 (unreported) the Tribunal refused the appeal in the face of "a bundle of correspondence between this country and Pakistan", which seem genuine (at 2).

sponsor and the claimed wife which impressed the adjudicator but the appeal was still dismissed. Where the correspondence in question covers the period before refusal of application by an ECO it is not unusual to find the authorities simply adverting to the existence of such evidence but preferring to draw no further inferences from it. Where it relates to the period immediately *after* the refusal of application it is common to find it being said that such evidence cannot carry much weight. In its evidence of the Home Affairs Committee UKIAS said that such correspondence was, in fact, "of crucial importance being almost conclusive evidence of the genuineness of the claimed relationship". This is because "there seems to be no plausible explanation as to why he [*i.e.* the sponsor] should still continue to write to them [his wife and children] in this way if they were not his real wife and children" addressing them always in the claimed relationship, particularly when he had lost all hope of bringing them here.[42] Official attitudes, however, belie this. Thus in *Hjera Bibi v. Entry Clearance Officer Islamabad* the Tribunal recounted:

> "The Appellants second round of appeal is that the adjudicator misdirected herself in not giving due weight to the contents of letters passed between the Appellant and the Sponsor. What the adjudicator said was 'I have been asked to take into account letters written to the sponsor from the appellant and from her family but these were written *after* the interview date and I must view them in this light'."[43] (Author's emphasis.)

Counsel for the applicants argued before the Tribunal that "the tone and the details of family life disclosed in them were consistent only with the existence of the relationship of husband and wife between the sponsor and the Appellant".[44] The Tribunal dismissed the appeal, however, replying: "It may be that as with *much of the other evidence* relied upon by Mr Hashmi [the applicants' representative], this evidence is consistent with the relationship *but it does not prove it*".[45] In *Tula Bibi v. Entry Clearance Officer Dacca* similarly, the adjudicator expressed the same view, saying: "A large quantity of documents were produced at the hearing consisting mainly of 56 family letters only 3 of which could be established as pre-dating the applications".[46]

---

[42] Memorandum by UKIAS to the *Fifth Report, op. cit.*, 100.

[43] TH/1040/75 (657) d. 19.3.76 (unreported) at 2.

[44] *ibid.*

[45] *ibid.*

[46] TH/48212/79 (2310) d. 18.3.82 (unreported) at 2. Another very revealing case is *Asha Bibi v. Entry Clearance Officer Dacca* TH/4650/76 (1081) d. 30.11.77 (unreported) where letters were produced and where even the ECO "accepted that there was strong documentary evidence to show that the sponsor had a wife and children of the names of the appellants". The appeal was still dismissed because the date of the marriage could not be pinpointed (at 4).

There was "no direct evidence to identify the persons" involved, he claimed.[47] These cases show that sometimes the submission of documentary evidence, in the form of private personal correspondence, is required to meet for a higher standard of proof than on a balance of probabilities.

(7) LAND DEEDS

Of all the documents likely to be tendered land transfer title deeds duly executed and naming the claimed wife as one of the parties, are the most reliable. The *Split Families* Report considers a land deed to be "of paramount importance as evidence".[48] Even the "Pakistan and Azad Kashmir" guidance referred to above,[49] accepted the probative value of land deeds *per se*. This is a public document proving the transfer of property between the parties mentioned in the document. If in such a genuine document an applicant (for example a wife) is identified as the vendee having the same address as that of the sponsor, this constitutes very cogent proof of the relationship. The *Split Families* report has stated that "in most cases where even the original of the land deed, bearing all the official seals and signatures and details of the registration, was produced", the immigration authorities attached no importance to the document at all.[50] Our own studies support this. In *Tula Bibi*, already considered, the adjudicator, dismissing the appeal, held that "although land deeds could generally be regarded as being reliable, one such document was not sufficient to discharge the burden of proof".[51] In *Marion Khatun v. Entry Clearance Officer Dacca* the appeal of the applicants was dismissed notwithstanding evidence of a land deed.[52] In *Koyrun Nessa v. Entry Clearance Officer Dacca*[53] the adjudicator latched on to the existence of

---

[47] *ibid.*

[48] The Report states that "the registration of land transfer deeds have been most systematically kept in the District Registrar's office, all over the country in the safest possible custody since 1797. A true copy of all land transaction deeds has been kept in large ledger books, duly endorsing the various official seals and the signature of the vendor and the witnesses for about two centuries in the various archives of the closely guarded rooms of the huge building of the District Registrar's Office. With special permission from the authorities we have been shown all the thousands of volumes of leather bound ledgers kept on iron shelves on the various floors, guarded by security men. On our request, to our surprise, we were also shown a copy of a document made exactly a hundred years ago." See *Split Families* Report, *op. cit.*, p. 23.

[49] See *supra*, p. 90.

[50] *Supra*, n.39, pp. 23–24.

[51] *Supra*, n.46, at 2.

[52] TH/31849/79 (1666) d. 5.12.79 (unreported), at 2.

[53] TH/2647/75 (790) d. 10.8.76 (unreported) at 3.

the discrepancies made by the principal applicant. Her representative argued, however, that these were inevitable in the circumstances considering that she was totally deaf. Evidence of a land deed and remittances going back 10 years showed that she was related. Again, the appeal was dismissed both by the adjudicator and the Tribunal. In *Phull Begum v. Entry Clearance Officer Dacca* equally, the principal applicant's representative argued that the sponsor who bought the land would not have done so for a woman who was not his wife. Incredibly, the Tribunal replied that, be that as it may, "No explanatory evidence . . . was adduced to prove that the transactions concerned the sponsor and the first appellant".[54]

The *de facto* treatment of what is generally regarded, even by immigration officials, to be the most reliable document in these and other cases, provides the most explicit evidence of the low priority given to documents produced by applicants abroad. No land deed, to the writer's knowledge, has been castigated as being a forgery by ECOs or the appellate authorities, and yet both manage to circumvent its implications by implementing or endorsing a refusal on obscure and untenable grounds. The example of land deeds as documentary proofs — in this case officially recognised — is the most telling in respect of the place of documents in the immigration process.

(8) Electoral Lists

If land transfer deeds can be disregarded then so can, arguably, any other document. Electoral lists or voters lists are prepared by government election commission officials and are maintained in the Election Commission's head office in each district as a public document.[55] The general public may inspect an electoral list and an official attested copy may be obtained. Voters lists are rarely produced by applicants in evidence before an ECO, or at the appeals stage.[56] This is curious because the probative value of such a document is high since it is made up by government officials based on information such as a person's address, relationship and age. The information is then printed in volumes and kept as a public document. In *Marion Khatun v. Entry Clearance Officer Dacca*,[57] however, a voters' list (as well

---

[54] TH/4255/75 (861) d. 8.12.76 (unreported), at 4.
[55] In Bangladesh this takes place under s.7(4)(2) of the Evidence Act 1872 as modified in 1963.
[56] In its investigation of 100 cases UKIAS only found evidence of one case where a voters list was submitted to an adjudicator. See *Split Families* Report, *op. cit.*, 22.
[57] TH/31849/79 (1666) d. 5.12.79 (unreported).

as a land deed and other documentary evidence) was produced before an adjudicator. Neither the adjudicator nor the Tribunal, who upheld the adjudicator's decision against the applicants, had anything to say about the importance that could properly be attached to such a document.

(9) OTHER MISCELLANEOUS DOCUMENTS

School certificates have also been ignored as in *Rajia Khatun v. Entry Clearance Officer Dacca*,[58] in which an appeal was dismissed without discussion of the value of school certificates as a means of identifying the child at school. In *Tula Bibi v. Entry Clearance Officer Dacca*[59] local vaccination records were left unassessed by the adjudicator. A pension and army book of a sponsor usually contains details of his dependent wife and children. This evidence comes from independent and reliable sources if it is obtained from proper custody in its original or duly certified form. It is infrequently produced in evidence, according to the *Split Families* Report, not because it is unavailable, but because its probative value is rarely appreciated.[60] In *Shafait Bi v.Entry Clearance Officer Islamabad*[61] however, one finds that a pension book was produced showing that the sponsor had served 17 years in the army. However, despite his representative emphasising its importance at all levels of the appeals process, both the adjudicator and the Tribunal disregarded this evidence and rejected the appeals on the basis of discrepancies. In the same way identity cards have not been evaluated for their evidential value. A striking case in this respect is *Hjera Bibi v. Entry Clearance Officer Islamabad*, in which the sponsor's claim for marriage allowance was accepted by the Inland Revenue and remittances were then sent by the sponsor to the claimed wife to whom an identity card was later issued. The Tribunal still rejected the appeal holding that this "may be regarded as consistent with their being man and wife but none of these matters *prove* the marriage."[62]

(10) CONCLUSIONS

It is clear from this analysis that the policy of disparaging documentary evidence cannot be justified in terms of widely existing fraud. In

---

[58] TH/93066/82 (2662) d. 8.4.83 (unreported).

[59] TI I/48214/79 (2310) d. 18.3.82 (unreported), at 2.

[60] *Split Families* Report, *op. cit.*, 27.

[61] TH/2900/73 (627) d. 16.3.76 (unreported), at 2–3.

[62] TH/1040/75 (657) d. 19.3.76 (unreported), at 4.

fact even official attitudes are not wholly consistent, which suggests
that there is no coherently worked out policy with regard to the
treatment of documents — save perhaps that most officials subscribe
to the view proclaimed by the various guidances that documents, on
the whole, are worthless. This lack of consistency is seen through a
number of mediums. One finds, for example, the Secretary of State
acceding in March 1976 "that it was often impossible for applicants
to produce satisfactory documentary evidence and it was therefore
necessary to question them".[63] Just a week later the Tribunal decided
in another case that documentary evidence in the form of remittance
slips and issue of identity card and other such documents did not
suffice as proof of fact of marriage because if the issue is one of
marriage, a genuine marriage certificate must be produced: "Had the
marriage taken place, as claimed, there should have been no difficulty
in producing positive credible evidence of the ceremony to the
ECO."[64] Another manifestation of the lack of consistency is that the
credence given to any set of documents has fluctuated from time to
time. If this is so, then immigration procedures can hardly be
justified as being necessary tools for the verification of the authenticity of genuine applicants. Thus in *Channan Bi v. Entry Clearance
Officer Islamabad*[65] further documentary evidence was produced before
the Tribunal which found:

> "All this additional evidence is very favourable to the appellant's case. On
> the other hand the discrepancies in the family tree and the reason for
> producing bogus birth certificates remain unexplained. Doubts therefore
> remain, as to the claimed relationship but if the appellants are the wife
> and children of the sponsor it is difficult to see what further evidence
> could have been adduced before us."[66]

So here were unexplained discrepancies relating not merely to
ancillary matters but to the family tree itself and there was evidence
of fraud in the form of bogus birth certificates. Yet the appeal was
allowed. Compare this with the case of *Begum Bi*,[67] above, where
there were no discrepancies regarding family matters; no pre-existing
fraud; receipts for bank remittances going back eight years; a previous
affidavit specifying the names of the children; evidence of passports;

[63] *Banti v. Entry Clearance Officer Delhi* TH/3216/74 (660) d. 11.3.76 (unreported), at 4.
[64] *Hjera Bibi v. Entry Clerance Officer Islamabad* TH/1040/75 (657) d. 18.3.76 (unreported), at 4.
[65] TH/2005/74 (545) d. 19.11.75 (unreported).
[66] *ibid.* at 5.
[67] *Supra*, n.34, at 5.

and photographs. In that case appeals were dismissed at all levels, the Tribunal explaining that the photographs failed to "resolve the question of identity" although it did accept that there was a Begum Bi and five children. Such cases abound.[68]

It is also manifestly clear that there has been a noticeable shift in official attitudes over the years. Thus in *Kamalinder Kaur v. Secretary of State for the Home Department*,[69] decided before the Immigration Act 1971 took effect, the Tribunal allowed the appeal on the basis that: "There is no evidence before us to cast any doubt on the authenticity of these two documents and we feel therefore that we must accept the documents as they stand."[70]

The evidence in this case related to an attestation by an Indian doctor that he had attended to the sponsor's first wife as she was dying which meant that his second wife was therefore genuine. In *Shiv Kaur v. Secretary of State for the Home Department* the Tribunal declared that "we must accept some, at any rate, of the additional evidence at its face value".[71] It is not known whether secret guidances of the kind that we have seen had been circulated among officials at posts overseas at this time, or whether scepticism of documentary evidence was as deep rooted as the later cases show.

There is no doubt, however, that statements such as that of the ECO in *Fultera Begum* 10 years later, are symptomatic of a decisive shift in official attitudes. The ECO in that case declared that although a marriage certificate "in the prescribed form" had been presented to him such documents "were not proof in themselves" because of the "facility with which they could be obtained."[72] Evidence that documents are prone to be regarded in this light proliferates at all levels and with regard to all documents. Thus as far as personal correspondences is concerned we have seen that a line is thrown between correspondence before and after the determination of the application. With regard to land deeds (exalted even by the secret guidances) the qualification is inserted in one case by an adjudicator that "although land deeds could generally be regarded as being reliable, one such document was not sufficient . . ."[73] In other cases such distinctions are dispensed with altogether.[74] Photographs are also rejected both by

[68] See, for example, the cases discussed above of *Tula Bibi* (*supra*, n.24), *Alam Bi* (*supra*, n.25), *Sundi Bibi* (*supra*, n.26) and *Phull Begum* (*supra*, n.31).
[69] Ex/203/710 d. 27.10.71 (unreported).
[70] *ibid.* at 4.
[71] TH/6116/71 d. 24.8.71 (unreported), at 6.
[72] *Supra*, n.19.
[73] *Tula Bibi*, *supra*, n.24.
[74] *Marion Khatun*, *supra*, n.57.

ECOs[75] and by the Tribunal even if "a likeness exists between the appellant as shown and the photograph attached to the declaration . . .".[76] Pension books, electoral lists and a variety of other documents suffer a similar fate.

This shift to which we have referred suggests that the variable content of the practices is a result of external pressures which bring themselves to bear upon the process of decision making. Although many of the guidances are demonstrably inaccurate they do regulate every aspect of the decision-making process by an official and many decisions are only explicable on the basis, not of the facts of a case, but of the guidances. This also helps to account for the shift over a number of years, but especially in the decade 1971 to 1981,[77] in the treatment of documents at all levels.

Finally, there is a lack of consistency in the present day cases. Of all the cases on documentary evidence examined by the writer there was only one kind of evidence which appeared to be accepted: an insurance endowment policy.[78] Here the Tribunal noted that the sponsor had been insured and in the event of his death the premium was to be payable to his wife, Mrs Alam Bi.[79] In its view this clinched the case for the appellants. But this does not square with the argument of "identity" which has been used in numerous other cases. Thus in *Tula Bibi* the adjudicator said:

> "A large quantity of documents were produced at the hearing consisting mainly of 56 family letters . . . There were local vaccination and marriage certificates and a family land deed . . . A report from the Salvation Army on field inquiries made in the Sponsor's village was produced. The

---

[75] *Begum Bi, supra*, n.34.
[76] *Nazir Begum, supra*, n.38.
[77] Compare for example, *Kamalinder Kaur v. Secretary of State for the Home Department* (*supra*, n.69) with *Fultera Begum* (*supra*, n.19) and *Tula Bibi* (*supra*, n.24). Another point to note is that if the demeanour of witnesses were to be properly considered there is much circumstantial evidence which the authorities could take into account but which never surfaces in the transcripts of these cases. For example, the UKIAS research team observed that an ECO would often note that the youngest child will have been brought to the interview "not because the child was required for the interview, but mainly because she is still being breast-fed. An observant ECO would also note that, after a considerable period of questioning, when the child tends to become somewhat restless, in utter desperation to keep the child quiet, the claimed mother starts breast-feeding the baby (while still replying to the questions of the ECO), scantily covering the face of the baby with one end of the sari." See *Split Families* Report, *op. cit.*, at 28.
[78] In the family reunion immigration cases, insurance policies were either found to have been made long before the application where the wife and some of the children were beneficiaries, or they were found to have been made by the sponsor with his wife and the children as beneficiaries to his wages in the event of accidental death.
[79] *Alam Bi, supra*, n.25 at 2.

representative had spoken to 3 villages who named persons bearing the same names as the sponsor's claimed family. There was *no direct evidence to identify* the persons mentioned as being those concerned in this appeal or to establish that further *deception* was or had been practised on that occasion. The adjudicator did not consider that report as conclusive evidence."[80] (Author's emphasis.)

The basis of this decision, that is — "how do we know that the woman and children identified in Bangladesh as the dependants of the sponsor in England, are the same on whose behalf evidence has been tendered at the hearing in London" — is currently the most popular argument employed by the appellate authorities. It is a sinister device and a catch-22 situation for the applicant because the Immigration Appeals Act 1969 laid down that no dependant may land without being in possession of an entry certificate. She cannot attend and give evidence at the hearing of her appeal against refusal of entry certificate. The appellate authorities can ask "How do we know?" but the kind of proof that they are demanding, in disregard of documentary evidence, can never be produced before them. In the case of *Tula Bibi* the applicants were fortunate because the Tribunal reversed the decision of the adjudicator because of the irrefutable findings of the Salvation Army. Other applicants have not fared well. In *Begum Bi*, for example, the Tribunal held that the evidence of photographs did not "resolve the question of identity".[81] In *Pritam Kaur v. Entry Clearance Officer Delhi*,[82] the sponsor, a man of over 60 years of age, wanted his wife to join him here. He was illiterate and had suffered an industrial accident some years ago as a result of which he claimed he did not remember well. When questioned about the discrepancies in his evidence he replied: "I am an old person and get confused." The adjudicator dismissed the appeal on the discrepancies. Before the Tribunal, two photographs of family groups were produced, one of which was claimed to have been taken 10 years ago before the sponsor came to England. This was not contested. The Tribunal accepted that one of the photographs included the "sponsor and a woman identified as Pritam Kaur" by the sponsor, his son-in-law living here and another witness appearing before the Tribunal. The Tribunal dismissed the appeal contending:

"The evidence of identification may be additional evidence linking the sponsor with Pritam Kaur . . . but it does not establish that the lady and

[80] *Supra*, n.24.
[81] *Supra*, n.34.
[82] TH/765/75 (809) d. 17.8.76 (unreported).

the young man who appeared before the EC were the person's identified in the photographs".[83]

Similarly in *Rashida Bi v. Visa Officer Islamabad* the adjudicator dismissed the appeal after remarking that:

"There seems to be a great probability that the sponsor married someone named Rashida Bi at sometime probably in July 1967, but the question for resolution is whether it was she who applied for an entry clearance certificate on April 24, 1972".[84]

These cases cannot be reconciled with the case of the insurance endowment policy discussed above. Yet the question is why should the issue of "identity" be so important in one set of cases but not in another?

A process of deductive reasoning may help answer this question. First, it is not the fear of being hoodwinked by unscrupulous applicants that leads officials to refuse an application, for genuine and officially authenticated documents have also been rejected all too readily.[85] Secondly, it is not a question of bogus applicants parodying genuine wives and children (as the guidance in Pakistan and Azad Kashmir suggested), because if proof is on a balance of probabilities, it is implausible to entertain the suspicion that a sponsor has been sending monies to a wife for the last 14 years, but now wishes to bring in another middle-aged woman with the complicity of the real wife and children who will, presumably, furnish the genuine marriage, birth and other documents.[86] The answer lies rather in the third possibility, and it is quite banal. It is seen in those cases where, for example, photographs have been identified of the sponsor with the claimed wife, as evidence which cannot be controverted — and yet the authorities have inquired, "how do we know that the woman applying is the same woman as in the photograph?" Through these devices, whether they be the "discrepancy system", concern with forgeries, or the issue of "identity" the entry of family members is kept at a "manageable" level as a matter of deliberate administrative choice and the majority of genuine applicants are turned away with the knowledge that they are genuine.

---

[83] *ibid.*, at 2–6.
[84] TH/12512/75 (1175) d. 3.3.78 (unreported), at 6.
[85] See *Begum Bi, supra*, n.34; *Nazir Begum, supra*, n.38; and *Fultera Begum, supra*, n.19.
[86] See especially *Monwara Begum v. Entry Clearance Officer Dacca* TH/1127/73 (585) d. 28.1.76 (unreported), at 94 and *Pritam Kaur v. Entry Clearance Officer New Delhi* TH/705/75 (809) (unreported), at 84.

Medical Evidence

Finally, in this chapter, we examine the unpalatable subject of medical examinations as a means of verifying the genuineness of applicants. This can basically be divided up, as far as cases in the 1980s were concerned, into an x-ray examination of an applicant and a more intensive personal medical examination, both of which we must here consider.

(1) MEDICAL EXAMINATIONS

(a) Background to the Yellowlees Report

The term "virginity tests" first surfaced in this country when on February 1, 1979 a report was published in the press of a medical examination made at Heathrow Airport concerning an Indian woman who wished to enter the United Kingdom in order to marry a man settled here. The immigration officer suspected that the woman might already be married and he referred her to a medical inspector with the intention of finding out whether she had borne any children. It seems that a personal examination of the woman then took place. Following the outrage a debate was held in Parliament on February 19, 1979.[87] A study of the medical records at the ports of entry showed that similar examinations had occurred on a few occasions during the previous eight years. During the debate the Home Secretary, Mr Merlyn Rees, announced that he had asked the Chief Medical Officer, Sir Henry Yellowlees, "to carry out a review of the objects and nature of all medical examinations in the immigration control context",[88] in the light of both the incident at Heathrow Airport and the concern that was equally expressed at that time regarding the use of X-rays to determine the age of applicants before issuing them with entry clearance.

In December 1980 the Home Affairs Committee on Race Relations and Immigration published, as *Immigration Topics*, Sir Yellowlees' report. It found that medical examinations were carried out "sympathetically, humanely, and with proper regard to the dignity of the person concerned".[89] The use of x-rays, it stated, "afford a fairly

---

[87] *H.C. Official Report* (5th series), Vol. 963 (February 19, 1979), Cols. 213–223.
[88] These were the terms of reference of Sir Michael Yellowlees, ACB, M.A., B.M., BCH, FRCP, MRCS, FFCM, as the Chief Medical Officer, and he was assisted by Dr N.J.B. Evans, the Deputy Chief Medical Officer at the Department of Health and Social Security. The Report was largely the work of the latter.
[89] Home Affairs Committee, Race Relations and Immigration Sub-Committee (1981), *Immigration Topics* (Minutes of Evidence), December 1980 H.C. 89), p. 6, para. 3.

accurate and acceptably safe method" for assessing age in the case of children but not for adult. Indeed the "Foreign Secretary had already given instructions to posts overseas not to refer adults for x-ray examination to assess age".[90]

(b) How Medical Examinations Work

In *Nasabat Jan v. Visa Officer Islamabad*[91] the Home Office was asked by the Tribunal to inquire about the circumstances leading up to the medical examination of the appellant in that case. The ECO in Islamabad sent a telex to the Home Office explaining the procedure for such examinations:

> "The applicant would be asked if she would be willing to undergo a medical examination. *If she agreed* she would be given one stock pro-forma letter addressed to her, stating *inter alia* that she had agreed to undergo a medical examination and that she should arrange to call on one of the doctors listed on the reverse side of the letter (on the reverse side, a list of three doctors with their addresses was given). The applicant would also be given a sealed envelope in which there was a second letter; this letter addressed to the doctor (unnamed), would show the applicant's name and passport number for identification purposes, and would request the doctor *to undertake certain medical examinations e.g.* an age estimate of the applicant on the basis of x-rays and her physical condition; an assessment of whether she had any trace of communicable disease, etc, . . .). The applicant would be told to give the sealed envelope to the doctor of her choice. Upon completion of the medical the doctor would send his or her report to the ECO who had signed both letters. The first letter (that addressed to the applicant) would be retained by the applicant, while the second (confidential) letter (is) retained by the doctor unless the ECO specifically asked for it to be returned to him".[92] (Author's emphasis.)

Serious ethical problems are raised through the adoption of this procedure, however. First, presumably medical examinations are only carried out where there is real doubt about the bona fides of an applicant which cannot be solved in any other way. To speak of consent suggests that the applicant has the right to choose and yet if she declines to oblige she is almost certain to be refused entry.[93] Secondly, the "consent" to medical examinations presumably entails

---

[90] *ibid.*
[91] TH/3584/74 (757) d. 17.6.76 (unreported).
[92] *ibid.*, at 5.
[93] In any event, the practice would be unlawful because the applicant would be acting under duress. As Sir Yellowlees said: "I do not think anyone consents happily to an examination of this sort." See *Immigration Topics, op. cit.*, p. 29.

consenting to any kind of examination which may be deemed appropriate in the circumstances and this could then validate even personal medical examinations like "virginity tests" which are surely objectionable. The basis of the Yellowless Report accordingly requires further examination.

(2) X-RAYS: POLICY, IMPLEMENTATION AND ACCURACY

(a) Shortcomings of the Yellowlees Report

The question of x-rays was not examined in depth in the Yellowlees Report. The subject was not discussed in the main body of the report but only described in the Appendix. The Report came to the conclusion that as far as children under 21 years were concerned x-rays "afford a fairly accurate and acceptably safe method" for age assessment. The subject is considerably more complex, however, since what x-ray examinations do is to estimate the chronological age of a person by using skeletal maturity techniques.[94] These techniques evaluate bone maturity but not chronological age. Chronological age is not necessarily linked with bone maturity,[95] in fact, it varies very much from country to country being dependent upon conditions of living, nutrition, climate and racial origin. Chronological age is thus different from "skeletal age" or "bone age" which is "a measure of how far a child has proceeded through the sequence of physical changes associated with adult maturity."[96] X-rays taken to determine "skeletal age" are useful for clinical purposes in assessing a child's growth to see whether the development of the child's skeletal system is advanced or retarded for his chronological age. If the age of a child is not already known, however, they only give a very loose approximation based on skeletal maturity.

How close then is this approximation? For a child of between 10 and 18 years the margin of error for most healthy British and American children is two years either side[97] of the actual age. Following the publication of his Report it was put to Sir Henry

[94] There are broadly two techniques: Atlas and Bone-Specified Scoring technique. See Dr N. Cameron, *The Estimation of Chronological Age* (University of London Press, 1981), p. 4.
[95] See Dr N. Cameron, *op. cit.*. Also see Rentoul and Glaister, *Medical Jurisprudence and Toxicology* (London, 12th ed.) pp. 79–80. The basic work used in Bangladesh is Bakshi's *Synopsis of Medical Jurisprudence* (3rd ed. 1980) which bears out this view at pp. 46–55. Also see *Split Families* Report *op. cit.*, p. 21.
[96] Memorandum by Lord Avebury to the *Fifth Report*, *op. cit.*, Vol. II, p. 158.
[97] *Loc. cit.*

Yellowlees that, "this means that the difference can be 3 years altogether, which means with a child who is said to be 18 but the bone x-ray shows that he might be 15 the margin of error would be enough to account for that difference."[98] Sir Henry concurred in this assessment. As a person gets older the margin of error spans wider, so that with someone over 21 years of age it is a futile exercise. This is reflected in Sir Yellowlees' assurance that the Foreign Secretary had taken steps to ensure that no adults would be so examined. It is also reflected in a case quoted in the *Split Families* Report, *Nessa and Others*, where Dr Jacobs, Consultant Radiologist, was called as an expert witness and contended that on the basis of the x-rays taken, the subject was over 25 but could also be as old as 55![99]

The second thing to note about x-rays is the ethical propriety of their use. In the normal course of life, x-rays are used for clinical purposes to determine "skeletal age" (as distinct from chronological age). The question is whether x-rays ought to be used for administrative purposes in the arena of immigration control. The British Medical Association, the World Health Organisation and the Department of Health and Social Security "Code of Practice" for radiation exposure condemn recourse to X-rays for administrative purposes. The British Medical Association considers its use, *inter alia*, to be "unethical"[1] in this regard. Yet the findings of the Yellowlees Report were that "it is ethical to carry out an x-ray estimation of bone age on a child . . ."[2]

Thirdly, the harmful effects of radiation cannot be overruled. Although the levels of radiation to which a person is exposed under a radiological examination are very low, it is not that the risk of harm is zero. Lord Avebury's memorandum to the Home Affairs Committee in 1982 also linked this with the context of the x-ray examination suggesting that, given the margin of error in most cases, "any radiation risk exceeds the expected benefits to immigration control".[3]

(b) Policy and Implementation

Given that x-rays are only used when everything else fails, clearly there ought to be a policy with regard to those "difficult" cases where

---

[98] *Immigration Topics*, *op. cit.*, p. 29, Q.149.
[99] *Split Families* Report, *op. cit.*, p. 32. The reference to the case is given as TH/20409/77.
[1] Memorandum by Lord Avebury to the *Fifth Report*, *op. cit.*, Vol. II, p. 158. Also see question by John Wheeler at p. 24, Q.103.
[2] *Immigration Topics*, *op. cit.*, Appendix 1, p. 3.
[3] *Supra*, n.96.

they are deemed necessary. Someone somewhere ought to be in a position of explaining that policy. For example, what importance should ECOs attach to medical evidence of an estimated age which does not correlate with the professed age? What age groups do posts overseas consider to be particularly suited among children for a radiological examination? It is not as if x-rays are a mere incidental practice in the immigration of dependants. The *Split Families* Report states that "In our survey of the grounds of refusal of the dependants' cases, medical age assessment lies manifestly the most prominent one".[4] It is estimated that in Bangladesh roughly 480 cases a year involve x-ray examinations, in Pakistan the figure is roughly over 400; and in India the practice ceased early in 1982. So, if with regard to children of a certain age group x-rays are definitely useful, why are they used in Bangladesh and Pakistan, but not in India? It seems that the matter is purely one of discretion with no strict policy being pursued. The discretion as to whether or not to use x-rays rests with each individual post. There is no overall policy so that a post can decide to either continue or drop the practice, as they did in India.[5] However, if age estimation is a matter of evidence, would it not eliminate an important part of that evidence if the practice were dropped? This question was put by Dr Dubs to Mr Adams, Assistant Under-Secretary of State in 1982. The reply given was that there was "a factor in India, and there is no point in neglecting this", whereby "in India there was a quite considerable amount of adverse comment in the press and so there is not the same controversy about this practice in Bangladesh".[6] Mr Lyon, another member of the Home Affairs Committee, interrupted to say that this only meant that in India the practice was not being used because, unlike Bangladesh, "there they are politically sensitive".[7] This exchange reveals that the practice of x-ray examination is not grounded in the sheer necessity for an evidential basis in an age assessment. Presumably, this is because officials at posts overseas are aware of the limited evidential value of x-ray examinations, but also, they may feel that in the vast majority of cases they can resort to other forms of evidence in order to decide the case on a balance of probabilities. So why resort to x-ray examinations at all? To answer this question it is instructive to look at the discussion of the Yellowlees Report by the Home Affairs Committee in 1980.

---

[4] *Split Families* Report, *op. cit.*, p. 31.
[5] *Fifth Report*, *op. cit.*, Vol. II, p. 47, Q.185 by Mr Dubs.
[6] *ibid.*, p. 47, Q.185 by Mr Adams.
[7] *ibid.*, p. 47, Q.186 by Mr Lyon.

(c) Accuracy and Inaccuracy: the use of x-ray evidence

Theoretically, at least, the Yellowlees Report is the basis of all current practices on medical examinations in the Indian sub-continent. When the Home Affairs Committee deliberated upon its findings x-ray examinations were also discussed. One particular contention by a Committee member that arose is worthy of note. Mr Alex Lyon, a former Minister for Immigration, stated that the bulk of the cases on children involved the x-ray of teenage boys of about 16 years. If there was a margin of error here of up to four years (*i.e.* two years on either side), "then it is really a useless assessment". Dr Evans, the chief architect of the Yellowlees Report, replied that that really depended on what one was trying to show. Mr Lyon argued that he had dealt with a lot of cases on x-ray examination but had "never seen an x-ray investigation which actually helped an immigrant to prove what he was saying. It has only been used to undermine his case".[8]

Mr Lyon's assertion that x-rays are only used to undermine the case of would-be immigrants was not adequately refuted either by Dr Evans or by Sir Yellowlees. The decided cases give proof that x-ray examinations do not help immigrants but have been used to hinder the fair consideration of applications.

These cases on wives and children may now be examined.

(d) Children

Most children that are x-rayed are teenage boys of about 16 years old. Many posts overseas take the view that there is a great incentive among people to bring in a teenage child of the extended family in order to work.[9] Thus in *Sawar Bi* the claimed wife and two children, a boy who professed to be 16, and a daughter sought to join the sponsor in the United Kingdom. In Islamabad the boy was sent for a radiologist examination. On the basis of x-rays his age was put at 12. The applications of all three were turned down on the grounds that a fraudulent attempt had been made to bring in someone who was not related as claimed. Before the Tribunal on appeal it was argued on their behalf that there was "substantial agreement" on detailed family matters given by all three and there was substantial documentary evidence of remittance receipts and income tax evidence. The appeals, however, were dismissed.[10] In view of the cogent documentary evidence the possibility of error in the medical evidence in this

---

[8] *ibid.*, p. 29, Q.146 by Mr Lyon.
[9] *Immigration Topics, op. cit.*, p. 29.
[10] *Sarwar Bi v. Secretary of State for the Home Department*, TH/23655/78 (1363)) d. 23.10.78 (unreported) at 3. In *Janhura Bibi, infra* (n.106) two children of about 17 and 14 years were refused in similar circumstances.

case cannot be overruled. In *Parveen Begum v. Visa Officer Islamabad* the claimed wife and her five children applied to join the sponsor. The visa officer in Islamabad accepted that apart from two boys all the applicants were related as claimed. Again he based this decision on the medical evidence with regard to their ages.[11]

More recently, evidence against the use of x-ray examinations has become stronger still. It has become increasingly clear that such evidence is not only unreliable *per se*, but it is used with the sole aim of endorsing a refusal by officials. Thus in *Santai Bibi v. Entry Clearance Officer Dacca*,[12] in 1980, three children sought to enter the United Kingdom with the claimed wife. In fact, both the ECO at the post in Dacca and the appellate authorities here, accepted on the evidence that the sponsor had the family members that he claimed he had.[13] The implausible doubt was entertained, however, that two of his own boys, the eldest, had been substituted for bogus ones.[14] The age of the two boys was given as about 16 years for the older one and about 12 years for the younger boy. A report by the Civil Surgeon in Sylhet estimated the age of the older boy at about 15 and the additional x-ray report by another doctor put the age at about 15 as well. For the younger child a report by the Civil Surgeon in Sylhet estimated his age at about 11 years and an additional x-ray report assessed the age to be about 10 or 11 years. It is to be noted here that both medical age assessments of the children fall well within the generally accepted margin of error. Three years later, however, in 1976, the British High Commission doctor in Sylhet, Dr Latiff, estimated the ages to be 15 years and 11 years respectively. It is not clear from the transcript of the case why, the x-ray examinations having been favourable, the applications of the entire family were not then allowed. Moreover, Dr Latiff's assessment was at variance with the assessment of two earlier doctors, working independently, whose findings were wholly consistent with each other. On the basis of the latest age assessment, the ECO found that the two boys were bogus and dismissed all the applications. The appeal to the adjudicator was also dismissed. Before the Tribunal it was argued first, that the rejection of the application and the decision of the adjudicator fell foul of the case of *Aftab Miah v. Secretary of State for the Home*

[11] TH/20235/77 (1285) d. 7.12.78 (unreported).
[12] TH I/42341/79 (1866) d. 23.9.80 (unreported).
[13] This acceptance was based on what can only be described as overwhelming proof in the form of tax relief claims since 1958 by the sponsor, land bought and letters exchanged, and remittances sent during this entire period.
[14] Again, the basis of this doubt lies in the secret guidances to officials which have been described earlier.

Department,[15] in which the Tribunal approved Glaister and Rentoul's *Medical Jurisprudence and Toxicology* in the estimation of a person's age within a range of two to three years; and secondly, that the adjudicator followed the questionable age estimates of Dr Latiff who was supposed to rely on Dr H.N. Bakshi's *Synopsis of Medical Jurisprudence*, but in his medical certificates it was apparent that he did not. Here was a substantial error of law both in the evaluation of evidence which was manifestly suspect and in the rejection of evidence which was patently sound. The Tribunal, however, not only dismissed the appeal but did so without any discussion of the appeal grounds.[16]

In *Ruqayah Begum v. Visa Officer Islamabad*[17] the evidence was once again interpreted in this way. Here the claimed wife's appeal was allowed but her three children were refused entry. The two boys, Khalil and Zafar, claimed to be 16 years old and 14 years old respectively. The ECO thought they looked younger and he subsequently proceeded to dismiss their applications after an age assessment based on "physical developments and x-rays". Before the adjudicator the appellants' representative tendered further medical evidence from two different doctors. In both cases the age estimates were well within the two to three year margin of error. These assessments were not disputed but the adjudicator still dismissed the appeals. On further appeal to the Tribunal a third age assessment was obtained from Dr P. Jacobs of the Royal Orthopaedic Hospital, Birmingham. Dr Jacobs estimated Khalil's age to be 14 to 15 years at the time when the first examination was undertaken, and Zafar's age to be 10 to 11 years. The sponsor was the sole witness at the hearing before the Tribunal and he adamantly maintained that both boys were his sons. He put in evidence a copy of his application for registration as a citizen of the United Kingdom and Colonies dated July 1971. This was almost a decade ago and he drew attention to the fact that in it he had mentioned both his wife and the two boys as members of his family. The Tribunal held that with regard to Khalil there was an age discrepancy of "some 16 months" and that this "caused disquiet". In the case of Zafar, there was an age discrepancy of "some two years two months . . . which caused grave suspicion". The Tribunal dismissed both appeals.[18]

---

[15] [1972] Imm. A.R. 185.
[16] *Santai Bibi v. Entry Clearance Officer Dacca* TH/42341/79 (1866) d. 23.9.80 (unreported), at 3–4.
[17] TH/30765/78 (1889) d. 30.10.80 (unreported).
[18] *ibid.*, at 2.

As far as the x-ray examination of girls is concerned the same approach is adopted. Cases of girls, however, are not as numerous as those of boys. As the *Split Families* Report explains, for a girl it is often used to consider the viability of her claimed marriage in the claimed year. If, on examination, she is found to be younger than she claims — for example, 14 or 15 years old — the claim of her marriage to the sponsor is found to be untenable and her application is refused.[19]

(e) Wives

The cases show that x-ray examination of wives was used by officials to the same end. In the case of children we have seen that even the safeguard of the two to three year margin of error is disregarded at posts overseas and by the appellate authorities in order to implement a refusal. In the case of wives, until x-rays were finally stopped in 1979, most cases involved women of between 35 to 45 years. As we have seen, an age assessment in such cases can give ludicrous results.[20] Nevertheless, they were used, with the result that they often led to a refusal. In *Janhura Bibi v. Entry Clearance Officer Islamabad*[21] the claimed wife was alleged to be 31 years of age by the sponsor. There were no discrepancies in the details that they gave regarding family and other matters. Following an x-ray examination her age was assessed to be about 45 years. The practice of age assessment in this case, however, went further because the doctor concerned (Dr Bassett) took into account other criteria as well, such as "Build; age; posture; gait; skin elasticity and tone; hair; memory".[22] If x-ray examination of a person over 21 years is highly unreliable, factors such as memory would appear to be doubly so, especially in the context of the Indian sub-continent.[23] In *Muhibun Nesa Khatun v. Entry Clearance Officer Dacca*[24] the claimed wife said that she was 38 years old. An x-ray examination led to her age being estimated at about 28 or 29 years. This conclusion was reached by Dr Latiff, the British High Commission doctor in Dacca,

> ". . . upon the ground that the union of the first *sacral vertebra* and the rest of the *sacrum* was 'almost completed'. Since this union completes at the

---

[19] *Immigration Control Procedures, op. cit.*, pp. 32–33. Note here the case of *Jofara Begum*, TH/46090/79 referred to at p. 33, n.1, where the ECO said, "Medical evidence indicated that the principal appellant was only 8 years old at the time of her stated marriage in 1950. She herself said she was 16 at the time of marriage".

[20] See also the *Split Families* Report, pp. 35–37.

[21] TH/3587/75 (695) d. 10.5.76 (unreported).

[22] *ibid.*, at 3.

[23] See *supra*, n.99, pp. 25–31.

[24] TH/15449/77 (1473) d. 23.3.79 (unreported).

latest at 30 years of age he concluded that she had not yet reached this age. If his estimate was even approximately right she could hardly have been the mother of the six claimed children."[25] (Author's emphasis.)

The *Split Families* Report shows how misconceived this approach is, however. In its discussion of x-ray examinations it states: "According to the opinion of the authorities it seems clear that there is no universal standard of determining the medical or skeletal age through radiological (x-ray) examination since the ossification and body union on which the skeletal examination is based varies from country to country."[26] The incidence of malnutrition and genetic factors are also significant. In the case before us, therefore, it is by no means clear that the union of the sacral vertebra with the rest of the sacrum takes place before the age of 30 years. The ECO, however, dismissed the appeal. Before the adjudicator further medical evidence was tendered by the appellant which showed her age to be between 30 and 35 years. This was naturally closer to her claimed age of 38 years. The adjudicator preferred to rely on Dr Latiff's earlier assessment and the appeal was dismissed. The appeal to the Tribunal saw yet another medical report based on an examination carried out some two years after the original one by Dr Latiff. This put the probable age at between 35 and 40 years. The Tribunal also considered the other evidence before it. In particular, it considered a Confirmation of Registration as a citizen issued eight years ago, which gave details of the sponsor's wife and children. The Tribunal, however, also chose to accept Dr Latiff's assessment despite the fact that not only were the latter reports consistent with the alleged age but they were both also consistent as between themselves. The Tribunal concluded: "There is some evidence of consistency of conduct in the sponsor's part but it does not of course necessarily connote that the woman shown on that document was the woman who presented herself before the ECO."[27]

Even as late as November 1979 middle-aged women were being x-rayed in the Indian sub-continent notwithstanding that the lid has been blown off the top of these practices by the "virginity tests" of February 1979. Thus in *Talibun Nessa v. Entry Clearance Officer Dacca*[28] the wife claimed to be 48 years old but Dr Latiff assessed her age to be about 36 years following an x-ray examination. Accordingly, the

[25] *ibid.*, at 2.
[26] *Split Families* Report, *op. cit.*, n.2.
[27] *Supra*, n.24, at 2–3.
[28] TH/31349/78 (1647) d. 8.11.79 (unreported).

application and the subsequent appeals were dismissed. In December 1979 the Tribunal heard of a wife who claimed to be 40 years old and was x-rayed. On the basis of all the evidence the Tribunal was satisfied that the sponsor had a wife by the name of the applicant but was not satisfied that the applicant was that wife.

True to the thesis adopted in this discussion that x-ray examinations are superfluous and not imperative to the effective implementation of immigration control, all posts in the Indian sub-continent have recently decided to abandon this practice. This decision appears to have been taken by the Home Office in 1982.[29] Medical examinations, in general, however, are still carried out.

(3) PERSONAL MEDICAL EXAMINATIONS

No degree of personal empathy by officials at posts overseas can help justify personal medical examinations. Admittedly, they have been rare over the years and have now been discontinued altogether. They show how far officials have been prepared to go in the past. The Home Office cannot escape criticism either for it is difficult to believe that they were unaware of what went on. The Heathrow Airport "virginity test" case of February 1979 was not the only case of its kind. In *Nasabat Jan*, mentioned earlier,[30] the applicant applied to join the sponsor as his second wife. She claimed to be 21 years of age but the Visa Officer considered her to be 17 years old. She agreed to undergo a medical examination "to show if there were any physical indications that she might be a married woman". Two doctors, working independently, examined the girl. One concluded that she had lived with her husband; the other, that she had not. The Tribunal hearing the case, noted how one doctor found that:

> "Her secondary sex characteristics were only just beginning to appear and she had not started menstruating. The hymen was intact. Doctor Malik in his medical report   stated that the appellant was 14/15 years old. Her hymen was ruptured, her vagina showed that she had had intercourse and the signs of marriage were positive. The appellant herself told the ECO that she had had sexual intercourse with the sponsor."

Perplexed, the Tribunal could only express consternation and concern at how two doctors working "on separate occasions on the *same*

---

[29] *Split Families* Report, *op. cit.*, p. 36, n.2. Also see *Immigration Control Procedures*, *op. cit.*, at p. 72.
[30] *Supra*, n.91.

day" could produce such conflicting reports. It allowed the appeal adding: "It would no doubt be a considerable ordeal for a girl from a village in Mirpur to be interrogated at length on such personal matters at the British High Commission."[31]

In fact, even after the Heathrow Airport incident of 1979, personal medical examinations were still taking place. The Government of the day was embarrassed over the incident at the time and appeared genuinely to regret it. On February 2, 1979 Mr Merlyn Rees, the Home Secretary, told the House that he had given instructions that immigration officers should not ask the medical inspector to examine passengers with a view to establishing whether they had borne children or had had sexual relations. This view was reiterated by Mr William Whitelaw as Home Secretary on November 13, 1980.[32] Mr Raison, the Immigration Minister, when questioned about it replied: "I do not myself think there is a great deal to be said about it . . . I think it is a piece of history."[33] In *Ambia Khatun v. Entry Clearance Officer Dacca*, however, the doctor carried out a "gynaecological examination" of the principal appellant on March 22, 1980. In his report the doctor also made reference to the appellant's obstetric history, and recorded her "as having two previous children, one male and one female".[34] The principal appellant's appeal was finally allowed by the Tribunal. In *Talibun Nessa*, the principal appellant was less fortunate. Dr Latiff of the British High Commission, Dacca, took an x-ray examination of the applicant but also found that "there was no greying of the principal appellant's hair and that the menopause had not started".[35] On this basis it was felt that she could not be 48 years of age and so her appeal was dismissed.

In conclusion, the following points need to be made. First, it is clear that contrary to what the Yellowlees Report concluded, such examinations by their very nature, cannot be carried out "sympathetically, humanely, and with proper regard to the dignity of the person concerned".[36] As the *Split Families* Report notes:

". . . it is sad to observe that so many women have had to go through a rather humiliating process of a thorough physical examination of a very

[31] *ibid.*, at p. 2–4. Once again it must be asked why ECOs want to know whether a woman is married or not. It seems that they consider this to be relevant because of the belief that a bogus wife may be brought in in preference to a real one, even though no evidence in support of this view has been produced.
[32] *Immigration Topics, op. cit.*, pp. 5–6.
[33] *ibid.*, p. 21–22, Q.83 by Mr Raison.
[34] TH/63386/80 (2956) d. 10.11.83 (unreported), at 3.
[35] *Supra*, n.28 at 3.
[36] See *supra*, p. 109.

intimate nature, for example, the configuration of the external genitals, *by a male doctor in every case* — practice (though regularly followed by the British High Commission) which would be considered abhorrent to public sentiment and the general custom of the country of the applicant."[37] (Author's emphasis.)

Secondly, the reliability of such evidence is, like x-ray evidence, highly suspect. This is seen not only in the case of *Nasabat Jan*[38] where two doctors found totally different facts, but also in the fact that it has been decided to discontinue this practice. Thirdly, and finally, it appears once more that there has been official delay in implementing policy decisions which have been for the benefit of immigrants at posts overseas. Mr Rees' declaration of February 2, 1979 clearly took its time in reaching the British High Commission in Dacca.

Conclusions

The evidence on both x-ray examinations and personal examinations shows that medical examinations of this kind have been used without logic or reason,[39] and the fact that they have now been abandoned is enough proof of this. The strongest proof, however, emerges from the cases that demonstrate that genuine applications have been deliberately refused through the manipulation of evidence. Where probative evidence exists this has been dismissed and where it does not, it has been "manufactured" in some highly dubious ways. Even politicians such as Richard Crossman who argued the case for compulsory entry clearance certificates on the basis of a quote on admissions, before the Immigration Appeals Act 1969 brought it into place, could not have foreseen hardships suffered to this degree by applicants. Still less would they have foreseen the difficulties faced by applicants in the appeals process, a subject which we must now consider in the next chapter. Before leaving this subject altogether, however, it should be noted that since the introduction of the DNA "Fingerprinting" tests in immigration control procedures in the late 1980s, disputed relationships for children are less likely to occur.

---

[37] *Split Families* Report, *op. cit.*, p. 37.
[38] *Supra*, n.31.
[39] Even Bakshi's *Synopsis of Medical Jurisprudence, op. cit.*, expressed doubts about the accuracy of age assessments over 30–35 years of age. (See *Split Families* Report, *op. cit.*, 36). While officials at posts overseas purport to use his methods of examination technique, they seem to have ignored this part of his work.

This would not help wives, but the breakthrough of the DNA blood test is such that a positive identification of a child's relationship can be made even when it is only possible for one parent to give a sample.[40] The Home Office published guidance notes to ECOs on this subject in February 1989 and for the first time there is a reference to blood tests in the appropriate circumstances as being "regarded as sufficient without further enquiry" or as being "regarded as presumptive."[41] At long last in 1990 the Government announced the DNA scheme for blood tests would no longer be privately paid for but from public funds in cases of doubt; medical technology was for once going to be used to aid applicants in their quest to prove their claims. The cost of entry clearance certificates to applicants, however, was to go up to help fund the provision of DNA blood testing.[42] A small price for immigrants — one could argue — given past hardships!

[40] *Split Families* Report, *op. cit.* p. 35.
[41] *ibid.*, p. 36.
[42] See Macdonald and Blake, *Macdonald's Immigration Law and Practice* (London, 3rd ed. 1991), p. 270.

Chapter Four

The Appeals Process

"This gentleman . . . represents our Inquiries Department. He gives clients all the information they need, and as our procedure is not very well known among the populace, a great deal of information is asked for. He has an answer to every question, if you ever feel like it you can try him out."

Kafka, *The Trial*

ECOs would not arguably be deciding cases in the manner described in the last chapter, with such awesome disregard of basic principles, if they did not have at least the general support of the immigration appellate authorities. This is a bold assertion to make, but the thesis of this work is that whatever may be the position today, this assertion was broadly true in the 1980s. Practically every issue that ECOs face at posts overseas is open to review by the immigration appellate authorities, since they have such wide-ranging powers to hear an appeal.[1] If they wished to express their disapproval of particular practices, they would have ample authority to do so.[2] The fact that a clear pattern of dubious decision making by ECOs persists, is arguably testimony to their having failed in this task during this period. Before this thesis can be advanced any further, however, it is necessary to look at the administrative structure of immigration appeals. Accordingly, in this chapter we first take a brief look at the framework of immigration appeals. Then we consider the appellate authorities own response to issues of the burden and standard of proof in immigration cases. We next consider, first those areas in

---

[1] These powers are enshrined in ss.19 and 20 of the Immigration Act 1971 as amended by s.5(1) of the Immigration Act 1988.
[2] The manner of the exercise of this discretion is discussed, see *infra*, pp. 135–139.

which the appellate authorities intervene to uphold the official findings of proof, and secondly, where they do not so intervene. Finally, we look at the judgments of the higher courts on how to evaluate issues of proof in immigration cases and their lack of effect on the appellate authorities in this sphere and during the period under consideration.

The Structure of Immigration Appeals

The structure of immigration appeals consists of a two-tier system of immigration adjudicators and an Immigration Appeals Tribunal (both being appointed by the Lord Chancellor). To these bodies appeals can be made against various decisions of immigration officers, ECOs and the Home Secretary. In the first instance appeals are normally heard by a single adjudicator with leave to appeal to the IAT, comprising one legally qualified chairperson and two lay persons. The system was set up following the Wilson Committee Report in 1967 whose main concern was one of "basic principle" that "however well administered the present control may be, it is fundamentally wrong and inconsistent with the rule of law that power to take decisions affecting a man's whole future should be vested in officers of the executive, from whose findings there is no appeal".[3] The Immigration Appeals Act 1969, as its name implies, gave effect to these recommendations and the present appellate machinery is now prescribed in Part II of the Immigration Act 1971 and its mechanics in secondary legislation: the Immigration Appeals (Procedure) Rules 1984 and the Immigration Appeals (Notices) Regulations 1984.[4]

In *Bahar v. Immigration Appeals Tribunal*[5] the IAT held that the Immigration Appeals (Procedure) Rules 1984 require adjudicators hearing appeals to undertake an interventionist and inquisitorial approach to the hearing. Accordingly, if representatives failed to ask witnesses questions which the adjudicator considered were important to enable him to arrive at the truth, he could, and should put such questions himself as adjudicators were not bound by the normal rules of evidence. Section 19 of the Immigration Act 1971 states that an "adjudicator may review any determination of a question of fact", or

---

[3] See *Report of the Committee on Immigration Appeals* (the "Wilson Committee"), Cmnd. 3387 (August 1987, at p. 28.
[4] See The Immigration Appeals (Notices) Regulations 1984, S.I. 1984 No. 2040 and Immigration Appeals (Procedure) Rules 1984, S.I. 1984 No. 2041.
[5] [1988] Imm. A.R. 574.

allow an appeal in respect of any "decision or action which involved the exercise of a discretion by the Secretary of State or an officer", on the grounds "that the discretion should have been exercised differently",[6] although recently restrictions on these extensive grounds of appeal have, it is respectfully submitted, been wrongly imposed by the higher courts. However, a decision or action that is in accordance with law cannot be reviewed. These powers are also extended to the Tribunal under section 19(4).[7] Section 20 further states, however, that "any party to appeal to an adjudicator may, if dissatisfied with his determination thereon, appeal to the Appeal Tribunal and the Tribunal may affirm the determination or make any other determination which could have been made by the adjudicator." These give the appellate structure very extensive opportunities to intervene and review a decision or action by an official, no matter how junior or senior, in the administrative hierarchy. We shall examine later the cumulative effect of these powers, but for the moment we must first consider the approach of the immigration appellate authorities to questions of proof. This is the first and primary hurdle that determines their intervention. If they cannot cross this in their minds, they cannot even begin to entertain satisfactorily claims to be "dissatisfied" by an appellant or arguments that a discretion "should have been exercised differently".

The Burden and Standard of Proof

(1) BURDEN OF PROOF

The burden of proof in immigration law, as in all forms of civil litigation, rests squarely on the person seeking an entitlement under the law. With regard to certain subsidiary matters — for instance, whether an applicant has changed his domicile — the burden is on the other party because of the presumption in English law against change of domicile.[8] Yet, there are many cases where the Tribunal has held erroneously the burden of proof on the question of domicile to be on the applicant.[9] Thus in *Fatima el Yach-Chiri v. Secretary of State*

---

[6] See section 19(1)(a)(i)–(ii). See the restrictions on appeal rights, however, in Juss, "Review and Appeal in Administrative Law: What is happening to the Right of Appeal in Immigration Law?" (1992) *Legal Stud* 3, pp. 364–376.
[7] Section 19(4) makes the whole of s.19 equally applicable to the Tribunal with the substitution of references to the Tribunal for references to an adjudicator.
[8] See *Winans v. Attorney General* [1904] A.C. 287.
[9] For example, see cases *Ghulam Sughre*, infra, n.26, and *Monwara Begum*, infra, n.69.

for the Home Department [10] the appellant, a citizen of Morocco, applied as a dependent wife of a sponsor who had been settled in the United Kingdom for 15 years. Her application was refused because the Home Secretary was not satisfied that the sponsor had capacity to marry her being already married once before. The question of capacity to marry depended upon whether the sponsor was domiciled in the United Kingdom having given up his original domicile of origin.[11] Before the Tribunal it was argued on his behalf that he had recently bought a plot of land in Morocco and erected a house on it and that this showed that he had not relinquished his original domicile of origin. In any case, however, it was submitted that under English law the onus was upon the Secretary of State to establish that a domicile of choice had been taken up by the sponsor in England. The Tribunal rejected these arguments with the bland statement that, "In our view the onus is upon the applicant in all cases to establish their eligibility under the immigration rules".[12] This is plainly incorrect and yet applicants have been unfairly excluded as a result of being unable to displace this burden.

(2) THE STANDARD OF PROOF

The standard of proof in immigration law has presented far more difficulties than even the burden of proof. It is clear that the test is one of "balance of probabilities", although one eminent academic lawyer has described this as a "nebulous expression of civil litigation".[13] According to the courts, the standard implies:

". . . a reasonable degree of probability, not so high as is required in a criminal case. If the evidence is such that the tribunal can say: 'We think it more probable than not', the burden is discharged, but if the probabilities are equal it is not".[14]

In immigration law there is "no possible reason for requiring a higher standard of proof . . . It would be unreasonable to assume", in the words of Lord Widgery, "that the Immigration Rules contemplate proof beyond dispute, or even beyond reasonable doubt".[15]

---

[10] TH/5500/79 (1922) d. 5.1.81 (unreported).
[11] As is well known, under Islamic Law, which applies in Morocco, a man may have four wives.
[12] *Supra*, n.10 at 3.
[13] Professor Hepple, "Judging Equal Rights", (1983) 36 *Current Legal Problems*, 76, at p. 80.
[14] *per* Lord Denning M.R. in *Miller v. Minister of Pensions* [1947] 2 All E.R. 372.
[15] *R v. Secretary of State for the Home Department, ex parte Hussein* [1975] Imm. A.R. 69.

However, in most immigration cases the standard has been far more exacting than this. In family settlement cases the deciding authority often does not ask whether it is more probable than not that the parties are related as claimed. Thus in *Nurej Bibi v. Entry Clearance Officer Dacca* the claimed wife and her four children wished to enter the United Kingdom to join the sponsor. The adjudicator and the Tribunal found as a fact the lady in question to be the mother of the four children. He found, however, that she had not proved that she "married the sponsor in 1957: nor has she proved on the balance of probabilities that she has married him at any later date or at all".[16] Moreover, documentary evidence is frequently not considered on the balance of probabilities. In *Koyrun Nessa v. Entry Clearance Officer Dacca* the Tribunal refused to be satisfied about the claimed relationships despite evidence at the hearing of land transfer documents and evidence of remittances even though it was not suggested that any of these documents were false.[17] Indeed, the Tribunal has in the past played a pivotal role in maintaining more exacting standards of proof in many immigration cases. In *Entry Clearance Officer Dacca v. Howayri Bibi* and *Jobril Uddin v. Entry Clearance Officer Dacca*[18] the Tribunal heard two appeals involving four members of the same family. These were the sponsor, Aziz Uddin, the claimed wife, Howayri Bibi, and their two claimed children, Jobril and Jalal who were boys aged 19 years and 15 years. The claimed wife was aged 42 years. Before the adjudicator, "a large quantity of documentary evidence, including correspondence" was produced. He allowed the appeal of the wife but dismissed that of the children. Before the Tribunal there were now two appeals; one by the two boys, Jobril and Jalal, against refusal by the adjudicator; the other by the ECO in Dacca against the finding that Howayri Bibi was related as claimed. The grounds of appeal of Jobril and Jalal were:

"(i) that one witness whose evidence was rejected by the Adjudicator knew both the sponsor and his wife in East Pakistan, particularly as his niece had married the sponsor's brother, (ii) that another witness could testify to knowing the sponsor's wife and her four children before that witness arrived to settle herself in the U.K. in 1969, and (iii) that the Appellant will seek leave to call evidence from one Muktar Ali who is the second cousin of the sponsor and has been principally in this country since 1966, as to the *fact* of the wedding, the *birth* of Jobril Uddin and the

---

[16] TH/6921/80 (2964) d. 21.11.83 (unreported), at 2. Also see *Jagir Kaur v. Entry Clearance Officer, New Delhi* TH/4221/73 d. 12.3.75 (unreported), at 2.
[17] TH/2647/75 (790) d. 10.8.76 (unreported), at 3.
[18] TH/41736/79 (2010) d. 3.3.81 (unreported).

existence of Jalal Uddin as part of the sponsor's family."[19] (Author's emphasis.)

The response of the Tribunal, after hearing the representations on behalf of Jobril and Jalal, was simply to say:

"At the hearing before this Tribunal Muktar Ali a nephew of the sponsor and the sponsor himself gave evidence and further documentary evidence, including correspondence was produced. *However, we find that this evidence does not carry the matter further one way or the other.*"[20] (Author's emphasis.)

With this, the appeals of both Jobril and Jalal were dismissed. In this case no cogent or coherent reasons were given by the Tribunal for its refusal of both applications. The decision has no probative value and the Tribunal's approach affords applicants no due process in any real sense in the making of immigration decisions and certainly falls far short of what the Wilson Committee ordained.

In fact, the Tribunal knew that this case had once before been before an adjudicator on appeal after the refusal of the application by an ECO six years ago in 1974 when the adjudicator had found that the sponsor was a married man but could not be certain that the woman who had applied to come was his wife. On the issue of identity he had dismissed her appeal. Six years later now the case had again come before the appellate authorities following a second application by the very same woman. The Tribunal looked at the adjudicator's reason for allowing her appeal and found that:

"The adjudicator who heard the parties' 1974 appeals accepts that Mr. Aziz Uddin is a married man. He thought it likely that Howayri Bibi was that wife. He was prevented and deterred from allowing her appeal because of the identity issue which had not been resolved to his satisfaction. Since then, however, Howayri Bibi has once more attended at the High Commission in Dacca. *The ECO has not suggested and there is no evidence to show that the principal appellant is not the same person who attended there in 1972. It follows that the identity issue has now become much less critical and cannot carry the same weight that it did 6 years ago.* Having applied to Howayri Bibi's claims as to her relationship to the sponsor the test to which I have referred earlier I find that *she is more probably who and what she claims to be* than otherwise. As she has to satisfy me solely upon the single issue, namely that, at some time she has married Mr. Aziz Uddin and is not divorced from him I find that she has discharged that burden and accordingly her appeal is allowed".[21] (Author's emphasis.)

---

[19] *ibid.* at 2–3.
[20] *ibid.*
[21] *ibid.* at 3.

The Adjudicator here was clearly applying the civil standard of proof of on "balance of probabilities" but the Tribunal rejected this reasoning, stating:

"We do not appreciate why he found the identity issue was less critical because 'there is no evidence to show that the principle appellant is not the same person who attended (the interview) there in 1972'. Because the appearances of the same person are separated by 6 years it does not follow that the person who appeared before the ECO in 1978, though the same person who appeared before him in 1972, is the person she claims to be. In this respect we find that the Adjudicator misdirected himself".[22]

In both cases, the Tribunal had overlooked that in addition to the same person appearing before the authorities, there was also other extrinsic evidence, namely, "a large quantity of documentary evidence" in 1972 and "further documentary evidence, including correspondence" before it now which the Tribunal did not comment upon, to say nothing of the testimonial evidence of witnesses that it simply rejected out of hand. As a result, the entire family of an immigrant sponsor in England was turned away by the Tribunal's decision in two separate appeals before it, without anyone concerned really understanding the reasons.

Most people representing immigrants on appeal know, in fact, that the proper standard of proof is not always applied. In *Walayat Begum v. Visa Officer Islamabad*[23] the issue was whether the first wife of the sponsor had died so as to enable him to marry the second time. The first wife's name was Manzoor Begum. On appeal, the Tribunal had before it the passport of Manzoor Begum which had not been available to the adjudicator. The Tribunal observed: "This is endorsed, 'The holder of this passport died. Passport has been cancelled and returned'".[24] Before the Tribunal it was argued on the appellant's behalf that had this passport been before the adjudicator he would not have dismissed her appeal to join the sponsor as his second wife. Two witnesses also gave evidence. The Tribunal held, however, that:

"There is no really *direct* or *solid evidence* that Manzoor Begum has died. The sponsor was not in Pakistan at the time of her alleged death and his letter to the Inland Revenue of November 13, 1971 reporting her death does not prove it. The appellants were there . . . but none of them give

---

[22] *ibid.* at 4.
[23] TH/13561/75 (191) d. 14.3.77 (unreported).
[24] *ibid.* at 4.

any convincing details of the illness from which she is alleged to have died, or of her death or burial. The applications for entry certificates were made over six years ago now".[25] (Author's emphasis.)

Here the claimed wife had waited six years while her case was being considered only to be told that she could not join the sponsor because what was required of her was "really direct or solid evidence" of Manzoor Begum's death. Here also the Tribunal would appear to be applying the wrong standard of proof. The case also shows that the treatment of official documents by the Tribunal is tinged with cynicism to say the least, and is not dissimilar to that of ECO's abroad.

(3) PROOF "BEYOND A SHADOW OF DOUBT"

If it is accepted that the Tribunal does not apply the proper standard of proof in immigration cases, what degree of proof then does it require for practical purposes? Is it evidence "beyond any reasonable doubt" as in criminal cases? It is difficult to give a definitive answer to this question, but before the Home Affairs Sub-Committee on Race Relations and Immigration in 1982, the main author of the UKIAS *Split Families* Report was questioned about the nature of the proof in the cases that his team had investigated while conducting field investigations in Bangladesh. He was asked whether the team had "found evidence that was so irrefutable that nobody looking at that case could have come to any other conclusion" but to allow the application. His answer was that in some situations a case has "reached the standard where you are satisfied beyond reasonable doubt, sometimes beyond a shadow of doubt".[26] Of the 45 cases that the team had originally investigated, "in quite a considerable number of the cases" there was irrefutable evidence in favour of the claimed relationship.[27] The *Split Families* Report is, however, essentially concerned with applications before ECOs. The question is whether

---

[25] *ibid.* at 5.
[26] *Fifth Report from the Home Affairs Committee* (1981–82 H.C. 90–I), Vol. II, p. 114, Q.328 by Mr. Lyon.
[27] *ibid.* at 115, Q.333 to Mr Choudhary. The cases that Mr Choudhary then drew attention to were case Nos. 2, 5, 7, 9, 15, 21 and 24 in the Appendix of the *Split Families* Report. The Director of UKIAS, Mr Fennals, emphasised that the evidence was not of any specific nature. There was, for example, "the almost intangible evidence which you cannot take with you to an interview, such as the photographs in the house of the sponsor and the appellant's children and the box in which the presents from the father were placed from Marks and Spencer and so on". *ibid.* p. 116, Q.342.

the same "irrefutable" and "beyond a shadow of doubt" evidence was required by the Tribunal. Logically, it may be said that the question is a false one in that clearly ECOs at posts overseas would not be deciding cases with the same persistence and consistency if they knew that they were going to be reversed by the Tribunal on appeal. Nevertheless, the Tribunal's activity in this area is worth probing into for the insights that it affords on the practice of deciding family settlement cases.

An early example of Tribunal practice is the Indian case of *Pritam Kaur v. Entry Clearance Officer New Delhi*[28] where the dates of birth and marriage of the sponsor and his wife were conflicting. The sponsor claimed that he had suffered an industrial accident from which he had never fully recovered and this affected his memory. Nonetheless, he was quite certain that he was over 60 years of age. His statements conflicted with what was recorded in his passport. As the Tribunal explained:

> "On his passport his date of birth is given as 1904 which makes him now about 72 . . . He attributed the date of birth shown on his passport to agents who had filled in the forms. He was sure he had been married about fifty years which is twenty-two years more than the principal Appellant's [*i.e.* the claimed wife's] version. His version of the number of years of the marriage is more in keeping with the age on his passport than with his own estimate of 60 but if he has been married for 50 years he must have been married in about 1926, and if the date of birth of the principal Appellant is correctly recorded in her application as 1927, before or at the same time as she was born".[29]

Undoubtedly there is a large discrepancy of dates here. It could be overlooked when one considers other aspects of this case. On a number of occasions adjudicators and the Tribunal itself have declared that concepts of time and distance do not impress themselves on the consciousness of rural dwellers from the Indian sub-continent.[30] The lenient approach taken in those cases contrasts sharply with the rigid attitude here. In addition, the appellate authorities are aware of the baleful role of agents who purport to help prospective immigrants. Yet, there was positive testimonial evidence in favour of the appeal. The Tribunal noted that the adjudicator had heard evidence from the sponsor's son-in-law who was settled in the United Kingdom. This witness testified to the existence of the said

---

[28] TH/765/75 (809) d. 17.8.76 (unreported).
[29] *ibid.* at 2.
[30] See *supra*, pp. 65–67.

relationship. He confirmed the sponsor's evidence and he estimated the claimed wife's age to be between 50 and 55 and the sponsor to be "four or five years older".[31] In fact, this was in line with the sponsor's own estimates. Another witness by the name of Harpal Singh had also appeared. The Tribunal said of him:

> "The Adjudicator was *impressed by his manner* — the witness appeared to him to be *'an extremely honest and straightforward man'*. Although not on intimate terms with the sponsor, *he had known him, Pritam Kaur and the family since childhood.* He assumed (though of course being only thirty years of age himself, was in no position to prove) that the sponsor and Pritam Kaur were married. He estimated the sponsor's age by reference to his own father who is 52 — he put the sponsor as being in his late fifties. Pritam Kaur he said was in her fifties".[32] (Author's emphasis.)

The Adjudicator had nevertheless dismissed the appeal because of the discrepancies stating:

> ". . . I would have expected the sponsor to have had a more accurate knowledge of ages of dates of birth of his children, even bearing in mind his illiteracy and his injuries which I am told he had suffered to his intestines. *It is always for the appellant to satisfy the ECO in these cases that she enjoys the relationship claimed".[33]* (Author's emphasis.)

On further appeal to the Tribunal more evidence was adduced. In particular, there were two family photographs. One of these was taken 10 years ago and was identified by the sponsor, his son-in-law, and by Harpal Singh to include the claimed wife and other family members. The Tribunal could still not be satisfied of the genuineness of the claim, declaring that: "it does not establish that the lady and young man who appeared before the Entry Clearance Officer were the persons identified in the photographs".[34]

At this stage the appellant's representative argued that "it would be safe for the Tribunal to direct that entry clearance should be granted if the persons who presented themselves to collect their certificates were the persons identified by the photographs". Remarkably, the Tribunal could not permit this: "We cannot do this. We can only make directions for issue of clearances if we allow the appeal and we can only allow the appeal if the appellants have discharged the burden of

---

[31] *Supra*, n.28 at 4. On the role of agents, see *e.g.* the case of *Amina Bibi v. Entry Clearance Officer Islamabad* TH/6906/74 (609) d. 12.2.76 (unreported).
[32] *ibid.* at 3.
[33] *Loc. cit.*
[34] *ibid.* at 6.

proof which lies upon them". Surely, however, the burden of proof on a balance of probabilities is amply satisfied in this instance.In fact the Tribunal went considerably further than this. It said:

> "The Adjudicator concluded his determination by saying that the first Appellant had clearly failed to discharge the burden of proof on her that she enjoyed the relationship claimed. *The same would be the case even if the lady who made the application to the ECO were identified as the lady in the photograph.* There is still no satisfactory documentary evidence of the marriage and there is no evidence from any witnesses of the ceremony".[35] (Author's emphasis.)

There is no doubt of a substantial error of law here. If the applicant applying at a post overseas is identified as being the same person as in the photograph which has in turn been variously identified by other witnesses as being that of the wife and child, then the relationships are established. There is no legal requirement at all that documentary evidence be adduced for any sort of case. In fact, it is unclear from this determination what standard of proof the Tribunal requires to be satisfied of the relationship, for if testimonial evidence as to the *fact of the marriage* is deemed insufficient to establish the relationship, it is difficult to see what testimonial evidence as to the *marriage ceremony* can do for the applicants.

This case affords a good example of how the Tribunal can turn down ostensibly genuine applications. The decision clearly encourages officials abroad to impose a stricter standard of proof than is in law necessary. The case demonstrates that notwithstanding the availability of cogent evidence in support of the claimed relationship, applicants are rejected on the issue of "identity". It is submitted that the correct approach in these circumstances is that once the fact of marriage is established it is not only improbable, but unreasonable, to assume that someone would wish to bring in a woman or child in preference to his own. Unless there is evidence to cast doubt upon the *bona fides* of the applicants, proof should not be required as to the specific question of "identity" otherwise some very absurd results will follow. In *Asha Bibi v. Entry Clearance Officer Dacca* the Tribunal had before it the following evidence:

> ". . . a certificate issued on September 23, 1953 granting Abdul Subhan, husband of Asha Bibi, citizenship of Pakistan;
> two wills made by the sponsor in 1971 and 1973 in which he referred to his wife Asha Bibi;

a certificate of the issue of a money order on March 19, 1964 for £25.10.0
payable to Mrs. Asha Bibi;
the letters produced showing strong evidence of relationship".[36]

Yet the Tribunal claimed here to be unsatisfied about the applicant's
"identity", when even the ECO had accepted the fact of the parties'
marriage. It is certainly improbable that a man would name his wife
as a beneficiary in his will and then bring in another lady by the
name of Asha Bibi in preference to her. However, the Tribunal
quoted with approval the submission of the ECO's representative
who said that he:

> ". . . accepted that there was *strong documentary evidence* to show that the
> sponsor had a wife and children of the names of the Appellants but he
> submitted that all the evidence pointed to a marriage in 1951. The
> sponsor, however, had throughout maintained that he married Asha Bibi
> in which case the lady who applied for an entry certificate could not be
> the sponsor's wife on the grounds of age alone".[37] (Author's emphasis.)

Because the Tribunal was "unable to decide on which of the many
dates put forward the marriage was likely to have taken place or to
estimate the age of the bride at the time of the marriage",[38] it
dismissed the appeal. Yet, in doing so it has applied an absolute
standard of proof.

In fact, the insistence on a higher, more exacting standard of proof
has been explicitly stated. In *Santai Bibi v. Entry Clearance Office Dacca*,
for instance, when faced with evidence of money remittances, tax
relief claims, land purchase transactions and personal correspondences, the adjudicator admitted that the sponsor had a wife and four
children in Bangladesh when he came to the United Kingdom in
1958: "But", he added, "I can find no conclusive evidence that these
appellants are his wife and children".[39] The appellants failed to get
the Tribunal on appeal to accept that the reference to "conclusive
evidence" was the application of a wholly wrong standard of proof.[40]

---

[36] TH/4650/76 (1081) d. 30.11.77 (unreported), at 4.
[37] *ibid.*
[38] *ibid.* at 4
[39] TH/42341/79 (1866) d. 23.9.80 (unreported), at 2.
[40] Even U.K. citizens attempting to have their wives join them here have had these
problems. In *Fehmida Begum v. Entry Clearance Officer Dacca* TH/80180/82 (2437) d.
26.8.82 (unreported) it was even observed that the "ECO noted that the sponsor had
given Fehmida Begum as his wife when he applied for citizenship for the U.K. and
Colonies on March 19, 1976", at p. 2, and yet, despite this information having being
given more than six years ago, doubts were raised in similar circumstances and the
appellant's appeal was dismissed.

Unsurprisingly in these circumstances — yet paradoxically — even when an applicant does meet these higher standards of proof he may still be rejected. There have been many cases where blood test reports have been adduced by the applicant. These have shown the blood grouping of the child in question to be the same as that of his parents. When coupled with other documentary and testimonial evidence there can be little doubt that the applicant child is related as claimed. In *Newa Khatun v. Entry Clearance Officer Dacca*[41] the Tribunal had before it for the first time two reports from the Medical College Sylhet which showed that the blood group for the child applicants were B positive, the same as their alleged father, the sponsor. In addition to a plethora of other evidence, it also had a report before it from the Assistant Director of the Immigration Advisory Service in Sylhet, who claimed that he had visited the sponsor's village and talked to his wife and children and was convinced that the relationship was established as claimed. The Tribunal, nevertheless, dismissed the appeal on the basis of discrepancies in the evidence of the applicants.

Restraint and Activism of the Immigration Appeals Tribunal

Should the Tribunal, properly speaking, in a case like *Newa Khatun*,[42] have intervened in favour of the adjudicator, given the evidence before it of blood test reports and the report of the Immigration Advisory Service, Sylhet? What is the proper function of an Appeals Tribunal in this respect? How does its approach in this case square with its approach in *Howayri Bibi*[43] (issue of identity held by adjudicator to be less critical in second application six years later) where the Tribunal did intervene, but this time against the interests of the intending immigrant, to reverse a decision by an adjudicator? Is there a principled and coherent approach to appellate decision making taken here by the IAT? If so, what is it? It is clear that as a specially-constituted administrative body under the Immigration Appeals Act 1969 to hear applications for immigration rights in the United Kingdom, it has undoubted regulatory and controlling tasks. What is it, however, that it seeks to regulate and control? In a comprehensive system of public law with a fully-fledged administrative justice system, such as in Australia, the answer to this question

---

[41] TH/41933/79 (2140) d. 24.8.81 (unreported). See also *Sarian Begum v. Entry Clearance Officer Dacca* TH/34811/78 (2038) d. 1.5.81 (unreported).
[42] *ibid.*
[43] *Supra*, n.18

would be rather more clear.[44] Is it the Tribunal's function to regulate and control immigration numbers as the legislation in this area is plainly designed to do, or is it the Tribunal's function to regulate and control possible official abuses of the exercise of a substantive public power, in a well structured and coherent way?[45] Or is it both of these things? The evidence in the discussion that follows is that the Tribunal in the exercise of its appellate function, has not been clear about these latter aims but has been disproportionately concerned with the control of immigration numbers. In so doing, it is submitted, the Tribunal has not helped, through the process of decision making, to create a code of good administrative practice (as for instance, the Court of Appeal has done in relation to the exercise of police powers under the Police and Criminal Evidence Act 1984).[46] It has not succeeded in establishing effective rules regarding the basic duties of public servants entrusted with the exercise of an important public power. The result has been that the official exercise of power has become, by and large, unaccountable because the Tribunal has overlooked the theoretical framework that underpins its essential role, which is that the system of appeals as an administrative remedy was instituted precisely to avoid the unfairness that can so easily creep into this area.[47]

To understand the Tribunal's essential role, we must once again turn to section 20 of the Immigration Act 1971. This suggests, as we saw earlier, that any party before an adjudicator who is "dissatisfied with [the] determination" may appeal to the Tribunal. For a long time it was felt that this only meant a right to appeal an adjudicator's finding on an error of law, not on the facts, but this is clearly wrong. In *R. v. Immigration Appeals Tribunal, ex p. Rashida Bi*[48] recently, the High Court went so far as to say that there was always a discretion in the Tribunal to grant leave to appeal against the determination of an adjudicator, even though under the Immigration Appeals (Procedure) Rules 1984 leave to appeal is required in all cases. It held that if an applicant contended that the adjudicator had misdirected himself on a point of law, the Tribunal had to reach a preliminary view on that

---

[44] See Partington, "The Reform of Public Law in Britain: Theoretical Problems and Practical Considerations", in *Law Legitimacy and the Courts* (ed. by McAuslan and McEldowney, London, 1985), p. 195.
[45] Juss, "Review and Appeal in Administrative Law – what is happening to the right of appeal in Immigration Law?, 12 *Legal Studies* 3, p.376.
[46] See Juss, "Suspect's Right and PACE : Can the Courts do the Balancing Trick?" (1990) 11 *Statute Law Review* 3, p. 225.
[47] See the *Wilson Committee Report, op. cit.*, p. 28.
[48] [1990] Imm. A.R. 348.

ground. After that it had to ask itself whether without that error of law (assuming that it was found to exist), the adjudicator could properly have made the determination he had made, in which case, if he would have come to a different conclusion, then the Tribunal had to grant leave. The Tribunal would always have a residual discretion to look at a case. If it concluded from this that, properly directing itself as to the law and looking at all the facts, it was reasonably likely that it would agree with the adjudicator, then leave would be refused, but otherwise it would be granted.

To sum up, what this means is that there is an undoubted overlap between the review powers of the immigration appellate authorities which are extensive, and the traditional supervisory jurisdiction of the High Court. The Court of Appeal, however, in a recent case involving deportation, held that Parliament could not have intended to leave the immigration appellate authorities with "a power equivalent to that of judicial review which would be coterminous and coextensive with the powers already exercised by the High Court, but without the necessity of obtaining leave" as this would be "a pointless duplication of jurisdiction".[49] This view clearly flies in the face of established authority, but it has been approved by the House of Lords in *R. v. Secretary of State for the Home Department, ex p. Oladehinde*, another case involving deportation.[50] The point is of obvious importance, but it does not affect the Tribunal's power to intervene for review of questions of fact to which the foregoing analysis continues to apply. Indeed, the power to review for errors of law also in all probability, still applies outside the specific deportation power at issue in *Oladehinde*.

What then is the proper ambit of the power under section 20 of the 1971 Act? Thanks to the intervention of the courts in earlier years this provision has been interpreted liberally by them to express the full amplitude of Tribunal power. In a case in 1980 Stephenson L.J. in the Court of Appeal said of section 20:

". . . the very wide words of section 20 of the Immigration Act do not so limit the powers of the Appeal Tribunal. That appellate authority hears an appeal from an adjudicator on the facts. *It can be as dissatisfied as an appellant with the determination of an adjudicator* and if, like the adjudicator on an appeal from a refusal of entry clearance, the Appeal Tribunal on reviewing the adjudicator's decisions on questions of fact comes to the conclusion

---

[49] *R. v. Secretary of State for the Home Department, ex p. Malhi* [1990] 2 W.L.R. 932, at 943.
[50] [1991] A.C. 254.

that those decisions were *plainly wrong*, it has the power and duty to review and to reverse both those decisions on facts on which the adjudicator's determination of the appeal is based, and therefore the determination itself. But I entertain not the smallest doubt that an appeal Tribunal would be *extremely sparing* in reviewing an adjudicator's decision *as to the credibility of a witness* or witnesses whom the adjudicator had heard and seen giving oral evidence and the Appeal Tribunal had not. It is trite law that an appellate authority of whatever kind can only substitute its view of a witness's credibility for the view that a court which had the advantage, denied to it, of seeing and hearing the witness, has formed for *compelling reasons*, and the cases in which it can do so must be rare".[51] (Author's emphasis.)

This description of the function of the IAT is clearly in line with the general role of appeal Tribunals and in *Entry Clearance Officer Dacca v. Rupjan Bibi* the IAT, referring to the judgement of Stephenson L.J. said, "we accept . . . that we should act under the guidelines laid down in *Alam Bi . . .*".[52] The "power and duty to review and to reverse" must definitely be exercised by the Tribunal where a determination "is plainly wrong". This would appear to be not dissimilar to what the courts, when reviewing the decision of an administrative body, have referred to as "a real error of law";[53] or in other instances, of an authority going "clearly wrong";[54] or making a "demonstrable error",[55] although as we noted earlier the House of Lords in *Oladehinde* has now restricted this view. For our purposes, it is important to note that if an adjudicator has been "plainly wrong" in his decision on the facts before him he thereby goes outside the law in reaching such a decision. The Tribunal, in this event, has a positive "duty to review" the determination and would itself be erring in law were it to refrain from doing so. Here it is incumbent upon the Tribunal to put that matter right.

In the same passage subsequently,[56] Stephenson L.J. went on to say that the Tribunal should be "extremely sparing in reviewing an adjudicator's decision" where the issue was that of the credibility of witnesses which the adjudicator had heard but the Tribunal had not.

---

[51] *R. v. Immigration Appeal Tribunal, ex parte Alam Bi* [1979–80] Imm. A.R. 146 at 149.
[52] TH/83535/83 (2539) d. 4.1.83 (unreported), at 6.
[53] *per* Lord Denning M.R. in *R. v. Industrial Injuries Commissioners, ex p. Amalgamated Engineering Union* [1966] 1 All E.R. 97, at 101. Also see *R. v. National Insurance Commissioners, ex p. Michael* [1976] 1 All E.R. 566, at 569.
[54] See *Boots the Chemists (New Zealand) v. Tews Pharmacy Ltd* [1969] N.Z.L.R. 890, at 905.
[55] *Re An Appeal from the Credit Tribunal by John Martin & Co. Ltd* [1974] 8 S.A.S.R. 237, at 267.
[56] *Supra*, n.51.

"The principle justification for any review at all", as Professor de Smith explained, "is that the second opinion is likely to be better than the first".[57] So if the matter is one on which the adjudicator is likely to be better informed than the Tribunal it should not lightly overturn his findings. This is so except where, as Stephenson L.J. explained, there are "compelling reasons" for the Tribunal to do so. This presumably means the gravity of an adjudicator's error.

(1) THE TRIBUNAL'S DECISION IN KHANMA JAN

The decision in *ex p. Alam Bi*[58] was especially important because it helped clarify a fundamental jurisdictional point which the Tribunal had thus far got wrong. Grant and Martin in their book, *Immigration Law and Practice*, refer to the case of *Khanma Jan v. Entry Clearance Officer Dacca*[59] as describing the Tribunal's pre-1980 position where the Tribunal said of itself that it:

". . . will not lightly overturn adjudicator's findings of fact, particularly where the adjudicators have the advantage of observing witnesses which the Tribunal has not. . . We apply the test of whether a *reasonable adjudicator properly directing himself* and applying his mind to the evidence before him, could have come to the conclusion reached by the adjudicator in this case".[60] (Author's emphasis.)

This means that the Tribunal was not concerned with the merits of a decision before it but merely with its legality. The question it was asking was not, "has the adjudicator got it right on the facts?" but, "Is he acting lawfully or unlawfully?" and this conception of the Tribunal's function was quite wrong as it consigned it to the role of a body of review, like the High Court, rather than an appeal body. Grant and Martin wrote then that the decision in *ex p. Alam Bi* means that "this approach must now be modified . . .".[61] However, as we shall see, this has simply not happened and there is in actual fact, no difference between the pre-1980 cases and the post-1980 cases following *ex p. Alam Bi*. This thesis needs examining.

---

[57] See de Smith, *Judicial Review of Administrative Action* (4th ed., London, 1980), p. 128.
[58] *Supra*, n.51.
[59] From Grant and Martin, *Immigration Law and Practice* (London, 1981), p. 309.
[60] See *ibid.*, p. 307. The writer has, however, found some earlier cases, such as *Zarda Begum v. Entry Clearance Officer Dacca* TH/2013/75 (808) d. 23.8.76 (unreported); *Joytun Bibi v. Entry Clearance Officer Dacca* TH/12582/77 (1324) d. 6.9.78 (unreported); and *Kamela Bibi v. Entry Clearance Officer Islamabad* TH/2696/785, (1505) d. 24.4.79 (unreported).
[61] Grant and Martin, *Loc. cit.*.

(2) THE PRE-1980 PRACTICE

The practice of the Tribunal before 1980 was wrong not only because it nullified its appellate jurisdiction but it was wrong also because it was exercised partially even on the premises of its own narrowly defined limits. Thus even though the Tribunal had declared that it would not "lightly overturn adjudicators' findings of fact" except where they were unreasonable, there are, in fact, a large number of manifestly unreasonable determinations which have not been reversed by the Tribunal. These determinations are all in favour either of an ECO or a visa officer. By contrast, there are cases where an adjudicator's finding on the evidence has been reversed all too easily by the Tribunal on appeal. These determinations are all in favour of the intending immigrant. The exercise of the reviewing power, albeit narrowly defined, has therefore been arbitrary and capricious with scant regard to issues of principle. To illustrate this point we first examine the cases where the Tribunal has intervened, then the cases where it has not intervened and then ask whether the Tribunal's approach in respect of both kinds of cases has been motivated by a desire to set aside wrongful determinations, or whether its motivation is to do with more external factors.

(a) Where the IAT does not intervene

Thus in *Marion Khatun v. Entry Clearance Officer Dacca* the adjudicator had before him "documentary evidence in the shape of a land deed, a voters list, and other evidence of remittances to Bangladesh".[62] We have already seen that land deeds constituting proof of a land transaction, and voters lists confirming a person's residence in an area, are public documents of the highest evidential value.[63] In fact, no cases involving these documents have ever come up before the authorities where the applicants have turned out to be bogus. The Tribunal in this case began by accepting that, "The appeal depended entirely upon the determination of questions of fact", but then concluded in a manner which made it quite clear that it had not taken note of the relevant evidence:

> ". . . it is not the function of the Tribunal to decide whether or not it would have made the same findings as the adjudicator. Rather is it its task to decide whether or not any adjudicator, properly directing himself,

---

[62] TH/31849/79 (1666) d. 5.12.79 (unreported).
[63] See *supra*, pp. 101–103.

could have reasonably come to the conclusions reached upon the evidence before him; and this is because the adjudicator has the advantage — which the Tribunal does not have — of seeing and hearing witnesses".[64]

Not only is this the application of the wrong legal test, but given the importance of those documents, unless their authenticity could be specifically impugned, the adjudicator should have come to no other conclusion but that the parties were, on a balance of probabilities, related as claimed, and the Tribunal on appeal should have so exercised its discretion to review.

Similarly in *Munir Begum v. Visa Officer Islamabad*[65] the "evidence tendered to the Tribunal consisted of two affidavits from persons who deponed that they knew the appellants well and that the claimed relationships were genuine, five birth certificates in respect of the children, two photographs, and an identity card". There was also further evidence of a large number of remittances sent by the sponsor to someone by the name of his claimed wife. None of this evidence was impugned. Here also the Tribunal said:

"There is no question of law in this case, the outcome of the appeal depending entirely upon the determination of questions of fact . . . The adjudicator who saw and heard the witnesses was in a better position than we are to determine the facts of this case. In our view his findings of fact were amply supported by the evidence and we can find no reason for interfering with them".[66]

The reluctance to interfere with an adjudicator's findings of fact, such as his assessment of the demeanour of witnesses before him, is obviously correct, but this reluctance should not extend to the adjudicator's failing to record the value of important documentary evidence on which the Tribunal can also now reach a view. In fact, in these circumstances it would have been plainly correct for it to have done so as a matter of law.[67]

In *Sarwar Bi v. Visa Officer Islamabad*[68] both the fact of the relationship and of identity was conclusively proved before the

---

[64] *Supra*, n.62 at 2.

[65] TH/10847/76 (1165) d. 30.3.78 (unreported).

[66] *ibid.* at 3.

[67] This has been repeatedly stated, and continues to be stated even now : see, *e.g. Raja Zafar Zia v. Secretary of State for the Home Department* [1993] Imm. A.R. 404; *Jagtar Saini v. Secretary of State for the Home Department* [1993] Imm. A.R. 96; *Entry Clearance Officer, Islamabad v. Ajaib Khan* [1993] Imm. A.R. 68; and *R. v. Immigration Appeal Tribunal, ex p. Iram Iqbal* [1993] Imm. A.R. 270. However, a refusal to follow this line has been consistently commonplace: see also *Joytun Bibi* TH/1258/77 (1324) d. 6.9.77 (unreported), at 3.

[68] TH/4896/76 (1361) d. 25.10.78 (unreported), at 3.

Tribunal. Here the claimed wife and daughter wished to join the sponsor. On the fact of relationship a letter from the Inland Revenue stated that a birth certificate showing the date of birth as October 9, 1972 was accepted by the Inland Revenue as having been genuinely issued. On the question of identity, the photographs of both the wife and daughter were identified by witnesses before the adjudicator. Their appeals against refusal of entry clearance, however, were dismissed both by the adjudicator and the Tribunal, the Tribunal declaring that it would only interfere with an adjudicator's determination if it was unreasonable. So here also the Tribunal did not intervene.

In *Monwara Begum v. Entry Clearance Officer Dacca* the adjudicator held that "there is a presumption that a person is domiciled in the country in which he resides"[69] and that the existing discrepancies must be cleared up by the appellant herself. Before the Tribunal the sponsor's son, also resident in this country, identified the appellant as his mother and the claimed wife of the sponsor. The adjudicator's refusal, however, was upheld by the Tribunal even though on the matter of domicile the presumption of law is always against a change of domicile, and if the change is alleged it must be proved with perfect clearness by the person alleging it.

In all the foregoing cases the Tribunal has wrongly prevented itself from intervening to correct an adjudicator's determination. In fact, in the second of these cases, in *Munir Begum*[70] where there were a large number of remittances, there was further evidence before the Tribunal which had not previously been put to the adjudicator, which made the Tribunal's approach of relying wholly on the adjudicator below all the more untenable. Its approach should have been that of an adjudicator in *Amena Khatun v. Entry Clearance Officer Dacca*[71] who, when hearing an appeal from the decision of an ECO, took a rather more liberal view of his role. Here the claimed wife, Amena Khatun and her four children applied to join the sponsor, Loylus Miah. The application was refused by the ECO and on appeal to the adjudicator, he said:

> "Of considerable evidential weight, . . . are fourteen letters, ranging in date from January 1975 to 1978, mostly from Amena Khatun to Loylus Miah. I am uncertain how many of these (if any), have been seen by the ECO, but in any event *I consider that I am as competent as he is to assess their*

[69] TH/1127/73 (585) d. 28.1.76 (unreported), at 3.
[70] *Supra*, n.65.
[71] TH/31081/78 (1698) d. 13.11.79 (unreported).

evidential weight, as contrasted with, *e.g.* certificates of birth or marriage, which can be verified by the issuing authority and may contain identifying features such as watermarks".[72] (Author's emphasis.)

Having considered the evidence before him thus, the adjudicator felt able to allow the appeal — an act that would clearly have been impossible had the adjudicator chosen to disentitle himself from looking into the case.

(b) Where the Tribunal intervenes

The Tribunal has not disentitled itself in this respect, or chosen to disapply its powers under section 20 of the 1971 Act, where the decision under appeal before it is not in favour of an immigration official, but in favour of an intending immigrant who has just been given the green light by an adjudicator below. Cases of this kind fall broadly under three heads: (i) where on facts, which are substantially the same as before an adjudicator, the Tribunal reaches a different conclusion; (ii) where, in the exercise of his jurisdiction, an adjudicator purports to rectify an error of law or a wrongful decision by an ECO; (iii) where an adjudicator's decision is based on his appraisal of witnesses before him. All three, but especially (i) and (iii) are areas in which the Tribunal makes a significant departure from its self-imposed rule of non-intervention. Once again, issues of principle are a casualty because in none of these cases are there "compelling reasons", (to adopt the language of *ex p. Alam Bi*[73]), to reverse a determination by an adjudicator, and in all of these cases, the Tribunal has itself erred in law in coming to the decision that it does.

(i) On the Facts. In *Visa Officer Islamabad v. Akhtar Begum* the Tribunal reversed a determination by an adjudicator on the same facts that were before the adjudicator, and thus found in favour of the Visa Officer:

". . . because a wedding photograph was produced. *The adjudicator considered that the photograph on the respondent's passport was that of the person shown in the wedding photograph.* He did however have a *slight doubt* about the matter and on looking at the same photograph we are by no means satisfied that they are the same person. Furthermore, it appears from the passport documents that the respondent is some three inches shorter than the sponsor but the wedding photograph indicates that the bride is at least a foot shorter than her husband".[74] (Author's emphasis.)

---

[72] *ibid.* at 2.
[73] *Supra*, n.51.
[74] TH/12567/77 (1537) d. 11.5.79 (unreported), at 4.

Not only does this reversal fail to apply the "balance of probabilities" test, but it is a very tenuous basis for correcting an adjudicator's decision on the same facts, particularly as it was accepted that the photograph in question was a "wedding photograph" and on which the adjudicator himself had only had a "slight doubt". Moreover, on the basis of *Alam Bi*,[75] can this be construed as a "compelling reason" for reversing an adjudicator's finding in favour of an individual?

(ii) On correcting an error of law or a wrongful decision. The case of *Visa Officer Islamabad v. Farzand Begum*[76] is disturbing because it shows how far adjudicators can be restrained if they wish to ensure that immigration officials consider applications in accordance with a fair procedure. In this case the claimed wife and her three children applied to join the sponsor, Fatha Sher. She had once previously applied to join the sponsor on January 18, 1971 and had been refused by the ECO on the basis of discrepancies with regard to the date of her marriage to the sponsor, and not — it should be it noted — with regard to the relationship itself. The second application, the subject of this appeal, was made six years later on March 17, 1977. The adjudicator allowed her appeal for the following reasons which included a substantial defect in the form of the explanatory statement:

> "Although the explanatory statement says that the appellants were present at the interview and were accompanied by the sponsor *there is no indication of any questions being put* to Mohd. Iqbal [*i.e.* one of the children] at all *nor any evidence as to his answers*. It is recorded that the ECO spoke separately to Fatha Sher in connection with the question as to whether the applicant had made a previous application but there is *no suggestion that any attempt was made to resolve or explain any of the discrepancies* or uncertainties that had arisen in the course of the firsth interview. The whole basis of the refusal on this occasion was the fact that Farzand Begum had been unable to produce any written or oral evidence to show why the first decision was wrong".[77] (Author's emphasis.)

The adjudicator had taken into account the fact that the sponsor, Fatha Sher, had gone to Pakistan to assist with the applicants' second application and found that the application had been considered in a prejudicial and unfair way by the ECO. He ended his statement

---

[75] *Supra*, n.51.
[76] TH/39036/78 (1672) D. 29.11.79 (unreported).
[77] *ibid.* at 3.

above by saying; "for these three reasons alone I consider it unsafe to leave this decision unaltered since the ECO's exercise of discretion was based upon both error and omission".[78] But the adjudicator, Mr Walters, also thought that when the first appeal was heard in 1972 by Mr Coley, another adjudicator, some facts may not have been properly evaluated. Mr Walter's feeling was that on the second occasion:

". . . had the Visa Officer questioned Fatha Sher he could have repeated the evidence he gave to Mr Coley in 1972 and resolved a number of points arising from the difference in the date claimed for the marriage by Farzand Begum when she made her first application".[79]

Such then was the extent of the irregularity in the handling of this case by the visa officer that he had not even discussed the discrepancies with the sponsor and the applicants and yet he had thought them important enough to be used as a ground for refusal. Mr Walters, however, found more in this case. He found that a marriage certificate produced was consistent with the sponsor's presence in Pakistan at the date of the marriage. He therefore concluded by saying:

"I cannot claim that all of these discrepancies and uncertainties of the first application are resolved but I have very grave doubts as to whether the correct decision was reached in 1971 and 1972".[80]

Thus, Mr Walters, the adjudicator, found two things: serious procedural anomalies of "error and omission" leading him to conclude that the visa officer's decision was "unsafe"; and he found, as a fact, on the basis of a marriage certificate and the location of the sponsor at the time of his marriage, the parties to be related as claimed. It was a determination arrived at after a carefully reasoned analysis of all the facts and all the evidence as it stood before Mr Walters. The visa officer appealed against this decision and the Tribunal allowed his appeal because it found that:

"The visa officer's further error regarding the date on which the Nikanama, [*i.e.* marriage certificate] purporting to show that the alleged marriage took place on 27 June 1968 was produced was not, in the view of the Tribunal, *of any material consequence* . . ." (Author's emphasis.)

---

[78] *ibid.* at 4.
[79] *ibid.* at 3.
[80] *ibid.* at 5.

Of Mr Walters, it said:

> "He appears to have decided in favour of the respondents *not by reason of any strength of the evidence* supporting their claim, but by reason of two errors in the explanatory statement and the lack of repetition by Fatha Sher to the visa officer of the unconvincing evidence he gave to Mr Coley in 1972".[81] (Author's emphasis.)

With respect, this cannot be right. It is not clear how the Tribunal can hold crucial evidence such as a marriage certificate not to be "of any material consequence" and yet in the same breath also say that the adjudicator's decision was "not by reason of any strength of the evidence", when it is precisely the strength of the evidence which the adjudicator was seeking to base his finding upon. Professor de Smith states that, "A tribunal which has made a finding of primary fact wholly unsupported by any of the primary facts found by it, will be held to have erred in point of law".[82] On these facts, who would be held to have erred in law, the adjudicator or the Tribunal? It is respectfully submitted that whilst it is conceded that the Tribunal has the power to intervene under section 20 to reverse a finding, it has been wrongly exercised on the facts in this case.

(iii) On the Demeanour of Witnesses. Adjudicators' findings have been reversed on appeal even though the witnesses who gave evidence before them have not been seen by the Tribunal. In *Visa Officer Islamabad v. Parveen Begum* the adjudicator disregarded the discrepancies because he was impressed by the witness. The sponsor, he said:

> ". . . was quite firm in his statements and he remained otherwise unshaken in cross-examination. Apart from his relying [sic] on a particular subject and save for his adamant denials of the undeniable I have no reason whatever to assume that he was untruthful".[83]

The adjudicator therefore suggested that the ECO could have referred the case to London for the interview of the sponsor so as to get to the bottom of the contentious issues and although he therefore allowed the appeal of the applicants, the Tribunal on appeal by the visa officer reversed this decision. On the question of referral to the United Kingdom, it said:

> "Entry Clearance Officers commonly — and very properly — do follow this course in cases where they feel that the application may be genuine

[81] *ibid.* at 6–7.
[82] See Professor de Smith, *supra*, n.57, p. 133.
[83] TH/15738/77 (1191) d. 24.4.78 (unreported), at 4.

but they are not entirely sure. In this particular case it is evident from the visa officer's explanatory statement that he considered that the discrepancies were such that this case was a 'non-starter' *ab initio*. This being so, it would have been a waste of time and public money to refer the matter to this country".[84]

Here again one finds the Tribunal frustrating an adjudicator's attempts to take a fairer approach towards the applicants, and to ensure that ECOs conduct their investigations properly.

In *Alam Bi* there was evidence before the adjudicator of family photographs, details of the children jotted down in the sponsor's diary, providing evidence of dependency going back some years. The adjudicator allowed the applicant's appeal but then on further appeal by the visa officer to the Tribunal, the Tribunal reversed this finding holding:

"Mr Shepherd [for the applicants] submitted that the Adjudicator had the benefit of seeing and hearing the sponsor and the witnesses in person but so, of course, did the Entry Clearance Officer apart from the non-family witnesses from Bradford who gave evidence to the Adjudicator but not to the ECO."[85]

Both the above cases are a departure from Stephenson L.J.'s lucid statement of the law in this area, that an adjudicator who has had the benefit of seeing and hearing witnesses should only normally be reversed if there are "compelling reasons" such as weighty documentary proof which it would not be right to ignore. These two cases, however, present other difficulties as well. It is evident that the Tribunal in these cases has spoken of adjudicators as if they were no different from ECOs. An adjudicator, however, sits in a judicial or a quasi-judicial capacity. The ECO is simply an agent of the Home Office amenable to its policy and subject to its direction. His assessment of evidence cannot carry the same, or even more, weight than an adjudicator's unless this involves consideration of facts which are uniquely known only to him. Furthermore, his view is not likely to prevail over an adjudicator's since in the nature of his function an adjudicator has more authority and is less likely to err whether on the facts, or on the law, whereas an ECO is pre-eminently concerned

---

[84] *ibid.*
[85] *Visa Officer Islamabad v. Alam Bi* TH/20164/79 (1373) d. 3.10.78 (unreported) at 4–5. This is the important *Alam Bi* case already discussed (at first instance) and where Stephenson L.J. explained the proper role and exercise of the Tribunal's discretion in respect of an appeal before it.

with the implementation of Home Office policy and is therefore more likely to present a one-sided view. The reality is that it is convenient for the Tribunal to decide cases in this way without due regard to legal niceties because of its general lack of sympathy for the intending immigrant. We shall examine this proposition fully in the next chapter, but it is a point that has not gone unrecognised by other commentators in this field, most notably by Professor Stephen Legomsky who wrote that, "In several decisions in which a literal interpretation would have benefitted the immigrant, the IAT departed from the clear language of the statute or rule to reach a result favourable to the Home Office".[86]

(c) Conclusions

What does the foregoing tell us? And what lessons are to be learnt from it? The doctrine of error of law in administrative law has been raised as a critical issue of law in this chapter, although it is quite illogical because it can apply differently to different adjudicative bodies, with the result that it is fraught with much difficulty. The courts apply it inconsistently under similar modes of judicial review,[87] since they may take into account the fact that "Parliament has not followed the usual practice of providing an appeal on points of law from an inferior tribunal, and may be less astute to detect errors of law on appeal".[88] Professor Felix Frankfurter explained in 1929 that it is for these reasons that judicial review of postal cases differs from that of land use cases or from that of immigration cases, because in each case it derives significance from the nature of the subject matter under review as well as from the agency which is reviewed.[89] However, this is only to say that the court's perception of an error of law is dependent upon its balancing of such disparate notions as justice, public interest, good administration and justiciability. The established principles of administrative law leave no doubt that an error of law arises where there is the following: "the application of a wrong legal test to the facts found", (virtually every case we have considered involving a higher standard of proof than is proper would fall under this category); "taking irrelevant considerations into account and failing to take relevant considerations into account", (in

---

[86] Legomsky, *Immigration and the Judiciary* (Oxford, 1978), p. 124.
[87] See Landis, *The Administrative Process* (Yale University Press, 1938), p. 144.
[88] See de Smith, *op. cit.*, p. 119.
[89] Frankfurter, "The Task of Administrative Law" (1929) 75 *Univ. of Panama L.R.* 64 and reprinted in *Law and Politics* (Occasional Papers of Felix Frankfurter 1913–1933, Macleish and Princhard, ed., 1939) pp. 236–237.

Sarwar Bi[90] appeals of applicants dismissed even though the fact of both relationship and identity conclusively proved before the Tribunal); "exercising a discretion on the basis of any other incorrect legal principles" (in *Monwara Begum*,[91] adjudicator erred in the law about domicile); "misdirection as to the burden of proof" (Tribunal saying in *Fatima el Yach Chiri*[92] that it was up to the sponsor to prove that he still retained his domicile of origin); "as well as arriving at a conclusion without any supporting evidence" (documentary evidence assumed to be bogus without any supporting evidence as in *Farzand Begum*[93] where marriage certificate not given any weight).[94]

In the same way, "if the drawing of an inference or the application of a statutory term is held or assumed to be a matter of fact for the 'tribunal' of first instance", it could still be found that the decision is erroneous if any of the defects above are present, "or if the inference or conclusion is one that no reasonable body of persons properly instructed in the law could arrive at".[95] The requirement that an applicant "satisfies an immigration officer" which appears in the Immigration Appeals Act 1969 is therefore the application of a statutory term by the immigration authorities. Whether or not an applicant is related as he or she claims is a matter of fact, not of law and if an ECO adjudicator, or Tribunal misconstrue the primary facts and reach a wrong decision they err in law. So in a case like *Farzand Begum*[96] it is not enough to say that the ECO has a duty (and not a discretion) to be satisfied and that if he is not so satisfied, he must reject the appeal.

Two cases bring these legal issues into sharper focus. The first is *Fatimax Kaniz v. Visa Officer Islamabad*[97] which was riddled with all the usual discrepancies in the evidence but where the appeal was allowed because a report was submitted by the Director of the *Immigrants Advisory Service of Pakistan* (IASP). The Tribunal said that the Director had "made a very thorough investigation of this case, visiting the District Health Officer's office, the appellants' schools, and their home. As a result of his investigations, which are fully described in his report, he was left in no doubt that this was a genuine claim . . ."[98] Compare this with *Rashida Bi v. Visa Officer Islamabad*

---

[90] *Supra*, n.68.
[91] *Supra*, n.69.
[92] *Supra*, n.10.
[93] *Supra*, n.76.
[94] de Smith, *op. cit.*, pp. 136–137.
[95] *ibid.* p. 137.
[96] *Supra*, n.76.
[97] TH/13304/77 (1403) d. 4.12.78 (unreported).
[98] *ibid.* at 2.

where there were again the usual discrepancies but the adjudicator, although dismissing the appeal, said that there was "a great probability that the sponsor married someone named Rashida Bi . . .".[99] Here also before the Tribunal a report by IASP was tendered in evidence in quite similar circumstances. The Tribunal acknowledged the report, recording that "it had been compiled over two years after the refusal of the visa officer". It included "an interview on 13 June 1977 of the appellants and sponsor in their own language at their village in Pakistan" which indicated that the applicants were related. However, on this occasion it said:

> "Had the statements of the sponsor and the first appellant and Danish Bi demonstrated the same consistency when interviewed by the visa officer as they now showed, their credibility might never have been in doubt . . . At the end of those interviews they were very properly given the opportunity to resolve the discrepancies, but remained silent. We do not accept that, having found their voices subsequent to the visa officer's refusal and publication of the adjudicator's reasons for his determination, their shaken credibility is now restored. There is a time and place for everything".[1]

This is a wholly arbitrary and unacceptable method of hearing appeals, the Tribunal not even doubting the existence of relationships as claimed, yet refusing the appeals because it was annoyed by the concerted effort of the applicants in attempting to prove their case.

One explanation for this capricious element in decision making is that the IAT is working under a system of strong pressure upon it to maintain a low success rate in appeals. Some have argued that this is a congenital defect in the system going back to the Wilson Committee with the emphasis being not upon substantive fairness but upon "reassuring"[2] immigrants which accounts for the variable content of decision making in immigration law.

The result is that the cases show that where a determination of an adjudicator had the effect of turning down the claim of an intending immigrant to entry into the United Kingdom, the chances of that determination being reversed on appeal were relatively slim. This was borne out by the figures in the 1980s. Only 18 per cent of immigrants' appeals against an adjudicator's determination were allowed by the Tribunal. The corresponding figure for the Secretary

---

[99] TH/12512/75 (1175) d. 3.3.78 (unreported).
[1] ibid. at 7, 9–10.
[2] Report of the Committee on Immigration Appeals Cmnd. 3387 (August 1987), pp. 19–20, para 62.

of State was 58 per cent per annum.[3] This was so even if an adjudicator had erred in law in coming to his decision. In contrast, the Tribunal would customarily intervene to upset an adjudicator's finding if the effect of that finding meant granting entry to an intending immigrant, even if the Tribunal's act in reversing an adjudicator's determination itself amounted to an error of law. The obvious instances were where an adjudicator's finding on a balance of probabilities had been altered to impose a higher standard of proof on the applicant.[4] In the same circumstances, the Tribunal would also countenance departing from certain strict rules which prescribe and go to the essence of its function. For example, in the absence of an error of law by an adjudicator, it had intervened to upset an adjudicator's finding based on the demeanour of witnesses that appeared before him but not before the Tribunal.[5]

Two general results have flowed from this practice. In the first place, the Tribunal has succeeded in restricting the entry of New Commonwealth immigrants into the United Kingdom because by deciding when, or when not, to intervene and by applying exacting standards of proof the Tribunal, as a body, has been especially instrumental in controlling the inflow of numbers.[6] In the second place, because Tribunals have much flexibility in how they conduct their business and are not bound by strict rules of evidence, the IAT has used this freedom to decide cases arbitrarily with the result that it has failed to play a procedurally more coherent and fair role in respect of its own appeal functions. This set the scene for the courts to step in on a number of occasions and to give guidance to the IAT on the proper exercise of this role. Whether their guidance has had the desired effect on Tribunal practice, however, is a different matter. This question is examined in the next section.

---

[3] See *The Pivot of the System*, A Briefing Paper on Immigration Appeals (Runnymede Trust, January 1981), pp. 15–16. Also see the Tables in Evans, *Immigration Law* (London 2nd ed., 1983), p. 364 compiled from statistical information given by the Secretary to the Immigration Appellate Authorities. See further the *UKIAS Annual Report* (1982–83), p. 9. These figures are also to be found in the publication of *Immigration Statistics* for the relevant years which is a publication by the Home Office of quarterly statistical bulletins. For more detailed information, see the Annual Command Paper, *e.g.* Cmnd. 8199 (1980).

[4] For example, see *Farzand Begum, supra*, n.76, and *Howayri Bibi, supra*, n.18.

[5] For example, see *Parveen Begum, supra*, n.83.

[6] Compare, for example, *Marion Khatun, supra*, n.62, where a land deed and other evidence was rejected by an adjudicator, with *Farzand Begum, supra* n.76, where a marriage certificate was accepted by an adjudicator. In the first case the Tribunal *declined to intervene* to reverse the adjudicator's rejection of evidence as compelling as names on a land deed; in the second case the Tribunal *did intervene to reverse* an adjudicator's finding that the marriage certificate indicated the existence of a valid marriage. In both cases the effect of the Tribunal's actions was to favour the Secretary of State but to reject the applicant's claim.

Guidance from the Courts and the Post-1980 Cases — Discretion to Disobey?

"The worst that can happen from opening the judicial doors in a doubtful case will be that a court will decide on the merits".

— K.C. Davis, *Discretionary Justice*, p. 230.

An important question here is whether the courts can be regarded as being relevant at all to the immigration process. This question has two quite different aspects. First, the courts may have been consigned to the periphery because they have themselves chosen to intervene only in very specific cases. This is a matter upon which some observers of the immigration scene have already commented,[7] but it is not something with which we are directly concerned in this work. Secondly, and more importantly from our point of view, the role of the courts may on the other hand, have been rendered nugatory because although they may have intervened to take corrective action in particular cases, their directions go largely unimplemented or ignored by subordinate bodies and authorities to whom they are directed. This is a far more serious matter because it leads to a state of affairs which can only be described as administrative lawlessness. It is something that has not been as widely commented upon as the first issue above,[8] but one with which we are fundamentally concerned because if the appellate authorities do not accept the legal controls on them, then it may well be that the only relevant controls are administrative and political. It also means that provided the Tribunal is determined enough it can continue to work within its own regulatory framework in derogation of express guidance from the courts. We begin by another look at *Ex p. Alam Bi*.[9]

---

[7] For example, see Evans, *op. cit.*, p. 418. More recently Legomsky has stated that "a general judicial conservatism is translated into a more specific judicial conservatism in immigration cases", *op. cit.*, p. 228.

[8] Legomsky does, however, refer to it but as was said at the outset, he was of the view that further more specific work was necessary, see p. 124 of his work. However, when he called for a further study, he did so in the context of *judicial* decisions. He said at p. 5 of his work that "the next logical step is to build on these works by studying, comprehensively *judicial decisions* falling within a carefully limited substantive sphere." This work, however, has been concerned with administrative decisions. Dummett and Nicol referred in their work to the *Subjects, Citizens, Aliens and Others* (*op. cit.*, p. 255) (London, 1990), "growing disregard for the findings of the appellate authorities" by the Home Office and its officials, but they have not focused as much on the nature of decision making by the immigration appellate authorities themselves.

[9] *Supra*, n.51.

(1) Ex p. Alam Bi and the Post-1980 Cases

Ex p. Alam Bi, it will be recalled, established that the Tribunal must play its proper role under section 20 of the 1971 Act and exercise its appellate jurisdiction to the full. It could alter an adjudicator's finding if it was "dissatisfied" with it; but had to do so if that determination was "plainly wrong". However, an adjudicator's determination based on his assessment of witnesses before him should only be altered if there were "compelling reasons" to do so.

The Court of Appeal judgement in *Ex p. Alam Bi* was given on April 23, 1980. A week later the IAT heard the case of *Bakshi Jan v. Visa Officer Islamabad*[10] where the sponsor, Mr Bahadur wanted his wife and children to join him here. The adjudicator heard evidence from him and three other witnesses and received additional documentary evidence. The entire transcript of this case is only one-and-a-half pages long. No account is given of what the witnesses said or what the documentary evidence consisted of and the adjudicator dismissed the appeal. Before the Tribunal it was argued that "the preponderance of the evidence established the claimed relationships". The Tribunal accepted, in fact, that evidence "was produced which we consider established that Mr Bahadur has a wife and two sons by the names of the appellants", but declined to reverse the adjudicator's determination on the grounds that:

> "The Tribunal will not interfere with an adjudicator's findings of fact unless it considers that no adjudicator, properly directing himself, could have come to the conclusions reached; or that additional evidence indicates that his decision was wrong".[11]

Even after *Ex p. Alam Bi*, therefore, the Tribunal was still not functioning as a proper appeals Tribunal, but only as a review body, and even here its exercise of jurisdiction was questionable.

Another case that followed close in the tracks of *Ex p. Alam Bi* is *Maya Bibi v. Entry Clearance Officer Dacca*.[12] Here the adjudicator had dismissed the appeal because of the discrepancies of which remarkably no details are given in his determination. He had heard before him the evidence of the sponsor and his alleged son, who had been settled in England since 1968. The Tribunal not only failed to examine the basis of the adjudicator's findings, but failed also to

---

[10] TH/21538/77 (1756) d. 30.4.80 (unreported).
[11] *ibid.* at 2.
[12] TH/31029/78 (1929) d. 12.1.81 (unreported), at 2.

ascertain for itself whether the sponsor and the alleged son were actually father and son as they claimed. It applied the usual formula that it would only reverse an adjudicator's determination if it was unreasonable.

The case of *Fatima el Yach Chiri*[13] has already been considered earlier in this chapter. It is, however, a good example that the Tribunal will not even interfere where an adjudicator has applied the wrong legal test. Here as we saw, the question was whether the sponsor had abandoned his domicile of origin and acquired one of choice in England. In English law there is a presumption against change of domicile. Consequently, the onus of proof is on the one who alleges the change of domicile. In this case the adjudicator wrongly concluded that the onus was upon applicants "in all cases to establish their eligibility". He found against the applicant because of the "sponsor's attitude on the subject during his testimony". However, apart from the fact that the burden of proof had been wrongly put on the applicant on this matter, it would appear that reference to the "sponsor's attitude" is insufficient as signifying a change of domicile. Here also the Tribunal concluded by affirming that it would only interfere if the decision under appeal was unreasonable.

Ex p. Alam Bi, therefore, appears to have been ignored or substantially ignored by the Tribunal as a guide to the exercise of its powers. Yet it is hardly conceivable that the same approach would have been taken on the facts by the Tribunal if the party to be benefited was not the intending immigrant, but the Home Office.

(2) EX P. MOTAHIR ALI

Yet, the following year in 1981, the High Court reiterated the rule in *Ex p. Alam Bi*. In *R. v. Immigration Appeals Tribunal, ex p. Motahir Ali*, Glidewell J. said: "The Tribunal's decision contains the phrase 'in the opinion of the Tribunal there was sufficient evidence to support the adjudicator's finding of fact.'"[14] With specific reference to this His Lordship said: "If the Tribunal does hear an appeal it is not, like this court, merely concerned to say whether there was evidence upon which the adjudicator's decision could properly have been made, or whether in some other way he had exceeded his jurisdiction." It could "hear appeals and allow them purely differing on the facts from the adjudicator."[15]

[13] *Supra*, n.10.
[14] January 29, 1981, QBD (unreported).
[15] *ibid*.

(3) THE DECISION IN EX P. ZAMAN

Both the Court decisions above still did not have the desired effect,[16] so the High Court sought in *R. v. Immigration Appeals Tribunal, ex p. Zaman*[17] on July 19, 1982 to re-state the correct position. The Court's ruling on the proper function of an appeal Tribunal is lucidly and emphatically given here leaving no doubt that the IAT's functions are not restricted to being that of a mere review body. Two children had lost their appeals before both an adjudicator and the Tribunal. On an application for judicial review to the Divisional Court, Woolf J., granting the application, said:

"Looking at section 20, it seems to me that, subject to the limitations which are placed upon the Tribunal to go into matters of credibility because they will not always see the witnesses, the right of appeal is the equivalent to that which was to be enjoyed where there *is the right to a rehearing*; that is to say, the Tribunal must consider the matter *de novo* on the material before it and *not restrict itself to the form of review which this court embarks upon when it is considering an application for judicial review.* That the Tribunal should recognise that this is its function can be of great importance to the appellants before it . . .".[18] (Author's emphasis.)

Woolf J. emphasised that "there is a heavy obligation upon the Tribunal to exercise properly the function which . . . is the proper function of an appeal Tribunal in those circumstances".[19] The Tribunal's approach in this case was strongly criticised by the Court as not fulfilling that obligation. It said of the Vice-President of the Tribunal:

". . . in giving his conclusions in dismissing the appeals of the two children, he said: 'The Tribunal has come to the conclusion that it would not be justified in interfering with the adjudicator's determination. It could only do so if it were to upset his findings of fact as to the date of the marriage and/or the number of children of the marriage born by 1970–71'. These findings were in its view supported by the evidence and were not unreasonable. Further the adjudicator heard the sponsor and he expressed the greatest doubt as to his credibility".[20]

---

[16] Ironically, the decision in *Alam Bi* was not actually favourable to the applicant himself and this may be one reason why the case did not have the desired effect. The Court of Appeal did say that "the ECO was in some respects in a better position than the adjudicator to assess the credibility of the sponsor" and decided against the applicant. See *supra*, n.51, at 154.
[17] [1982] Imm. A.R. 61, QBD.
[18] *ibid.* at 84.
[19] *ibid.* at 64.
[20] *ibid.*

This conclusion, used as a formula in many other cases, was what the Court took exception to. The Tribunal was failing to perform its proper function. It was not approaching the evidence *de novo* but was viewing it purely as a matter of law, and this approach was "too narrow and one which is not in accordance with the statutory provisions".[21] The Court then explained at length how the IAT should be dealing with these questions:

> "It is perfectly proper for the Tribunal to have regard to the view which the adjudicator formed of the witnesses who gave evidence before him; however, it is *not right for the Tribunal to refuse to interfere with an adjudicator's assessment of a matter such as the number of children at a particular date,* . . . purely because the adjudicator could reasonably take the view which he did of that evidence. *What the Tribunal should do is to look at that material in the same way as the adjudicator had to look at it.* The Tribunal is well equipped as the adjudicator to do that. It should then ask itself whether it would have come to that same conclusion. If the Tribunal comes to the same conclusion, then of course it would uphold the adjudicator's decision. If, on the other hand, it formed a different view, then in appropriate circumstances it would allow the appeal".[22] (Author's emphasis.)

If there were any doubts about this question in *Ex p. Alam Bi* this ruling must be seen as having wholly clarified them.[23] It is, in fact, quite in line with what was said in *Ex p. Alam Bi*. Did these decisions seep down to the practices of the IAT? Did the IAT taken any notice of them?

As with *Alam Bi* and *Motahir Ali*, *Ex p. Zaman* had little effect on Tribunal practice. Errors of law were still made by adjudicators and the Tribunal continued to follow its policy of non-intervention for the most part. Thus in *Sarwar Jan v. Visa Officer Islamabad* it was contended on the appellants' behalf that:

> ". . . a letter from the Chief Inspector of Taxes dated 25 August 1981 showed that details given to the tax authorities by the sponsor accorded with his claim. It confirmed that he had made claims for all the appellants and stopped claiming for his first wife after he married his second wife".[24]

This evidence must count as proof of the relationship beyond any reasonable doubt. However, the Tribunal failed to evaluate it and

---

[21] *ibid.* at 3.
[22] *ibid.* at pp. 64–65.
[23] It should not go unsaid that this, in fact, is completely in line with an adjudicator's analysis of his own role in *Amena Khatun, supra,* n.71.
[24] TH/88353/81 (2607) d. 14.2.83 (unreported), at 2.

failed to examine the case *de novo*. The sponsor was not interviewed to try to see why it was that the adjudicator had not been satisfied. Instead, the case ended with the usual statement by the Tribunal that it would "not lightly interfere with an adjudicator's finding of fact in such cases".[25] Rendered six months after the Divisional Court's judgement in *Ex p. Zaman*, this case gives especial cause for concern.

Even where the Tribunal has gone through the motions of examining the evidence as it should, it is clear that this act is often perfunctorily undertaken and the applicant is not getting the benefit of having his case heard on full appeal the second time. In *Ghulam Sughre v. Visa Officer Islamabad*,[26] heard by the Tribunal in November 1983, there seems to have been evidence beyond any shadow of doubt that the parties were related as claimed. Without giving any credible reasons, the evidence was rejected. The adjudicator dismissed the appeal on some astonishing grounds. For example, he said: "There is absence of personal correspondence and the evidence of remittances to the principal appellant . . ." In fact, there was evidence of remittances which pre-dated the application in October 1973 — 10 years earlier. The adjudicator also erred on the question of domicile. He said:

> "I am of the opinion that the sponsor had acquired an English domicile of choice at least by 1968. He said in evidence 'From my first arrival I was considering applying for British Nationality' and he did in 1971".[27]

It is well established, however, that domicile and citizenship do not necessarily go hand in hand. The Tribunal in *Khatun*[28] and others recognised this when it said: "Domicile is different from citizenship; a change of citizenship does not necessarily involve a change of domicile, though it may be some evidence to demonstrate such a change".[29] The adjudicator also confined his reasoning only to the discrepancies, many of which were plainly no such thing. Thus he

---

[25] *ibid.*

[26] TH/96117/82 (2925) d. 28.11.83 (unreported).

[27] *ibid.* at 3.

[28] *Supra*, n.71.

[29] Quoted by the Tribunal in *Sufia Khatun v. Entry Clerance Officer Dacca* TH/89275/82 (2793) d. 13.7.83 (unreported) at p. 3. Indeed, in *Re Flynn* [1968] 1 All E.R. 49, the defendant, the film actor Errol Flynn, made a declaration about his domicile to someone who was acting on his behalf in negotiations with the authorities over his passport and citizenship. Megarry J. held that he "would treat it with great caution, standing as it does with little or no extraneous indication of intention to support it", at 60, and this decision purported to follow that of Lord Scarman in *Re Fuld* [1966] 2 W.L.R. 717, where his Lordship said that so serious a matter as the acquisition of a domicile of choice is "not to be lightly inferred . . .", at 731.

remarked that "There is considerable inconsistency as to who arranged the marriage". It was pointed out before the Tribunal, however, that "as many people are involved in arranging a marriage no weight should be placed on that so-called discrepancy". Finally, the adjudicator was wrong in declaring that there was no rule which permits a person to bring in more than one wife to the United Kingdom.

Before the Tribunal all these matters were raised. It was also submitted that the adjudicator ignored very positive evidence in the form of remittances and evidence with regard to blood grouping of the children, and the acceptance by the Inland Revenue of the applicants as being the family of the sponsor. The Tribunal gave its decision curtly:

> "We are conscious of the fact that the adjudicator, unlike ourselves, made his findings after seeing how the sponsor gave his evidence. We regard the discrepancies which he outlined *as being significant and for the most part unresolved.*
> We find that the blood reports and the fact that the sponsor has persisted in this claim over a number of years are factors in support of the appellant's case.
> Looking at the evidence as a whole we are not satisfied on a balance of probabilities that either appellant is related to the sponsor as claimed.
> We agree with Mr Drabu that only if the relationship were established should the issue of domicile become relevant".[30] (Author's emphasis.)

The decision is given in terms merely of assertions or conclusions and not reasons as such. In fact, they are quite illogical when read through and it is quite clear that the evidence has not really been considered. The statement that the discrepancies are significant and unresolved is not borne out by the evidence because as we have seen most of these were only so-called discrepancies. Even if they are significant the Tribunal does not explain why it regards them so. In the next statement, in fact, it emphasises how strong the case of the applicants is by referring to positive blood reports and the determination of the sponsor over many years to bring his family here. It seems extraordinary that the Tribunal should then remain dissatisfied with the standard of proof here. Failure of the Tribunal to explain this shows that adverse determinations by adjudicators have continued to be rubber-stamped on further appeal despite the clarification of the law in *ex p. Zaman*.

---

[30] *Sufia Khatun, ibid.* at 4.

A bizarre case in this respect is *Choudhary v. Entry Clearance Officer Dacca* where an adjudicator was shown a forged marriage certificate of the sponsor with wrong details entered on it as to family matters. Despite the adjudicator being told that the certificate was false he nevertheless went ahead and used it as a basis for his refusal. On further appeal the Tribunal heard that the adjudicator had erred in taking into account a forged marriage certificate when knowing it to be such, but the Tribunal held that he "was perfectly entitled" to take it into account "since it had been produced on behalf of the appellants".[31]

An even more absurd case is *Visa Officer Islamabad v. Manzoor Begum*[32] which is ultimately very revealing on the nature and purposes of immigration law as traditionally seen. Here Mrs Begum made an application with her son, Tanvir for an entry clearance certificate in order to join her husband who was settled in the United Kingdom. This was in October 1977. Her status and the child's status, as wife and son of someone settled in Britain was proved and her application was therefore granted. However, as she was expecting another child she decided not to go to the United Kingdom until after the birth of her child. In the meantime, her entry certificate expired after six months. Her second child was then born whereupon she made another application. The visa officer refused this application because in his view there were certain discrepancies in the answers to the questions asked by him so he came to the conclusion that she was not related to her sponsoring husband in the United Kingdom as claimed.

Mrs Begum appealed to an adjudicator who decided from the explanatory statement that "nothing except the discrepancies" were against her. To him this seemed an insufficient basis for refusal. Nor could he find any evidence that "the first entry certificate was obtained by deception or concealment of material facts". Furthermore, he believed "it could well be argued that an estoppel arises in the circumstances" and so he allowed the appeal both of Mrs Begum and her two children. The visa officer thereupon further appealed to the IAT which, despite the guidance given by the courts in *ex p. Alam Bi* and *ex p. Motahir Ali*, reversed the adjudicator's determination without an investigation of the visa officer's decision. It chose rather, to decide the appeal on the basis that "the doctrine of estoppel could not operate against the Secretary of State because he had power to change his mind" and that "similarly the doctrine of *res judicata* has no application in immigration entry and immigration departments".[33]

[31] TH/77768/81 (2532) d. 12.1.83 (unreported), at 3.
[32] TH/83002/81 (2341) d. 10.5.82 (unreported).
[33] *ibid.* at 20.

One is bound to ask in these circumstances, whether the application for an entry certificate or an appeal thereafter, is simply a mechanical exercise undertaken perfunctorily or whether it is a more meaningful exercise engaging in a search for truth — the truth about the parties' claimed relationship to each other. Cases such as these, where the search for discrepancies or other stumbling blocks is simply a quest for a peg on which to hang a decision maker's refusal of an application, suggest that the system is operating at all levels with a totally different purpose in mind, which is not that of ascertaining eligibility of applicants but of ensuring their "ineligibility" wherever possible. If this is so, it makes the case for an even more stringent supervision by the courts all the more unassailable. Otherwise, the law here can only be brought into further disrepute.

Conclusions

Despite the very clear directions given in *ex p. Alam Bi*, *ex p. Zaman* and *ex p. Motahir Ali* to the immigration appellate authorities, it is evident that legal control by the courts of immigration control is at best superficial. The aberrant nature of appellate decision making suggests that the primary controls in this jurisdiction are political. The Tribunal's compliance in *Rupjan Bibi* that "we accept . . . that we should act under the guidelines laid down in *Alam Bi*"[34] cannot be regarded as being anything more than lip-service to a legal ideal, in the period that is under consideration in this work, since the decided cases are irreconcilable with the required judicious conduct of appeal hearings which the courts have advocated in this field. The question remains why the Tribunal should reverse the decision of an adjudicator in one case but not in another, where there is manifestly an error of law requiring correction.[35] Why should the Tribunal refuse to acknowledge the probative value in evidence of a genuine marriage certificate,[36] yet mystifyingly regard as relevant a bogus marriage certificate that has been withdrawn from evidence by the applicants?[37] Why does it intervene to gainsay an adjudicator's assessment of a witness account in one case[38] but not another?[39] Most importantly,

---

[34] *Supra*, n.52.
[35] Compare *Akhtar Begum, supra,* n.74 with *Monwara Begum, supra,* n.69.
[36] Compare *Farzand Begum, supra,* n.76 with *Choudhary, supra,* n.31.
[37] Compare *Parveen Begum, supra,* n.83 with *Alam Bi, supra,* n.85.
[38] See *Parveen Begum, supra,* n.83.
[39] See *Alam Bi, supra,* n.85, p. 147 and *Bakshi Jan, supra,* n.10.

why has it ignored court judgments that are favourable to the intending immigrant in terms of their effect? The answer to these questions lies in the realms of fundamental value judgments that all decision makers make when considering the merits of a case that is being argued before them. It does not lie in the formal provisions of technical law the application of which would have been made all too clear to them time and time again through the statute books and the various legal precedents.

After the arrival of Professor Jackson as Chairman at the IAT in late 1983, the quality of Tribunal decision making was considerably enhanced and it has been going up ever since. It seems, however, that the Tribunal still did not accept even then, that a hearing before it implied a hearing *de novo* both on the facts and the law.[40] So what are these value judgments? To understand that, we must turn to the next chapter.

---

[40] See, *e.g. Ghulam Sughre, supra,* n.26.

Chapter Five

Unfencing Legal Thought

"Law is endowed with its own discrete, integral history, its own 'science', and its own values, which are all treated as a single block sealed off from general social history, from politics, and from morality. The habits of mind appropriate, within narrow limits, to the procedures of law courts in the most stable legal systems have been expanded to provide legal theory and ideology with an entire system of thought and values. This procedure has served its own ends very well: it aims at preserving law from irrelevant considerations, but it has ended by fencing legal thinking off from all contact with the rest of historical thought and experience."

J.N. Shklar, *Legalism* (1964) pp. 2–3

In this chapter we make an attempt at understanding Tribunal decisions described in the last chapter as being arbitrary. We find that these decisions can be rationalised on the basis of their time and context. If we examine the period before 1973 when the Immigration Act 1971 came into effect we find that many appellate decisions were quite liberal and one could not necessarily speak of these cases, as Professor Legomsky has done of the present cases, as embodying "the typically conservative results of the immigration cases".[1] Many Tribunal decisions were prepared to give would-be immigrants the benefit of the doubt.[2] That, however, changed markedly with a change in government policy in 1971. It is correct here to say therefore, as Professor Legomsky has done, "that there is a positive correlation between a general political conservatism and a specific tendency to view immigration in an unsympathetic light".[3] This may

---

[1] Legomsky, *Immigration and the Judiciary* (Oxford, 1978), p. 228.
[2] This was even true in the few years immediately following the 1971 Act before attitudes hardened. See, for example, the cases at pp. 164–167 *supra*.
[3] Legomsky, *op. cit.*, at pp. 232–233.

be regarded as a particularly glib assertion if Tribunals are viewed simply as a vehicle for the implementation of government policy. One Home Secretary, Mr Reginald Maudling said: "I have never seen the sense of administrative law in our country, because it is only someone else taking the government's decision for them. I cannot see that [tribunals] are better qualified if it is not a legal but a practical matter."[4] This view cannot today be regarded as valid, even if ever it was in the past, for Tribunals are expected to hear appeals impartially and in a judicial spirit.[5] Yet even if in the very nature of things there is an undoubted relationship between politics and the law, when does this correlation become unhealthy? We answer this question in this chapter by saying that the correlation became unhealthy when basic questions of proof began to be dealt with arbitrarily, and when the Tribunal correspondingly began to develop certain specific doctrines such as the "discrepancy system" with a view to implementing particular policy ends. This chapter is divided into two: the first part looks at the earlier, pre-1973 cases, the later part looks at the post-1973 cases.

Administrative Justice In Immigration Law — A Scarlet Pimpernel?

Wives and children who wished to join their husbands in the United Kingdom stood a better chance of doing so in the years before 1971 than afterwards. Even though the Immigration Act 1971 did not set out to formally curtail the rights of wives of children of men settled here, but in fact expressly preserved those rights,[6] more stringent requirements of proof were applied in the years following 1973 than in those preceding it. A discrepancy as to when the marriage took place or when a certain child of the marriage was born, was much more important after 1973 than before it. Similarly, although documentation is much better today in the sub-continent than it was 25 years ago, a marriage certificate was more readily accepted as proof of marriage then, than it is today. How could the evaluation of truth have changed over the years. In *Liversidge v. Anderson*, Lord Atkin, in his celebrated dissenting judgment, cautioned against such fluctuations of mood:

---

[4] *Official Report*, Standing Committee B (May 15, 1971), Col. 1508.
[5] This has been true at least since the (1957) *Report of the Franks Committee on Administrative Tribunals*, which emphasised the need for openness in the procedures of decision making affecting individual rights (see Cmnd. 218).
[6] See p. 42, *supra*, and the reference to section 1(5) of the Immigration Act 1971.

"I know of only one authority which might justify the suggested method of construction. 'When I use a word', said Humpty Dumpty in rather a scornful tone, 'it means just what I choose it to mean, neither more or less'. 'The question is', said Alice, 'whether you can make words mean different things'. 'The question is', said Humpty Dumpty, 'which is to be master — that's all'."[7]

After 1971 the appellate authorities pursued a policy of increased rigorism to ensure that, in accordance with the politics of the law during this time, the further entry of new Commonwealth immigrants was restricted as a matter of a deliberate policy. All the obstacles confronting prospective immigrants, such as when or whether the benefit of the doubt should be given to them in difficult cases, the shortcomings of documentary proofs in the sub-continent, the "discrepancy system" and concerns over the identity of applicants, will now be considered in relation to these two separate periods.

(1) The individual and the "Benefit of the Doubt"

Generally in the earlier cases, the individual was given the benefit of the doubt in difficult matters of proof. In *Manzoor Begum v. Secretary of State for the Home Department*,[8] the sponsor had claimed tax allowance for his claimed wife and children for the last 10 years. The Tribunal was prepared to overlook the discrepancies to say, "we are prepared to give the Appellants the benefit of any doubts that remain and to find on the balance of probabilities that they are the wife and son of Mohd. Hayet [the Sponsor]".[9] In *A.M. Patel v. Secretary of State for the Home Department*,[10] the Tribunal allowed the appeal of the applicants although all the doubts about the relationship claimed "had not been resolved". In *Secretary of State for the Home Department v. Rabia Bi* the Tribunal again upheld the claim of the applicant even though it felt that "it is not possible to feel any certainty about the relationship of the parties concerned."[11] In fact, in *Akbar Jan v. Secretary of State for the Home Department*,[12] one gets an important glimpse of how different the attitude of the Tribunal was in the earlier cases when it said:

---

7 [1941] 3 All E.R. 338, at 361.
8 Ex/9/71 d. 8.3.71 (unreported).
9 *ibid.* at 4.
10 Ex/11/71 d. 25.1.72 (unreported).
11 TH/2528/71 d. 17.3.72 (unreported), at 3.
12 TH/2152/71 d. 23.3.72 (unreported).

"There are a number of discrepancies which have not been satisfactorily explained but the explanatory statement of the ECO was prepared a long time after the Appellants were interviewed and by another officer. Although no doubt inevitable in the circumstances this is not altogether satisfactory and we consider it might well be unfair to rely upon it entirely at this stage. At the same time there are a number of documents which have not been challenged, in particular, evidence of fairly substantial remittances over a long period, which raise a presumption that the first named Appellant is the wife of Mohd. Azam [*i.e.* the sponsor]. In all these circumstances we consider that the Appellants should be given the benefit of any doubt and we therefore allow the appeal."[13]

This suggestion that "the appellants should be given the benefit of any doubt" is a most noteworthy feature of the earlier cases as it is totally absent in all the present-day cases that we have discussed in this work. It is also a key to the general attitude of the Tribunal before 1973 showing that the Tribunal was more concerned to protect due-process rights and entitlements of individuals under the law and to apply proper standards of proof.[14]

(2) REMITTANCES AS PROOF OF RELATIONSHIP

In the earlier cases appeals have even been allowed simply on the basis of evidence of remittances produced by the sponsor showing that money had been sent to the claimed wife and children. Of course, as we saw in the last chapter, nowadays evidence of remittances alone is unlikely to lead to success for a would-be immigrant.[15] Even where there is evidence of remittances going back 15 years this is deemed insufficient to prove the alleged relationship.[16] In the case just considered, *Akbar Jan*, evidence of remittances seems to have played a crucial role, however. Similarly, in *Said Bi v. Secretary of State for the Home Department*,[17] the claimed wife's appeal succeeded primarily because of the remittances. The Home Office representative also stated that having seen the remittances he thought it right to concede that the wife was related as claimed. This is quite unusual today.

---

[13] *Akhbar Jan, supra*, n.12, at 4.
[14] Other cases may also be considered such as *Raja Blegum* (TH/417/71) d. 23.3.72 (unreported).
[15] *Supra*, pp. 134–135.
[16] *Soydun Nessa v. Entry Clerance Officer Dacca* TH/64047/80 (2214) d. 7.12.81 (unreported) *supra*, p. 134 and *Tula Bibi v. Entry Clerance Officer Dacca* TH/48214/79 (2310) d. 18.3.83 (unreported) where there was evidence of 38 remittances going back 14 years; *supra*, p. 134.
[17] TH/875/71 d. 5.5.72 (unreported).

(3) Documents: the "Face-Value Test"

The corollary of accepting the probative value of evidence of remittances is the general acceptance of documentary evidence at its face value. This means that unless there is evidence to the contrary documents are presumed to be genuine and to have been genuinely issued. Thus in *Shiv Kaur v. Secretary of State for the Home Department*,[18] the Tribunal remarked:

> "It has been submitted to us that in countries where there is a serious lack of records statements by officials are often compiled from notes of what they have been told by the parties for such statements. This may well be so but in this case *there is no evidence before* us that the priest and headman (who submitted evidence that the claimed wife was related to the sponsor) prepared their statements in this way. We accept that the further evidence before us does not specifically deal with some of the discrepancies already in evidence and which remain unresolved. However, we consider that we must accept some, at any rate, of the additional evidence at its face value and *we accordingly find that on the balance of probabilities*, the Appellants are the wife and dependant child of Mr Darshan Singh [*i.e.* the sponsor]".[19] (Author's emphasis.)

In the same way, in *Kamalinder Kaur v. Secretary of State for the Home Department*,[20] the Tribunal had before it some documents, including a death certificate. It held: "There is no evidence before us to cast any doubt on the authenticity of those two documents and we feel therefore that we must accept the documents as they stand."[21] This may be compared with some of the present day cases where the authorities have openly disparaged public documents from the Indian sub-continent.[22]

(4) Discrepancies or Just Human Failing?

Equally, there is evidence that often a less serious view was taken of discrepancies then, as compared to today. We have already seen, for example, how in *Akbar Jan* the Tribunal upheld the applicants' claim

---

[18] TH/616/71 d. 24.8.71 (unreported).
[19] *ibid.* at 6.
[20] Ex/203/71 d. 27.10.71 (unreported).
[21] *ibid.* at 4.
[22] Again, comparison may be made with the cases already discussed: *Nazir Begum* TH/338500/78 (1655) d. 19.10.79 (unreported), *supra*, p. 94; *Fultera Begum* TH/64779/80 (2221) d. 4.12.81 (unreported) *supra*, p. 94; *Rajia Khatun* TH/93066/82 (2662) d. 8.4.83 (unreported) *supra*, p. 95).

despite the fact that the discrepancies had not been satisfactorily explained.[23] In *Imitaz Begum v. Secretary of State for the Home Department*,[24] the claimed wife and her child had been refused entry certificate because their accounts as to the accommodation in which they lived, the domestic animals that they owned and the crops grown on their land, differed. The Tribunal allowed their appeal because two cousins of the sponsor who were also resident in England provided the necessary corroborative evidence. It concluded that "Without such evidence this appeal would have been dismissed . . . even though the discrepancies referred to earlier have not been satisfactorily explained."[25] In fact, a number of cases were allowed on appeal in 1978 when the 1971 Act was fully in force. It appears that these cases succeeded not because the discrepancies were any less important than in other cases or because they had been explained away, but because the Tribunal preferred to attach more weight to the positive evidence in the cases.[26] This spurt, however, did not last very long but it provides an instructive example of how the "discrepancy system" can be, and indeed has been, discarded by the Tribunal even in more recent years.

(v) PROOF OF "IDENTITY"

Finally, the question of "identity" for applicants was not a major hurdle before 1973. Provided there was enough extrinsic evidence to prove the relationship on a balance of probabilities further evidence as to the identity of the persons applying was not normally required. In fact, in one case when an adjudicator refused the appeal on this ground, the Tribunal on further appeal upheld the applicant's claim. The adjudicator had referred to a "fairly weak *prime facie* case" and to the unresolved discrepancies. Although he dismissed the appeal, he added: "I dislike coming to this conclusion because . . . I can think of no reason why a man should wish to bring to the United Kingdom a woman who is not his wife." The Tribunal *allowed* it because, in addressing itself to the same question of why a sponsor would wish to bring into this country someone who is not his wife, it concluded: "We cannot think of a reason in this case".[27]

---

[23] *Supra*, see n.12. Also see n.8, *supra*, for the case of *Manzoor Begum*.
[24] *Imitiaz Begum v. Secretary of State for the Home Department* TH/1032/1971 d. 25.6.71 (unreported).
[25] *ibid.* at 3.
[26] See *Sarwar Begum* TH/9141/76 (1266) d. 12.7.78 (unreported); *Murtar Begum* TH/13431/77 (1270) d. 17.7.81 (unreported; *Nazir Begum* TH/12844/75 (1276) d. 7.7.78 (unreported); and *Razina Begum* TH/1689/77 (1289) D. 14.8.78 (unreported).
[27] *Nazir Begum v. Secretary of State for the Home Department* TH/2729/71 (10) d. 16.6.72 (unreported).

Law-making Through Adjudication: The Later Cases

In the years following 1973, there was a significant change in the way that the Tribunal handled some of the central issues of law and fact that we have discussed above. This is not to say that the change can be rigidly compartmentalised into cases before 1973 and cases after. But it does mean that all the major problems that we have discussed in this work with regard to dependency applications — the existence of discrepancies, fear of possible bogus applications, and fraudulent tax claims on the Inland Revenue — were dealt with in a markedly different way by the end of the decade. Underlying this change was a shift in priorities and emphases in the weight attached to such basic considerations as the individual interest, the public interest, departmental interest and what and what was not considered justiciable in immigration control. By the end of the decade, the Immigration Tribunal played a more robust role in the development of immigration control policies. How that role differed from the earlier, pre-1973 cases, can best be described by looking at its conduct in a number of specific instances over this period.

(1) THE DISCREPANCY SYSTEM AND "THE RULE IN MAYARUN NESSA"

As we have seen,[28] the greatest contention in entry clearance procedures currently rages over what has been called "the discrepancy system". In contrast to the earlier cases, discussed above, the later cases show that the Tribunal began to take a very strict and uncompromising view of discrepancies to the point that it required absolute certitude on all matters. The high-point of this approach, and change in attitude, was the phenomenon of the now discredited "rule in *Mayarun Nessa*" which was based on a decision of that name in July 1978.[29] The decision laid that the parties must provide clear proof not only as to the fact of marriage but also as to the precise date of such an event. Adjudicators who allowed appeals simply on proof of the fact of marriage were now said to have taken a mistaken approach. The decision seemed to confirm the worst fears of those that had believed for some time now that the standard of proof applied by the Tribunal was far higher than the civil standard. The Tribunal reprimanded the adjudicator for allowing the appeal because

---

[28] *Supra*, pp. 62–67.
[29] *Entry Clearance Officer Dacca v. Mayarun Nessa* TH/20291/77 (1318) d. 18.7.78 (unreported)

as ". . . It had not been established that the claimed marriage took place in 1958, he should . . ., like the ECO, not have been satisfied that Mayarun Nessa was the genuine wife . . ."[30]

Such a ruling, however, is open to question. First, ECOs have a duty not just to stand at the bench and listen to what intending immigrants have to say but also to investigate matters that arise before them.[31] It would be a mistake to say that an ECO has an activist role and an adjudicator on appeal a merely passive one. Adjudicators are equally empowered to probe into matters further and get at the truth. Secondly, it is submitted that the decision is contrary to law. The only burden upon applicants is to show that they are related as claimed in the circumstances. Dates of marriage and birth are only relevant in so far as they throw light on this question. Nonetheless, the decision was immediately seen by adjudicators and immigration officials as establishing a new precedent. Adjudicators began to refuse appeals where the claimed wife and the sponsor were unclear about the date of the marriage or gave discrepant answers. In fact, according to the UKIAS *Split Families* Report, it was at this time that medical age assessments began to be increasingly used in order to determine the true age of the wife, even though as we have seen such evidence was in itself quite unreliable. The Report states:

"During the catastrophic period of the so-called 'Mayarun Nessa Rule', many adjudicators, it seems, were obsessed with the idea of discovering whether the principal appellant was really married in the year as claimed, and in doing so the medical age estimate by the respondent was taken as useful evidence. As a result, we reckon *hundreds of cases were dismissed* on the basis of such medical age assessment".[32] (Author's emphasis.)

Seeing the refusal rate rise on these grounds the Tribunal then relented and sought rather belatedly to restore the correct legal position. Thus in *Bibi Barkat v. Visa Officer Islamabad* the adjudicator said typically:

I am satisfied that the sponsor is married to Barkat Bibi but that he married her at a later date than claimed. The respondent concedes this possibility in his submission. But I am precluded by the rule in *Mayarun*

---

[30] *ibid.* at 4.
[31] See *Visa Officer Islamabad v. Khadaja Bi* TH/26083/78 (1971) d. 10.7.79 (unreported), p. 3. Now also see *Bahar v. IAT* [1988] Imm. A.R. 574 and *R. v. IAT, ex p. Rashida Bi* [1990] Imm. A.R. 348.
[32] *Split Families* Report, *op. cit.*, p. 36.

Nessa . . . from assuming this to be so . . . and therefore cannot allow her appeal."[33] (Author's emphasis.)

The Tribunal, on further appeal, reversed this determination, holding that under the immigration rules the wife of a person who is settled in the United Kingdom is to be admitted for settlement: "That is the relevant immigration rule and no decision of this Tribunal can be read as amending it or substituting a different rule."[34] *Mayarun Nessa*, it was claimed, had been "misapplied". In that case, the Tribunal explained:

> "The adjudicator's determination was set aside because the evidence did not support a finding that the parties were ever married. What has to be established in cases of this type is that the applicant is indeed the wife of the sponsor. It is not essential, as a matter of law, to pinpoint the date of the marriage, . . . There must, however, in every case be evidence sufficient to establish the relationship claimed. In *Mayarun Nessa* that evidence was lacking".[35] (Author's emphasis.)

This does not, however, account for the Tribunal's assertion in *Mayarun Nessa*, that, "As the adjudicator found that it had not been established that the claimed marriage took place in 1958, he should in our view, like the ECO, not have been satisfied that Mayarun Nessa was the genuine wife".[36] In fact, it was precisely because of this tendentious statement that adjudicator's refused so many cases.

The snow-ball effect of the decision continued uncurbed, however. The situation was viewed seriously enough for the Tribunal to hold a specially-constituted hearing in *Monwara Begum v. Entry Clearance Officer Dacca*. It explained:

> "This appeal was set down for hearing before three full-time chairman of the Tribunal because there have been a number of cases recently in which adjudicators have stated that they are applying the 'rule' or 'principle' in the case of Mayarun Nessa. We wish to make it abundantly clear *that there is no such rule and no such principle*."[37] (Author's emphasis.)

---

[33] *Bibi Barkat v. Visa Officer Islamabad* TH/36849/78 (1761) d. 8.5.80 (unreported).

[34] At the time the applicable rules were: *Statement of Immigration Rules for Control of Entry*. EEC and Other Non-Commonwealth Nationals (January 25, 1973), H.C. 81, para. 36.

[35] *Supra*, n.33 at 2.

[36] *Supra*, nn.29 and 30.

[37] TH/29451/78 (1823) d. 21.8.80 (unreported), at 2. The three full-time Chairmen were D.L. Neve, P.N. Dalton and R. Hooton.

Adjudicators again, however, continued to apply the "rule". In many subsequent cases, the Tribunal has found it necessary to repeatedly restate the correct legal position. Thus in *Jaigun Bibi v. Entry Clearance Officer Dacca* the Tribunal remarked that "the decision in the case of *Mayarun Nessa* appears to have been misconstrued by adjudicators".[38] In *Ruqayah Begum v. Visa Officer islamabad*[39] and *Minara Begum v. Entry Clearance Officer Dacca*[40] the Tribunal allowed the applicants' appeals once again because the adjudicator had applied *Mayarun Nessa*. However, despite the repeated admonitions by the Tribunal, one finds that the "rule" was being applied by adjudicators at least as late as May 1983.[41] This was almost five years after the original decision in *Mayarun Nessa*. The disturbing question that is raised once again, therefore, is why it has taken so long to bring home to adjudicators and immigration officials changes in law that are favourable to intending immigrants. Once it was discovered that *Mayarun Nessa* was being applied by adjudicators and that it ought not to have been, the proper thing to have done was to inform adjudicators by internal circular rather than hope to affect individual cases piecemeal on appeal to the Tribunal. Since not all refusals by the adjudicator find their way to the Tribunal on subsequent appeal. Failure to take the appropriate steps can be attributed either to the inefficiency of the system or to a deliberate policy of allowing refusals to be made by adjudicators in genuine cases.

There remains one final ironic twist to this episode, however. It is by no means clear that every adjudicator had heard of the Tribunal decision in *Mayarun Nessa* or was applying it in the manner suggested. One adjudicator has informed the writer that he had never heard of the decision and had never refused a case simply because the date of the sponsor's marriage could not be accurately pinpointed.[42]

Is this then, the end of *Mayarun Nessa*? In *Shoriful Nessa v. Entry Clearance Officer Dacca*,[43] decided over two years after *Mayarun Nessa* in 1980, the Tribunal itself expressly purported to follow *Mayarun Nessa*. This is bound, surely, to be read as impliedly sanctioning the practice of adjudicators based upon that decision. In *Shoriful Nessa* the Tribunal held that in accordance with its decision in *Mayarun Nessa*

---

[38] TH/277223/78 (1872) d. 27.10.80 (unreported), at 2.
[39] TH/30765/78 (1889) d. 30.10.80 (unreported).
[40] TH/4747/79 (1887) d. 30.10.80. (unreported).
[41] See *Rufjan Bibi v. Entry Clearance Officer Dacca* TH/64692/80 (2722) d. 23.5.83 (unreported).
[42] Personal communication from Dr David Pearl when part-time immigration adjudicator (now H.H. Judge David Pearl and Chief Adjudicator).
[43] TH/37927/78 (1908) d. 19.11.80 (unreported).

in 1978 an appeal must be dismissed if the marriage was not on the given date or on any "alternative date" which "has been satisfactorily established". Such a suggestion, however, would appear to require a degree of specificity in time which is not a requirement under the immigration rules.[44] The sponsor in this case was questioned about the death of his father in relation to the time of his marriage, both events having taken place over 20 years ago. The Tribunal held:

"The appellant's case largely stands or falls on the date of the marriage of the sponsor and Shoriful Nessa being 1955. As in *Mayarun Nessa*, so here, because it has not been satisfactorily established that this marriage took place when claimed and no alternative date has been satisfactorily established, the ECO and the adjudicator in the instant case were properly not satisfied that Shoriful Nessa is the genuine wife of the sponsor."[45]

The decision makes it quite plain that there is, or was such a thing as "the rule in *Mayarun Nessa*". According to this rule even if the fact of marriage is not in doubt an appeal must be dismissed if the given date, or any alternative date of marriage, cannot be accurately established on the evidence. This is bound to lead to the refusal of many genuine cases, not only because documentation in the Indian sub-continent being what it is, the appropriate evidence may often be lacking, but also because the decision is not based on the law. The immigration rules have never specified that the date of marriage be accurately ascertained for to do so would be asking for proof beyond all reasonable doubt, and yet the injustice for the appellant in this case, who was a naturalised British subject and had been one for the last 10 years, must have been abundantly clear to the Tribunal.

(2) FRAUD AND THE DEVELOPING DOCTRINE OF "IDENTITY"

As with "discrepancies", a similar restrictive doctrine was developed by the Tribunal in the "fraud" cases. Here also a chronological review of the decisions over the last decade makes fascinating reading and allows for very similar inferences to be drawn. It appears that a general change in appellate decision making took place at both tiers after 1977. There is little doubt that this change emanated from the Tribunal. The nature of this change and the circumstances in which it took place gave further credence to the view that the decision-making process, at a given time, is not dependent upon the evidence

---

[44] See *Statement of Immigration Rules for Control on Entry*, Commonwealth Citizens (January 25, 1973); H.C. 70, paras 41 and 43.
[45] See n.43, *supra*, at 2–3.

per se, but upon such imponderables as the political and legal climate in which decision making occurs.

Twenty years ago it was by no means settled that adjudicators and the Tribunal could dismiss applicants' appeals on the question of "identity" in the face of cogent documentary and testimonial evidence. In fact, many adjudicators were prepared to accept that the fact of the sponsor's marriage having been established on the evidence, the woman that he would seek to bring in would be his wife and not an impostor. In the years to come this position changed, not because there was any evidence to the contrary, but because the Tribunal directed that it should. Today, as we have seen, this argument has gained much currency with the appellate authorities and constitutes a major ground for refusal of appeals by intending immigrants.[46]

Thus in 1972 in *Secretary of State for the Home Department v. Rabia Bi* the sponsor succeeded on the evidence in gaining entry for his wife despite the Tribunal's observation that "it is not possible to feel any certainty about the relationship of the parties concerned".[47] Even in 1975 cases such as *Zarina Begum v. Entry Clearance Officer Islamabad*[48] were not uncommon. Here the appeal against the adjudicator's adverse decision was only allowed by the Tribunal because it was found that the Inland Revenue had, after considerable investigation, finally accepted the sponsor's claim for money remittances sent to his family. The Tribunal assumed that the persons who were now applying were the sponsor's true wife and children. In 1977 the Tribunal reversed a number of determinations by adjudicators on the grounds that the identity of the claimed wife had not been accurately established. In *Entry Clearance Officer Dacca v. Sofina Khatun*[49] the adjudicator allowed the appeal of the claimed wife explaining that: ". . . there is a great incentive for the sponsor to bring to the United Kingdom two male teenagers who may well be related in another way, whereas *there is little incentive for him to bring a middle-aged lady unless she is related* to him as claimed." (Author's emphasis.) The Tribunal, however, reversed the adjudicator's decision contending that: "His conclusion that 'there is little incentive for him [*i.e.* the sponsor], to bring a middle-aged lady unless she is related as claimed' *is pure speculation* not based on the evidence."[50] (Author's emphasis.)

---

[46] *Supra*, pp. 165–173.
[47] TH/2528/71 d. 17.3.72 (unreported), at 3.
[48] TH/1670/73 (505) d. 20.8.75 (unreported).
[49] TH/1726/76 (1924) d. 1.9.77 (unreported).
[50] *ibid.* at 2–3.

Similarly, in *Manzoor Begum* the fact of the marriage was not challenged by the ECO. The date of the marriage was established as being 1950 and even the dates of birth of the children were ascertained. A photograph of the wife was also produced in evidence. The adjudicator allowed the appeal on the grounds that, "it seems somewhat far-fetched to suggest that Ajaib Khan [*i.e.* the sponsor], would encourage the admission of a person of that age and background if she were not his wife". This decision was also reversed by the Tribunal as it found it "impossible to say where the truth lies".[51]

"The evidence of the principal appellant in almost every respect is at variance with the other evidence, including important documentary evidence. Mr Hashmi (her representative) has suggested that she was confused and was not being deceitful in her statements to the ECO. *I accept from the evidence that Mohd. Khaliq (the sponsor) is married to a person by the name of Akhtar Jan* (the principal appellant). He has made several visits to Pakistan and it is not unreasonable that he should have *children of the ages of the minor appellants*. In considering whether the principal appellant is Akhtar Jan, it must be asked why should the sponsor wish to bring over a person other than his true wife. *It is more credible to accept Mr Hashmi's explanation that* the principal appellant was extremely nervous and that her mis-statements are to be attributed to this factor than to suggest that she is an impostor". (Author's emphasis.)

On appeal by the ECO the Tribunal reversed this determination. In the Tribunal's view the adjudicator had proceeded wrongly:

"The adjudicator has attached importance to the question why the sponsor should wish to bring over a person other than his wife but *experience in appeals* in these family cases shows that *impostors have undoubtedly been put forward*."[52] (Author's emphasis.)

This is a familiar syndrome. We have encountered it already in the utterances of the Home Affairs Committee in 1982,[53] in the evidence of the Foreign and Commonwealth Office before it,[54] and in a more caricatured form, in the dossier prepared by the British High Commission in Dacca in October 1976. But in neither of these cases was it ever proved that sponsors brought in bogus wives or bogus

---

[51] *Entry Clearance Officer Islamabad v. Manzoor Begum* TH/8677/76 (1034) d. 26.9.77 (unreported), at 3–4.
[52] *Visa Officer Islamabad v. Akhtar Jan* TH/7606/76 (1051) d. 21.10.77 (unreported), at 4–5.
[53] *Supra*, p. 83.
[54] *Supra*, p. 84.

children in preference *to real ones*. The Tribunal's basis for decision in this case, however, suggests that the appellate authorities are often open to the same beliefs and feelings about intending immigrants as are subordinate immigration officials at posts overseas, who are not performing judicial or quasi-judicial functions, but are acting at the direction of the Home Office.

Thus in *Fatima Bibi v. Entry Clearance Officer Islamabad*[55] the adjudicator referring to the appellant's representative said:

"He questioned what possible motive could there be for attempting to bring a woman and two children into the U.K. if not his wife and his own children. It is a sad commentary to say that impersonation does *frequently* take place in immigration matters, the would-be immigrants being unable for one reason or another to secure entry in their true identities."[56]

The adjudicator's decision in this basis was left unaltered by the Tribunal. Again, in *Maqbool Jan v. Entry Clearance Officer Islamabad*[57] the adjudicator refused to consider counsel's argument that there could be no possible motive for the sponsor to bring in a middle-aged woman who was not his wife, on the grounds that this was a "rhetorical submission".[58] The basis of all these decisions is the suspicion that substitution of genuine wives and children occurs on a large scale. Yet the evidence shows that the appellate authorities have taken this idea to extraordinary and ludicrous lengths. In *Monwara Begum v. Entry Clearance Officer Dacca*,[59] for example, the sponsor took his son of a previous marriage to meet his second wife in Bangladesh whom he had married in 1964. When the question of identity was raised before him he argued that if the claimed wife and the appellant "are not one and the same person it would have been highly dangerous for the sponsor to have taken his son to Bangladesh to go to meet Monwara Begum and then for his son to meet a different lady on her arrival in the U.K." The Tribunal was not persuaded by this. In its view:

". . . the marriage between the sponsor and Monwara Begum took place in 1964. The sponsor's son did not go to Bangladesh and meet the lady introduced to him by the sponsor as Monwara Begum until 1974 by which time a 'switch' if it may be so termed, could have taken place."[60]

---

[55] TH/1504/73 (440) d. 6.3.75 (unreported).
[56] *ibid.*, at 3.
[57] TH/20755/77 (1640) d. 25.10.79 (unreported).
[58] *ibid.*, at 3.
[59] TH/1127/73 (585) d. 28.1.76 (unreported).
[60] *ibid.*, at 5.

Such decisions defy all logic and rationality. The notion of a "switch" is based on pure speculation, not evidence. Yet good evidence is casually rejected by the Tribunal. How can an applicant possibly prove his identity in such circumstances? It is as if the decision to refuse has already been made before the evidence is heard. The result of these decisions by the IAT is that by the end of the 1970s the mould had been set. On the whole, adjudicators were no longer to be found allowing appeals of claimed wives even if they were convinced about the improbability of substitution in these circumstances.[61] The doctrine of "identity" became firmly installed and little importance was ascribed to documentary and testimonial evidence in most appeal cases.[62] In 1978 a batch of cases succeeded on appeal but only because the Tribunal overlooked the usual obstacles that it had itself created over the years in the exercise of its function, and some cases were allowed even though the usual discrepancies remained unresolved.[63] In one case even the requirement of "identity" was waived. In *Zeenat Bibi v. Visa Officer Islamabad* the Tribunal said that the marriage in question is "a marriage of a young couple and no motive is apparent for the sponsor wishing to bring to the U.K. as his wife someone who is not his wife".[64] However, if it can be applied to young couples, why not also to a middle-aged wife? Surely, the argument is far more appropriate in respect of middle-aged wives.

(3) The "Sylhet Tax Pattern" and Other False Claims

In the "Sylhet Tax Pattern" cases there was also a shift in policy attitudes. Here again, the stringency was imposed by the Tribunal. This is remarkable because the Tribunal has often said that those immigrants who are caught up in this situation should "come clean" and make a tax confession. This would clear the slate and help the authorities to expedite the processing of their claim. They should not try to cover up or live up to the lie. However, many intending immigrants were afraid to do this because once it is known that they have indulged in a purported tax fraud, this is viewed odiously by the authorities and they are refused admission.[65] This has serious implications because it is questionable whether the Tribunal should

---

[61] Where, in a case like *Farzand Begum*, an appeal was allowed by an adjudicator, it was subsequently reversed by the Tribunal. See *supra*, pp. 144–146.

[62] *Supra*, pp. 131–133 and 141 for the examples of *Munir Begum* and *Pritam Kaur*.

[63] See n.26, *supra*.

[64] TH/7113/76 (unreported) at 3.

[65] See pp. 77–85 *supra*, but especially the case of *Choudhary* at p. 82.

be concerned to punish would-be immigrants by refusal rather than consider their eligibility on their merits. Under the law they are only mandated to consider whether the parties are related as claimed.

In one case an adjudicator found that although a fictitious name had been submitted to the authorities long ago, the sponsor did now have a real wife and three children. He allowed their appeal on this basis. The Tribunal did not dispute the authenticity of the claims but said that because a fictitious name had been lodged the claim should be dismissed:

> "It seems to us that this matter should be decided as a matter of practicality. When an ECO issues entry clearance he does so by stamping an entry in the passport. Had the ECO in this case stamped such an entry in the passport produced by the principal appellant he would have been granting entry clearance in the name of somebody other than the principal appellant. In our view he was right to refuse to do so and consequently the adjudicator was in error in allowing the appeal."[66]

The Tribunal recommended that all the appellants make "fresh application for entry clearance in their proper names and satisfy the ECO that they are the same persons who applied for entry clearance on 1 February 1978". It added, "We appreciate that this may involve a delay of some 18 months but this is the *penalty* which has to be paid for the fraudulent conduct of the sponsor *vis-à-vis* the Inland Revenue in this country".[67] It is clear from a case such as this that not only does the Tribunal engage in a punitive exercise here — even though the subject of tax fraud is a matter expressly between the tax authorities in this country and the sponsor, and the Inland Revenue has in many cases decided not to prosecute, because there was no defrauding being done in the event — the Tribunal is actively here adding to the delay of genuine cases, which is the first and most pre-eminent concern of all separated families. Even before the difficulties of discrepancies and documentary evidence begin to arise and the parties are required to begin to prepare for them — even before the parties get started — they are required to wait in the queue for lengthy periods of time. The refusal, and, as the Tribunal says, the consequences that it will inevitably entail, are, however, considered to be just retribution for the purported fraud and untruthful behaviour. Similarly, in *Khalida Begum v. Visa Officer Islamabad* the Tribunal simply said, "We do not feel disposed to grant this application since

---

[66] *Entry Clearance Officer Dacca v. Khanam* TH/60512/80 (2381) d. 15.2.82 (unreported).
[67] *ibid.*, at 2–3.

the sponsor admits to having told serious lies about his family",[68] and overlooked the accompanying evidence in support of the application, and the same approach was taken in *Fatima Bibi*,[69] in *Banti*,[70] and in *Sarwar Bi*.[71]

Conclusions

This chapter shows that the immigration cases discussed here cannot be understood on the basis of rationally assessed, objective criteria. The keys to understanding these cases are subjective standards and value judgments made by individual Tribunals in individual cases. Even in 1978, after the imposition of stringent standards of proof by the Tribunal following the period after 1973, it was possible to witness a batch of cases that were all allowed on appeal by the Tribunal in favour of the intending immigrant. Attempts at objective rationalisation, therefore, are subject to considerable bedevilment. Subjective rationalisation within the context of the immigration system is much easier and practicable, but it presents theoretical problems of principle.

If Tribunals faced with difficult questions of proof in a specialised area for which they alone have been specially constituted to deal with, were to ask what in the circumstances would be "fair" or "reasonable" or "legally right" for them to hold on a balance of probabilities, many of these problems which at first sight appear elusive could be handled in an expert rather than amateurish way. Many of the cases in this chapter could have been taken on judicial review before the High Court. That would have led to further delay and expense for the applicant. However, the Court is bound to have advocated the observance of objective standards of decision making.

Instead, what we see is that the net substantive content of administrative justice has changed for aspiring entrants in the last 20 years, although in the particular cases under discussion, the substantive law which established the rights and duties between the State and individual, have not. The purpose of adjudication is to give "the affected person a peculiar kind of participation in the decision, that of

[68] TH/13310/71 (1529) (unreported), at 2.
[69] *Fatima Bibi v. Visa Officer Islamabad* TH/1504/73 (440) d. 6.3.75 (unreported), at 3.
[70] *Banti v. Visa Officer Islamabad* TH/3216/74 (668) d. 11.3.76 (unreported), at 2.
[71] *Sarwar Bi v. Visa Officer Islamabad* TH/4896/79 (1361) d. 25.10.78 (unreported), at 3.

presenting proofs and reasoned arguments for a decision in his favour", says one American writer.[72] To this end, important developments have taken place in administrative procedure recently which have affected the adjudication of disputes between parties. As another writer explained, the most important of these has been:

> ". . . the recognition that an administrative decision is not a narrow contest between two parties but a determination of what ought to be done in the public interest in a particular case. This has led to the decision-maker taking a more active part than the courts in the gathering of material on which to reach decision and also to wider participation before the decision by persons who are not the parties to the dispute."

But the underlying impetus for all this has been to get better adjudication and the belief that "participation cannot take place meaningfully without information" and so is "interrelated with the demand for open government at all levels."[73] These developments then, make it inappropriate that, in the words of Professor Jowell, "an appeal to power, private interests, or political expediency" be made during the process. An adjudicator in the dispute will be "bound to evaluate the relative merits of claims in the light of accepted techniques for determining their importance and weight, by reference to authoritative guides, irrespective of his personal view of the result."[74] Yet the reality has been shown in this chapter to be different.

This chapter makes it plain, however, that despite the important legal developments in adjudication that have taken place these past years, the evaluation of the "relative merits of claims" of prospective entrants have not been undertaken "in the light of accepted techniques for determining their importance and weight". It would appear that the importance accorded to the relative merits has fluctuated over the years. This being so, it is submitted that the more pertinent considerations regarding adjudication in immigration law are essentially the political ones. Much can be learnt by looking at the values that are advanced in this area and the sort of accountability that is sought from the State. The concepts of justice and the degree of inefficiency that is tolerated from the State at the expense of fairness tell us much more about immigration control and immigration law than the legal rules and rules of administrative procedure.

---

[72] Fuller, "The Forms and Limits of Adjudication" (1978) 92 Harvard L.R. 353.
[73] G. Ganz, *Administrative Procedures* (London, 1974), pp. 1–2.
[74] J. Jowell, "The Legal Control of Administrative Discretion" [1993] *Public Law* 178.

We are able to learn what the practical limitations are of statutory rights in such a context. For a fuller exposition of these ideas we must turn to the final chapter.

Chapter Six

Conclusions

"We know that 1 in 5.4 cases — around 1400 cases last year — succeeded on appeal . . . no-one can be tolerably certain that future statistics will more likely show that it has been got wrong in one out of two cases, or one out of three, because . . . without the opportunity to have a decision scrutinised, arbitrariness tends to become part of the decision process."

Lord Ackner (*Hansard*, H.L., February 16, 1993)

For too long now strict immigration control has been presented by the State as a de-politicised and as a politically neutral exercise that politicians of all parties are agreed upon. This work demonstrates the contrary to be the case. The State has an interest in presenting the control of immigration in this way because this is an ideal way of deflecting political opposition from those adversely affected by it, thereby avoiding challenge to the behavioural and cultural assumptions upon which immigration control is founded. This work shows that such a technique is today insufficent in itself in neutering the opposition and widespread dissatisfaction with a process of law that does not meet with the proper expectations of the actual consumers of the law, through the mere adoption of formally enshrined procedures.

This has obvious consequences that are not always fully appreciated. Thus, the idea that there is a formal review of the decision-making process through a system of immigration appeals is clearly intended to emphasise the concept of procedural fairness by deflecting attention away from substantive injustice, but it is very questionable whether anyone, who is genuinely related as claimed, has ever gone away from an appeal hearing thinking that their case has been fairly considered, and with genuine empathy, just because of the

183

appeals system. Similarly, the idea that the conflict between the appellant and the State can be treated, through the appeals system, as being capable of resolution through completely formal and rational means, without the intrusion of value judgments, is equally flawed given the fact that the entire immigration process is replete with assumptions about immigrant culture and behaviour that have never been scientifically proven. Finally, the belief inherent in the adjudication process, that each appellants case can be treated as an isolated individual case, so that there is no challenge to the underlying ideology of immigration control by collective political protest, is clearly also mistaken given the grave disquiet demonstrated over individual cases in the press, media and the relevant immigrant communities. Each one of these three assumptions, moreover, fails to take into account the cultural alienation that is caused through the existing immigration process, even if there is no overt political opposition to immigration control, through the failure to adopt culturally sensitive techniques of dispute resolution.

The entry clearance system should be abolished for the wives and children of Commonwealth citizens and for others settled here. It was after all been dropped for immigrants from Eastern Europe for reasons that are entirely political.[1] It is hardly therefore a question of principle that has to be preserved at all costs. In fact, given its potential for injustice more countries should be taken out from the scheme, not more put in. Applicants, it is submitted, should be permitted to assist in the verification of claims by travelling to the United Kingdom and attending the appeal hearing to give evidence and all behavioural assumptions in the law should be carefully scrutinised by officials carrying out decisions. The adjudictive process should promote the values of participation, dignity and trust discussed at the outset of this work. The proposed reforms by the Home Affairs Committee Report in 1990, that we discussed at the

---

[1] In fact, the Home Affairs Committee on June 7, 1990 said that, "Like all politicians in the West, we welcome the monumental changes in Eastern Europe in the last year. We have no doubt that the process of democratisation will be aided by exchanges at all levels between our countries. For this reason we welcome Mr Langdon's confirmation that European Community Ministers are actively considering whether visas should continue to be required for Eastern European countries. The Government has already announced that nationals of the German Democratic Republic will not need visas from June 8, 1990. We wish to see more developments like this." This indicates the possibilities that are open provided that there is the political will to seize them. There is, in fact, nothing axiomatic about the imposition of visa controls as this passage only too well demonstrates. (See Home Affairs Committee Report on *Administrative Delays in the Immigration and Nationality Department* (June 7, 1990), H.C. 319., p. xii, at para. 31).

outset,[2] are not in themselves sufficient to dispel present concerns, as the detailed analyses in this study well show, and were in any event already disregarded in 1986 as unrealistic by Vaughan Bevan in his work, *The Development of British Immigration Law*, when he wrote that "the provision of extra ECOs and prospects of that are theoretical, whichever of the major parties is in power".[3] Subsequent events, as we saw, have more than vindicated this sceptical view. Bevan advocated a number of reforms in this area, including the application of time limits within which entry clearance applications must be considered by the Home Office subject to financial compensation for non-compliance, an entry certificate once granted to be conclusive proof of entitlement to enter, dependant applications to be initiated by United Kingdom sponsors with ready access to advisory services for guidance, and that an appeal should not be confined to facts which existed at the time of the original decision.[4]

Indeed, given that the immigration appellate authorities are required to take an inquisitorial rather than an adversarial approach to the hearing, it is odd that they should be confined to facts as found earlier[5] rather than later, *such* as the birth of another child to the alleged wife. In fact, if the quest be that of a search for truth or a search for eligibility rather than a search for untruths and ineligibility amongst applicants, the standard of proof that dependants have to satisfy could be lowered with a specific direction that untruths in themselves are of no consequence, *but* relevant only in the overall weight of the evidence. This would ensure that a genuine wife or a genuine[6] child would suffer no detriment if in order to secure entry they had to have recourse to fabricated documents, provided only that the genuineness of their case was apparent in other ways.[7] This would be a significant reform and far more realistic because it would not require the allocation of additional financial resources to an area that is of low priority in the Home Office.

Such a reform is already evident in refugee law where the concern of the international community has so focused as to ensure that the

---

[2] *Supra*, pp. 48–51.

[3] V. Bevan, *op. cit.*, p. 174.

[4] *ibid.*, p. 175.

[5] This was established in *R. v. IAT, ex p. Kotecha* [1983] 2 All E.R. 289; *R. v. IAT, ex p. Bastiampillai* [1983] 2 All E.R. 844; and *R. v. IAT, ex p. Weerasuriya* [1983] 1 All E.R. 195.

[6] After all, this is exactly what many adjudicators, and even the Tribunal, were doing in the earlier cases when they were assessing the evidence in the round and concluding that the case was genuine despite its many shortcomings.

[7] For example, the Home Affairs Committee in 1980–1981 specifically recommended that adjudicators be told that the existence of discrepancies is not *per se* determinative of the issues one way or the other: see *infra*, at n.42.

rules and practices are facilitative and enabling rather than restrictive and disabling. If one is as serious about the re-uunification of separated families, as these rules suggest one is about protecting the rights of refugees, then a similar approach is needed to the entry of dependent relatives in our domestic law. The Geneva Convention of 1951 Relating to the Status of Refugees, as amended by the Protocol to the Convention 1967, is the basic law on the subject of refugees. Originally, the Convention was concerned to protect peoples who were displaced following the Second World War. The Protocol now ensures that no person may be expelled or returned to the frontier of a territory or territories where his or her life or freedom may be threatened because of the race, religion, nationality, membership of a particular social group, or political opinion[8] of such a person. The threat to such a person must be "owing to a well founded fear of being persecuted" for these reasons. But what does an applicant have to prove to demonstrate "a well founded fear"?

In *R. v. Secretary of State for the Home Department, ex p. Sivakumaran*[9] the House of Lords held that the Secretary of State should look at the objective facts and consider whether there was a real likelihood of persecution for a Convention reason, but it soon transpired that the way that this was to be interpreted and applied in practice showed that in reality the applicant would succeed if this was shown on less than a balance of probabilities, because Lord Keith said that, "if the examination shows that persecution *might* indeed take place then the fear is well founded" (author's emphasis). In fact, their Lordships approved the words of Lord Diplock in *Fernandez v. Government of Singapore*[10] when he said that "a reasonable chance" would suffice.[11] Indeed, it has even been held that a person who is not involved in any act of political opposition against a government may nevertheless be prosecuted by it for perceived opinions or for membership of a social group,[12] although Home Office Presenting Officers continue to present cases on the basis that some political involvement is necessary. Nevertheless, the law in this area is a good example of how legal rights can be expounded in an expansive and liberal way in appropriate types of cases.

Yet it is not appreciated how easily such a humane approach can also — and indeed should — be applied to the rights of dependent

---

[8] See Article 1 as amended by the Protocol.
[9] [1988] A.C. 958.
[10] [1971] 2 All E.R. 691.
[11] See Lord Keith in *Ex p. Sivakumaran, supra* n.9, at 994.
[12] See *Duodu* (5803) (unreported). Also see *Otchere* [1988] Imm. A.R. 21.

relatives wishing to join someone in this country. The Wilson Committee was quite clear that compulsory entry certificates for Commonwealth citizens were to be avoided. The initial justification for their introduction on a voluntary basis was "for the convenience of Commonwealth citizens".[13] This convenience would clearly be offset if they were made mandatory because then they would simply be a visa requirement "under another name."[14] As this study shows those fears have been amply borne out by subsequent events where mandatory entry certification has turned out to be nothing more than the indefensible imposition of a quota on the entry of New Commonwealth immigrants and where official arguments in support of such mechanisms as the "discrepancy system", the "Sylhet Tax Pattern", the delays, the rejection of genuine documents, and the so-called "medical evidence" have simply been a ruse that has allowed such a quota to be put into effect.[15] The authorities applied a higher standard of proof in practice than even the one legally sanctioned. They required conclusive and incontrovertible proof that the sponsor prove that the woman who was applying was his wife, and the child his child. Yet the figures disclosed by the FCO, whilst showing that a potential existed for fraud because of the Sylhet Tax Pattern, did not prove that any attempt was made to bring in a bogus wife.[16] In fact, even when such proof existed an application would not necessarily be allowed.

The clearest proof in the existence of a quota lies in the way that the figures fluctuated over the years. Under Mr Alex Lyon, the Labour Minister of State for Immigration, there was a remarkable increase of over 90 per cent in the rate of processing applications between February 1974 and early 1976, and in Dacca and Islamabad the number of applications granted rose five-fold.[17] This happened

[13] The Home Secretary, Mr James Callaghan, *Hansard*, H.C. (May 1, 1969) at cols. 1631, 1633.

[14] Wilson Committee, *op. cit.*, p. 22, para. 70.

[15] The earliest sign of the possible introductions of an informed quota came from Richard Crossman when the issue of mandatory entry certification was being debated (see *supra*, at 5). Once it was introduced queues were then allowed to develop which became the essence of the operation of informal quotas (see *supra*, at 6). The Government itself admitted then that it is an "inevitable inconvenience" contrary to all the public announcements at time of the introduction of the scheme when it was being hailed as being in the interest of the genuine immigrant (see *supra*, at 13). Finally, the Home Affairs Committee in 1989–1990 on *Administrative Delays in the Immigration and Nationality Department* itself said that a "poor service gives rise to understandable suspicion that bureaucratic delay is an instrument of control" (*op. cit.*, p. xxi, para 62).

[16] *Supra*, p. 84.

[17] See *First Report from the Select Committee on Race Relations and Immigration*, Annexes and Minutes of Proceedings (1977–1978) H.C. 303–I, pp. 107–110.

because Mr Lyon gave instructions while in the Indian sub-continent to immigration officers that the proper test for all dependants to satisfy was proof on a balance of probabilities. Unbeknown to him, the Divisional Court of the Queen's Bench had already decided in a case in 1972 that the standard of proof contemplated by the immigration rules was the civil standard, on a balance of probabilities, and not proof beyond reasonable doubt. In 1975 and the first half of 1976 the ratio of applications refused to applications granted fell at Dacca from 1:16 to 1:6, and at Islamabad from 1:23 to 1:5.

However, following his own visit to the Indian sub-continent in November/December 1975, Mr Enoch Powell published the Hawley Report which accused Mr Lyon of lowering standards, because "it was previous practice to insist on proof on bona fides beyond reasonable doubt", but that now "too many doubtful cases have been allowed through following the new measures". Mr Lyon was then removed from office in June 1976 because of the disquiet caused by his measures, even though they were wholly in conformity with the Divisional Court's own ruling of the law which he did not know about. The refusal rate did not just return to one where the erroneous test of "beyond all reasonable doubt" was being applied but became even higher than it was in 1974, before Mr Lyon arrived at the Home Office (in the second half of 1976 this was nearly 1:1 in Dacca and 1:2 in Islamabad).[18] The Hawley Report gave some indication of how this completely unwarranted surge in the refusal rate would have occurred when it adverted to the anxiety of officials at posts abroad, that if they "considered that there was an end in sight, there would be less uneasiness felt about pushing through dependants' cases with increased despatch". It is clear, therefore, from this that the whole exercise was far removed from any orderly application of the law. The considerations were wholly political and extra-legal and the process of decision making unprincipled and arbitrary. Mr Lyon had no doubt that this was now the case when after leaving office he remarked that it was "absurd that in Dacca in the last quarter of 1976 only 481 applications were granted out of 2,168 processed", as it was impossible to maintain that 75 per cent of the cases were bogus.[19] It was to prevent precisely these difficulties that he had taken the trouble to tell officials in the sub-continent that "the question of numbers being admitted to the United Kingdom is

---

[18] *ibid.* See also Memorandum by JCWI at p. 193, paras 24–26. The Divisional Court's ruling was in *R. v Secretary of State for the Home Department, ex p. Hussein* [1975] Imm. A.R. 69.
[19] *ibid.*, at 114–115.

one for the government, and you need not concern yourself with it".[20] Failure to heed this advice was bound to lead to arbitrary decision making and it was small wonder that it had happened if there was scant regard for legalese because of an inappropriate preoccupation with the imposition of an informal quota. The existence of an informal quota was hinted at also by the Home Affairs Committee in 1982 when it said:

"Further evidence suggesting that the system might be inaccurate are the variations in refusal rates . . . In Dacca, the refusal rate for wives in 1981 was 21 per cent, similar to Pakistan, but in 1977 that rate was 47 per cent. The refusal rate for children in Dacca was 65 per cent in 1977, and in 1981 was 33 per cent. Overall, the rate there has fallen from 60 per cent in 1977 to 30 per cent in 1981."[21]

In four years the rates of refusal had been halved. Once again it is hardly credible that this may be justified on objective criteria alone. We may thus conclude that for these reasons procedural reforms alone, like those advocated by Wilson, can never hope to preserve let alone enhance the substantive rights of applicants. Essentially, this is why Wilson failed.

Yet no single person who was in a position of high responsibility and authority has raised these issues in the way that Mr Alex Lyon did from the early 1970s through to the mid-1980s. In 1977 he told the Home Affairs Committee:

"I think there is a *real case for increasing the flow*. If wives and children are to come to this country, and they *have the statutory right to come*, it is better that they come when the children are young so that they go through the whole school curriculum than they should come when they are in their secondary school age, *having waited another seven years*. If I am right in saying that there is 100,000 or less to come, at the rate which they were coming before I went to the sub-continent it would take something like ten years to clear them. I have managed, partly by increasing the Entry

---

[20] *Op. cit.* In fact, *The Guardian* reported on April 2, 1984 that, "It has been known for senior Home Office officials to remark openly to colleagues that it was a good thing that the Conservatives, with their tougher line on immigration, were now in power and that Mr Alex Lyon — a Liberal Minister once in charge of immigration — was sacked.
[21] See *Fifth Report, op. cit.*, Vol. I, p. xvii, para. 44. Confirmation of the existence of a quota has since come from a confidential Home Office briefing to Ministers which states that if the Government acknowledged publicly "a policy of deliberate delay without legislation giving powers to impose quotas" it would run the risk of legal action in British Courts and under the European Convention on Human Rights. See *The Guardian*, March 21, 1985.

Clearance Officer's but partly by *applying different standards to the rate of interviewing*, to increase the rate by something like 50 per cent so that the time limit now is down to about seven years. I think it could be reduced still further . . . I think in many ways of that sort *you could end the commitment much more quickly*. If you could tell the people of Britain, if they are concerned about immigration, and everybody tells me that they are. This is going to end. We are going to honour our commitments but it is going to end within three or four years,m and that is demonstrably true from the figures', I think they may be prepared to accept an increase in the flow in the interim."[22] (Author's emphasis.)

Less than five years afterwards the Home Affairs Committee itself recognised in its 1981–1982 Report the fact of declining immigration numbers, and as we noted at the outset, this particular commitment of wives and children had itself by the 1990s come to an end as prophesied by Mr Lyon. But the Home Affairs Committee itself had in previous years stopped short of outright condemnation of unfair immigration practices as it did in its 1990 Report. In fact, it had just as much been pre-eminently concerned with numbers.

Thus its most radical proposals came in its 1977–1978 Report when it recommended a system of "internal controls" when it sat to examine "the assumptions made by the Government about potential immigration."[23] This is important because even in 1981–1982 when it undertook the most thorough appraisal of the entry clearance system, which forms the subject-matter of this study, it continued to be concerned about "new commitments" from second-generation immigrants. Indeed, its purposes in setting up an inquiry at this time were not the delays which wives and children of immigrants settled here have endured, since "if these were the only or major cause of concern over immigration from the sub-continent, *there would have been little justification* for our having undertaken a major inquiry" (author's emphasis). The Committee declared that the inquiry was instituted because "concern persists for other reasons, one of which is that although immigration is declining *new commitments are emerging through second generation immigrants marrying the sub-continent*"[24] (author's emphasis). This indicates that the Committee, whilst in the event expressing criticism of entry clearance procedures, was not ultimately concerned so much with the hardships suffered by intending immigrants but with the numbers of new arrivals.

---

[22] See *First Report, op. cit.*, p. 111.
[23] *ibid.*, p. 187.
[24] *Fifth Report, op. cit.*, Vol. I, at p. v, para. 2.

It is important to recognise the distinction here because the difference in emphasis and stress in what one is setting out to do, means a difference in *intent*, and a difference in the *effect* of what one is doing. This is then all too determinative of the consequences. It makes inevitable the preconceived notions that administrators have in immigration control and it explains why the adherence to established legal norms becomes so difficult. Mr Lyon was quick to spot this distinction, as is seen from his exchange with the then Minister of State for Immigration, Mr Timothy Raison: Mr Lyon asked: "do you regard it as some kind of problem that people are born here or living here go abroad and marry," especially as such a practice had been going on for over a hundred years between the English aristocracy and the Americans? He asked: "why is a continuing marriage commitment necessarily a difficulty or a problem because it has been going on for generations?" The crucial thing was whether the wave of migration that started in the mid 1950s from the New Commonwealth had ended or not. It was a mistake to think that it had, not simply because new marriages were taking place since these had been going on for many generations anyway. In fact, the incidence of marriages taking place in the sub-continent would be relatively large only initially, but this would subside in time after people had been here a few years.[25] Recently, the Divisional Court exposed such falsehoods yet again in *Ex p. Iqbal* when it quashed the decision of the Tribunal refusing leave to appeal to a Pakistani man in an arranged marriage because the Tribunal felt that the primary purpose of his marrying here was not for love but for entry into the United Kingdom. The Divisional Court disagreed, holding:

> "To draw an analogy with English society at the turn of the century, the fact that an American heiress was so keen to be a duchess that she was prepared to marry an Englishman whom she did not love would not lead one to suppose that the primary purpose of the marriage was for her to obtain admission to the U.K. She may have been after his title and be after her money."[26]

Given the existence of such misconceptions the Home Affairs Sub-Committee on Race Relations and Immigration consistently failed up until the 1990s to recognise that the basic attitude of immigration officials to their work is wrong. The complaints against the "discrepancy system", the "Sylhet Tax Pattern", documentary evidence

---

[25] *ibid.*, Vol. II, p. 140; see Qs 466, 469 and 490.
[26] Mr Justice Schiemann in *R. v. IAT, ex p. Iram Iqbal* [1993] Imm. A.R. 270 at 276.

and medical examinations highlight the primary importance of
official attitudes which prevent decisions on entry clearance applications being fair and proper. Yet, the Committee did earnestly
recommend the *Split Families* research project to ECOs, but did so
most notably, "not because we feel their attitude is wrong but to
improve further their ability to appreciate the difficulties of applicants". The Committee found "a strong commitment by ECOs and
their seniors to recognising the difficulties facing applicants in
proving their relationships and in some circumstances giving them
the benefit of any doubt". In its view they "do a first class job in
extremely difficult circumstances".[27] It may well be that the Committee did genuinely find this after watching ECOs work and after
holding lengthy discussions with them. But our investigations point
generally to different conclusions. Both the unpublished CRE Report
and the UKIAS *Split Families* Report written after several months of
field investigations in Bangladesh, came to this conclusion. In fact,
several years ago Mr Lyon put the same view to the Committee:

> "When you talk about an impartial official doing his work, there is nobody,
> apart from, possibly Dr Shirley Summerskill or Mr David Lane, who has
> had, just by the accident of nature, as great an opportunity of seeing what
> goes on in immigration as I had. I could see it from both sides. I could see
> it not only from the official side, which I used to have to do in reviewing
> something like 1500 cases a year, but also from the view of the commu-
> nities by going around and talking to individuals who had been refused, or
> their wives had been refused, and getting their side of the picture too."[28]

It was not long before this view was vindicated in the higher courts,
and that of the Home Affairs Committee disproven, because in March
1984 in a case heard by judicial review both Donaldson M.R. and Fox
L.J. spoke with regret about the attitude of officials.[29] In order to
establish whether an applicant had entered fraudulently and therefore
as an illegal immigrant, Donaldson M.R. explained how:

> ". . . the British High Commission, on instructions from the Home
> Office, mounted what can only be described as an 'expedition' to the
> applicant's home village of Holimbur. There were no less than four entry
> clearance officers involved, travelling in two Land Rovers. For the last
> three miles they had to walk and cross two rivers, one by boat and the
> other by way of what is described as a rather precarious bamboo bridge."[30]

[27] *Fifth Report, op. cit.*, Vol. I, pp. xviii–xix, para. 48.
[28] *First Report, op. cit.*, p. 111.
[29] *Ali v. Secretary of State for the Home Department* [1984] 1 All E.R. 1009.
[30] *ibid.*, at 1014.

In fact, the photograph of the applicant which they took with them was taken eight years before when he was 16. In the village they went to the family compound and there interviewed people. Donaldson M.R. explained that:

> "So far as identification was concerned, one villager in this compound identified the applicant as Fozlu, but the rest said that he was Momin. The report relies heavily on this identification as Fozlu and dismisses the contrary identifications with the words, 'The rest of the family all agreed with the sponsors story as naturally they would'."

There was little doubt from this that "the entry clearance officers did not go to the village with an open mind. They clearly believed their informants and were going there in order to establish that the applicant was Fozlu and not Momin.[31] They were not inquiring, so much as seeking confirmation for a preconceived view."[32] Fox L.J. was left with no doubt that "they were not engaged on an independent judicial inquiry."[33] With this, their Lordships had little difficulty in highlighting all the problematic areas that we have discussed in relation to entry clearance procedures, such as how discrepancies can be misleading,[34] the role of inter-family jealousies,[35] the difficulties in adducing evidence in such societies,[36] the problems associated with fraud and the "Sylhet Tax Pattern"[37] and the unfortunate practice of severe cross-examination before adjudicators and the Tribunal.[38]

The clear failure of the Home Affairs Committee in explicitly recognising these problems (in the same way as the courts) and expressing its disapproval, has meant that the reforms advocated by the Committee have made little impact upon those to whom they were directed. This is especially so given that the Committee's pre-eminent concern was with "new commitments". It is unsurprising therefore that in 1990 the Committee was having to make more or less the same recommendations that had been made a decade earlier with practically no effect. This suggests that if little had changed then little would change in the future, unless there was a fundamental shift in attitude to the whole business of immigration control. In 1980–1981 the Committee did say that once the present queues had

---

[31] *ibid.*, at 1014.
[32] *ibid.*, at 1015.
[33] *ibid.*, at 1016.
[34] *ibid.*, at 1012n and p, and at 1015c.
[35] *ibid.*, at 1011h.
[36] *ibid.*, at 1013c and p, and at 1015c.
[37] *ibid.*, at 1012h.
[38] *ibid.*, at 1017c.

been cleared up "the Government should not permit anything approaching similar delays to recur",[39] and yet found itself making the same recommendation in 1990–1938.[40] It also recommended then that "the Home Office should speed up the interview of sponsors in this country to reduce the delay between the deferral of the case to the Home Office and the interview of the sponsor, subject to the sponsor replying promptly, to a maximum of three months."[41]

Yet the fact that some of its recommendations did not meet with the required changes should not detract from their importance, for in reality the Committee recognised the essence of the criticisms made in this work all too clearly: this is the irony of the Report. Thus the Committee expressly recognised that there was a problem with regard to discrepancies which led to the refusal of genuine applicants. It said: "We recommend that adjudicators should be explicitly instructed to come to their conclusions on the basis of the balance of probabilities, even if they consider a *discrepancy* has not been resolved.[42] (Author's emphasis.) Similarly, on fraud it was also concerned that genuine applicants should not be refused. In the "Sylhet Tax Pattern" cases often a wife would not admit that she was trying to cover up for family members that had been falsely declared by the sponsor. She would not tell the truth unless she had "direct instructions from the husband" telling her to do so. In such circumstances the Committee emphasised that ECOs should not refuse an entire family because they are suspicious of one member of it: a split decision refusing just one member may be the right one, particularly where the ECO is satisfied that the applicant may be telling lies but if the truth were told she should be entitled to come". (Author's emphasis.)[43]

These then were the three major areas of concern that we discussed. However, the Committee also made other recommendations. In particular, it suggested that more resources be made available by the government in at least three areas: better advisory services for applicants; a more thorough investigative role by officials abroad; and better representation for applicants at the appeals level. All three areas would require more money. As for the first area, it said that it was "impressed by the UKIAS role" and so recommended that the FCO "provide funds for a second representative in Sylhet

---

[39] *Fifth Report*, op. cit., Vol. I, p. xvi, para. 4.
[40] See the Committee's Recommendations in *Administrative Delays in the Immigration and Nationality Department*, op. cit., p. xxii, paras 9, 10, 11, 12, 14, 15, 19 and 21.
[41] *Fifth Report*, op. cit., Vol. I, p. xxii, para. 60.
[42] *ibid.*, p. xxv, para. 66.
[43] *ibid.*, p. xx, para. 53.

with proper clerical support for the sole purpose of advising applicants on filling in forms and on the acceptability of any documentation they have."[44]

For a more thorough investigative role by officials, it recommended that more village visits be undertaken because they "add greatly the accuracy of the entry clearance procedure". It said: "We recommend that ECOs undertaking village visits should be fully aware *of the many important observations made by UKIAS in their research project* and that in all three countries more village visits should be undertaken". (author's emphasis.)[45]

And on more effective representation in appeals, the Committee recommended "that the Home Office take careful *account of UKIAS's difficulties* and consider whether extra resources should be made available to them in the short-term". (author's emphasis.)[46]

However, by the end of the decade not only were village visits rare through increased financial stringency, but by the beginning of the next decade UKIAS had been reduced to a crippling state by the government. This was a sad end for a body that had been set up during Harold Wilson's second administration in 1970 and had subsequently operated quite effectively from its 10 offices in London, Glasgow, Manchester, Birmingham, Leeds and Cardiff, providing advice and legal representation for about 2000 families a month on an annual government grant of 1.5 million. It happened because the Government decided in July 1991 to force the service to expand and become the monopoly supplier of legal assistance for new immigrants. At the same time, it decided to withdraw the "green form" legal aid system of public funding from all independent solicitors. UKIAS was therefore forced to accept a monopoly of immigration services which it refused to do, whereupon the Home Office in a letter of October 7, 1991 told the service that "this must throw a question mark over the funding you already receive". In January 1992, the Home Office stripped the service of its asylum work[47] after it failed to agree a new constitution and hived off that work to another body, the Refugee Asylum Unit. This was obviously a long cry away from the esteem with which the Home Affairs Committee viewed UKIAS in 1981–1982 and the recommendations it had made to safeguard its role at the time.

---

[44] *ibid.*, p. xxi, para. 57.
[45] *ibid.*, p. xxii, para. 59.
[46] *ibid.*, p. xxiii, para. 62. It ended by suggesting that "our conclusions on the entry clearance system — will clearly require extra resources" (p. xiii, para. 133) which as we have seen is exactly what the Committee in 1989–1990 called for (at p. xviii, para. 50, and p. xxii).
[47] See *The Guardian*, May 13, 1992.

In this general milieu, the role of the adjudicating authorities also
naturally suffers. Immigration law in the tribunals is seen not as
"law" but "lore" because it has been possible at the end of the day to
be able to justify almost any decision, no matter how arbitrary or
capricious. This is in spite of the fact that many of the great advances
made in English administrative law in the 1980s were made on the
backs of immigration cases as they were argued on judicial review in
the higher courts.[48] Yet there is no doubt that in some areas,
particularly the marriage and family cases, an immigration tribunal
can often if it wishes come to any decision that it likes. This problem
is not necessarily unique to the immigration tribunals, as the early
history of adjudication of disputes through Tribunals well demonstrates, and which comprised the subject-matter of Lord Scarman's
Hamlyn Lectures in 1974. In his *English Law — A New Dimension*,[49]
Lord Scarman warned of the "great modern challenges to the law's
flexibility in the pursuit of survival" that arose from the rapid
increase since the Second World War in state intervention and
regulation of areas that were hitherto considered to be outside its
scope. His Lordship inquired whether such activities as industrial
relations, the social security system and the control of land use "are
to be regulated in accordance with a law interpreted within a unified
legal system", or extra-legally in accordance with some "specialised
system of control isolated from the general legal system" heralding a
"move away from a general legal system to specialised and detached
systems."[50] In consequence, "should this happen there would be little
value in discussing the technical questions of administrative law:
society would quickly move away from the constitutional position of
legal control to one of administrative control."[51] The pivot of such a
system then would not be the rule of law, but "administrative and
political controls themselves beyond the reach of the law".[52]

Others around that time held a similar view. Lord Gardiner
described the Supplementary Benefit Appeal Tribunals as the lowest
form of tribunal life.[53] Professor Katherine Bell was inclined to be no

[48] For example, see *Khawaja v. Secretary of State for the Home Department* [1984] A.C. 74;
R. v. Secretary of State for the Home Department, ex p. Asif Mahmood Khan [1984] 1 W.L.R.
1337; *Att.-Gen. of Hong Kong v. Ng Yuen Shiu* [1983] 2 A.C. 629; *R. v. IAT, ex p. Jonah*
[1985] Imm. A.R. 7; *R. v. IAT, ex p. Zaman* [1982] Imm. A.R. 61; *R. v. Secretary of State
for the Home Department, ex p. Swati* [1986] 1 All E.R. 717; *R. v. IAT, ex p. Bastiampillai*
[1983] 2 All E.R. 844.
[49] Leslie Scarman, *English Law — A New Dimension* (Hamlyn Lectures, London, 1974)
p. 35.
[50] *ibid.*, pp. 61–62.
[51] *ibid.*, p. 72.
[52] *ibid.*, p. 73.
[53] *H.C. Official Report* (5th series) Vol. 353 (July 9, 1974) Col. 511.

more charitable when she described them as "not yet full, independent, adjudicatory bodies following a clear judicial process — which
in the post-Franks era has come to be accepted and expected as the
essential hallmark of a tribunal."[54] Many English welfare lawyers
looking at these Tribunals felt that they had escaped the post war
trend towards formalisation and that they should now be judi-
cialised.[55] Yet only a few years later a direct right of appeal was
provided from the Supplementary Benefits Appeal Tribunal to the
High Court on a point of law.[56] This did not, however, prevent
Professor H.W.R. Wade from remarking that even today, "Tribunals
are so diverse in their nature that, although considerable progress has
been made towards procedural uniformity, there is nothing as yet
resembling a common code of procedure and there are exceptions to
almost every rule".[57] For example, "the only tribunals with power to
affect personal liberty, are immigration tribunals and mental health
review tribunals"[58] yet in the case of the former there is no right of
appeal to a court of law at all.

It is in this respect that it can be asserted that the position of the
immigration tribunals is peculiarly unique in the current context of
administrative adjudications, because even allowing for the oddity of
what Lord Hailsham described as, "the proliferation since the war of
tribunals of all sorts outside the ordinary structure of the courts"
which are "seldom bound by strict rules of evidence or procedure",[59]
the extensive degree of importance ascribed to departmental interest
remains a most distinguishing feature of this area. This is illustrated
by the dissenting opinion of Professor Jackson in the leading
marriage case of *Vinod Bhatia v. Entry Clearance Officer New Delhi*,[60]
where he admonished the decision of the majority members with the
words that, "It is not for the Tribunal to act as a surrogate for the
Secretary of State" because this was an area where the "individual
rights of British citizens are at stake". The "law must be construed
bearing in mind the balance to be struck between the powers of the

---

[54] See *Research Study on SBATs*: Review of Main Findings, Conclusions,' Recommendations (1975, HMSO), p. 26.
[55] See, for example, Harlow and Rawlings, *Law and Administration* (London, 1984),
Chap. 19.
[56] By an order under section 15(3) of the Tribunals and Inquiries Act 1971: see
Supplementary Benefits Appeal Tribunals: A Guide to Procedure (HMSO, 1977), Chap. 7.
[57] H.W.R. Wade, *Administrative Law* (Oxford, 5th ed., 1982), p. 804.
[58] *ibid.*, p. 809.
[59] Lord Hailsham, *Hamlyn Revisited: The British Legal System Today* (Hamlyn Lectures,
London, 1983), p. 42.
[60] *Vinod Bhatia v. Entry Clearance Officer New Delhi* TH/11935/83 (3456) d. 31.8.84
(unreported).

Secretary of State and the responsibility to British citizens *and to potential immigrants*". (Author's emphasis.)[61]

Other observers of the immigration scene in the 1980s took a kindred view. Harlow and Rawlings maintained that, "The appellate authorities, especially the precedent, forming IAT, have not merely umpired according to pre-existing rules but have *actively developed Home Office policies* to limit immigration. In short, they have not played a 'neutral' role."[62] Professor J.M. Evans expressed the view, as someone now based in Canada, that:

> "A person whose knowledge of English public law was limited to immigration cases would hardly guess that in the last 20 years or so *the courts* have transformed the principles of administrative law and demonstrated a remarkable readiness to *defend individual rights from governmental encroachment* by subjecting the literal interpretation of statutes to common law doctrines of fairness, reasonableness and legality, and to other presumptions of statutory construction which are derived from *a view that favour a limited role for government*." (Author's emphasis.)[63]

It is for this reason that Ian Macdonald had no doubt, as a foremost practitioner and author in this field, that:

> "It would certainly be open to an *activist appellate authority*, which was responsive to the interest and needs of the immigrant community, *to change the whole tenor and trend of immigration law* and practice, provided it also had the support of the High Court judiciary. In the early days some adjudicators were clearly seen to be trying to temper the rougher edges of immigration controls as they applied in individual cases, *but their efforts were largely frustrated*." (Author's emphasis.)[64]

What this means is that the ball is firmly in the court of the immigration appellate authorities: for most immigration cases they must take the initiative; they must play a more activist role; they must promulgate fairer immigration practices. The question of High Court support only arises once they have demonstrated an ability to distance themselves from pervasive departmental influences. Only then may they meaningfully turn to the higher courts for support. However, the evidence is that throughout the 1980s it is the higher courts who have been pointing the appellate authorities in the right

---

[61] *ibid.*, at 1–2 and 9.
[62] Harlow and Rawlings, *op. cit.*, p. 519. Also see Grant and Martin, *op. cit.*, at p. 355.
[63] J.M. Evans, *op. cit.*, p. 418.
[64] Ian Macdonald, *Immigration Law and Practice* (London, 1st ed., 1983), p. 4.

direction. This direction has not consistently been followed because the appellate authorities have sometimes been under pressure to give vent to departmental interest. In doing so they have frustrated the proper exercise of their functions. The evidence in this respect is manifestly clear. Many of the cases surveyed in this work point unmistakably to that conclusion, and it is a view also echoed by Professor J.M. Evans. Indeed, in the 1990s the higher courts have continued to expand the canvas of administrative law.[65] It is not, therefore, so much their support that is in question.[66]

Nevertheless, even if the higher courts were opposed to the appellate authorities assuming a more robust role, this is likely to be temporary. It is difficult to see how the Courts, even with initial scepticism, could resist an exercise of appellate discretion that was undertaken in a principled and coherent way. The appellate authorities are bound to meet with a measure of success in formulating fairer practices and they are bound to be able to check possible official abuses by a government department. There must first, however, be a fundamental shift towards a more equalitarian approach, by which it is meant that the immigration authorities must seek to ensure that the values of parity and equity are protected in a substantive sense in their quest to find facts accurately, and this can only be done if they are culturally aware. There must be a recognition of the social facts and of social data in the adjudicative process. This is not a novel idea. Law may be an instrument of social control or it may be an instrument of social justice. In some regulatory contexts, such as family law and welfare law, it is preeminently an instrument of social justice.[67] In immigration law it has been the former. It is not suggested that the law should give up its control function in immigration law, but a move to a more equalitarian basis would mean that it would also be concerned with doing justice. To do this, it must apprise itself of the circumstantial facts firmly and squarely.

The requirement of cultural sensitivity is only another way saying that facts must be socially grounded. The idea had been more eloquently expressed already in 1983 by Professor Bob Hepple in his inaugural lecture at the University of London.[68] He argued for a

---

[65] For example, see the case of *M. v Home Office and Kenneth Baker* [1992] 2 W.L.R. 73, or the tenor of the judicial approach in the decision of Mr Justice Sedley in *R. v. Secretary of State for the Home Department, ex p. Abdi, The Times,* March 10, 1994.
[66] See Richard Gordon Q.C., "The Awakened Conscience of the Nation", [1994] March/April, 8. The major exception to this is, of course, the case of *R. v. Secretary of State for the Home Department, ex p. Oladehinde* [1991] A.C. 254.
[67] See, for example, S. Juss in the (1988) 47 *Cambridge Law Journal* 516.
[68] Professor Hepple, "Judging Equal Rights" (1983) 36 *Current Legal Problems* 71–86.

system of public law adjudication. The traditional British system of adjudication of disputes was between private individuals. Here the emphasis was on formal legal rules. However, in public law litigation the lawyer had to go beyond the rules and look at the social facts. British lawyers had already started to look at the United States for guidance in this respect where the system was more fully developed. They did so in relation to the meaning of "discrimination" in the sex and race discrimination legislation which, as Lustgarten explains, was "one of the very few occasions in parliamentary history when the meaning of a statute, has been explained by reference to the case law of another nation".[69] According to Professor Hepple, American judges have a tendency "to turn social problems into judicial ones of due process, equal protection and civil rights."[70] In the public law context this results in their taking:

". . . judicial notice of [social] facts, without formal evidence — what Jerome Frank disparagingly called 'cocktail hour knowledge'. There has been increasing use of statisticians, particularly in the development of discrimination law. By contrast, the Employment Appeal Tribunal has firmly set itself against the use of elaborate statistical evidence."[71]

The difficulty then is that in this country "The Courts and Tribunals were expected to achieve their regulatory tasks by adopting methods of fact finding especially of *social facts*, and by methods of evaluation which are *outside the usual compass* of civil adjudication in Britain" (author's emphasis). There is therefore a "mismatch between the structure of the judicial process and the purposive social engineering which the Courts and Tribunal are occasionally asked to perform". This has to change, according to Professor Hepple, and he concludes that:

"Whether lawyers, including judges, like it or not, they are going to have to equip themselves, to deal with the social facts which lie behind

---

[69] L. Lustgarten, "Legal Control of Racial Discrimination" (London, 1978), p. 5. He is referring to the parliamentary debates at H.C. Official Report (5th series) Standing Committee B, Vol. 48 (April 22, 1975), Col. 48.
[70] Hepple, *op. cit.*, p. 84. Also see J. Frank, "The Lawyer's Role in Modern Society" (1955) 4 *Journal of Public Law* 1, 16.
[71] Hepple, *op. cit.* Professor Hepple further pointed out that even in the historic case of *Brown v. Board of Education*, 347 U.S. 483; 74 S.Ct. 686 (1956) where the "separate but equal" doctrine of *Plessy v. Ferguson* was struck down, this was not done on the basis of a common sense or intuitive belief about the effects or racial segregation, but in the Court's findings of fact of seven social science studies that to separate children "from others of similar age and qualification solely because of their race generates a feeling of inferiority as to their status in the community . . .".

legislative policies of this kind. In the modern areas of legal regulation, such as consumer protection, environmental control, business and labour relations . . . the lawyer cannot limit himself to the logical organisation of rules and principles. He has to be able to handle empirical social data and to identify efficient social policies. His primary materials are no longer law reports, *but reports of social investigations*, and studies of the social and economic effect of legislation."[72] (Author's emphasis.)

The reports of social investigations that we have considered in this work, such as the UKIAS *Split Families* report and the four-year study by the Commission of Racial Equality, were so important in terms of being determinative of the truth of relationships concerned, that the Home Affairs Committee recommended them for guidance to ECOs. In this instance, therefore, a consideration of the social facts achieved what the formal application of the rules plainly did not. In fact, it is clear that Professor Hepple's approach would not have been radical for the immigration tribunals because this must have been one of the few areas of the law in early years where adjudicators were actively going down the empirical road. We are referring here, of course, to the pre-1973 cases, particularly those involving such apparently insoluble questions as "identity". In these cases appeals were allowed even where there was a "fairly weak prima facie case" and where there were the usual unresolved discrepancies.[73] Quite simply, the adjudicators took account of the local conditions. This changed when the IAT failed to provide the necessary support. Questions of "identity" now became a problem that was so intractable that no amount of reasonable evidence could help solve.

It is here that Professor Hepple's observations can be useful to the appellate authorities. Of the issue is whether a sponsor aged between 40 to 60 years is married or unmarried and there is no marriage certificate, then it is essential to go beyond the rules and give some consideration to the society that he comes from. The precise concept of the standard of proof applicable will alter accordingly and may even acquire a different meaning altogether. For example, sociological studies have shown that in Sylhet in Bangladesh almost every male does marry. Only 0.15 of the rural male population has never been married by the age of 45–49 years.[74] This suggests that it is improbable that a sponsor of those years in the United Kingdom will be unmarried. Similar studies show that the substitution of a real wife for a false one never really takes place once the existence of the

---

[72] *Brown v. Board of Education, supra*, n.71, at 84.
[73] *Supra*, p. 168. Also, see generally pp. 165–168.
[74] See JCWI Memorandum to the *Fifth Report, op. cit.*, at p. 60.

marriage is accepted because of the "community sanctions"[75] in that society. As for the wider use of statistical evidence, it is often assumed by the authorities that a woman who appears to have been 13 years old at marriage cannot be the mother of older children (born when she would have been over 14 years of age). Yet statistical studies show that the average age at marriage of women born in the 1940s was 11 years old. Twenty years later it had gone up only to about 13 years old. This is despite the fact that it has been illegal to marry under the age of 16 in the sub-continent ever since the Child Marriage Restraint Act 1929.[76] If the appellate authorities were to take such social facts on board they could then actually formulate clear guidelines for given sets of cases before them such as the "Sylhet Tax Pattern" and cases where there appears to be some fraud. This would help ultimately with the evaluation of the standard of proof which is so critically important here.

Such a sea-change is unlikely to happen, however, if only because it would require a re-examination of fundamental value systems in immigration law. The analyses in this work show that many decisions are unfair not because they are based on the law but because they have regard to irrelevant circumstances outside the law. They are unreasonable. This, of course, is the converse of the argument above, that in appropriate cases regard must be had to matters outside the formal legal rules. The difference, however, is that a recourse to social facts or statistical information is objectively verifiable and is for that reason relevant to the question of proof, whereas a resort to some unsubstantiated and arbitrary preconception or value outside the law is not. Many immigration decisions that we analysed in this study can only be comprehended on this basis. Yet it is heresy to say so because it is not the accepted way of looking at legal situations. English law regards law as autonomous and the function of lawyers is deemed to be analytical purely in respect of the decision before them.

This view was challenged by K.C. Davis who has been regarded as having "profoundly altered the way in which scholars regard administrative law".[77] Davis argued that there was "a considerable degree of intellectual dishonesty"[78] about this approach. In England he said:

"The typical judge, barrister, solicitor, teacher or student responds with consternation to an inquiry into the soundness of the policies embodied

---

[75] *Supra*, p. 75.
[76] See JCWI Memorandum to the *Fifth Report, op. cit.*, pp. 60–62.
[77] See Baldwin and Hawkins, "Discretionary Justice — Davis Reconsidered [1984] *Public Law* 580. Also now see Hawkins, *The Uses of Discretion* (Oxford, 1992) for a development of the ideas in that article.
[78] Davis, "The Future of Judge-Made Public Law in England: A problem of practical jurisprudence" (1961) 61, Col.L.R. 216.

in a judicial decision, and, if he persists, the inquirer is gently reminded that judges do not consider policy questions and that only Parliament can change the law."[79]

This gives a misleading picture of how the law works. More recently, Baldwin and Hawkins have argued that "a proper appraisal of discretionary justice must recognise the part played in decision-making by moral, political, organisational, and economic values, in addition to legal ones".[80] This is because:

". . . what is regarded as a 'decision' actually consists of two very different components. We typically regard a legal decision as concerning action, e.g. arrest, sentence or settlement. More subtle, however, are the prior decisions to be made in defining the 'facts' or matters deemed relevant to the decision. 'Facts' in legal cases are by no means self-evident, but have to be matters for interpretation by decision-makers. Some of the central concepts in legal decisions, such as 'crime' or 'record', 'culpability' or 'compliance', often involve considerable interpretative work by a decision-maker, *because the exercise of discretion involves a search for meaning*."[81] (Author's emphasis.)

If that is true then this has enormous implications. It means that subordinate civil servants working at posts overseas would feel entitled to reject Mr Lyon's policy because, as Mr Enoch Powell said, "if they considered that there was an end in sight, there would be less uneasiness felt about pushing through dependants' cases with increased despatch."[82] But more importantly, it means that an adjudicator who hears a case is not just influenced by the logical organisation of rules and principles, or the evidence before him, or with the evaluation of proof — all of which are within the law — but with the extra-legal consideration also of whether or not his decision properly arrived at, with due consideration of the merits, is going to be reversed on appeal by the Tribunal. Indeed, it may even be said that his evaluation of the legal rules, the evidence and proof is itself determined by how he regards the Tribunal will exercise its discretion on appeal. To that extent, decision making does, to use Lord Scarman's phrase, take place in a "specialised and detached systems"[83] fenced off from the external influences of the courts. The evidence in this study bears this out because throughout the period that has been

---

[79] *ibid.*, p. 202.
[80] Baldwin and Hawkins, *op. cit.*, p. 580.
[81] *ibid.*, p. 584.
[82] *Supra*, p. 188.
[83] *Supra*, p. 196.

reviewed the law on entry of wives and children of Commonwealth citizens settled here remained unchanged since immigration controls were first introduced for them in 1962, but after 1973 they found it difficult to exercise their legal rights simply because the Tribunal decreed that there must now be additional proof as to the "identity" of the person applying. Yet adjudicators had earlier allowed cases freely if they were satisfied as to the sponsor's claimed relationship; that is, if they were satisfied on a balance of probabilities that there was a wife in existence of the sponsor, and that the person applying was likely to be that wife. Now, however, if they did this they were likely to have their determinations reversed on appeal.[84]

This failure to abide by the law raises fundamental questions of legal theory. If the decisions are made extra-legally on the basis, not of established legal norms and principles, but the perceived requirements of public interest, then is that a sufficient justification or raison d'être for decision making in that particular regulatory context, or is it still necessary to seek to reconcile such a process with the wider tenets of the legal system? The problem may be stated as follows. Anglo-American legal thought is deeply rooted in the Rule of Law model as an ideal model of legal authority. Dicey defined this, *inter alia*, as "the absolute supremacy or predominance of regular law as opposed to the influence of arbitrary power, and excludes the existence of arbitrariness, . . . or . . . wide discretionary authority on the part of government".[85] This formulation has been variously adopted subsequently. Professor F. Hayek defines the Rule of Law as connoting that "government in all its actions is bound by rules fixed and announced beforehand — rules which make it possible to foresee with fair certainty how the authority will use its coercive powers in given circumstances . . .".[86] Thus what the Rule of Law model says is that government must adhere to strict rules of law.

However, this characterisation of legal authority has been refuted as being an inaccurate analysis of legal structures in human society. Professor K.C. Davis has remarked that:

"No legal system in world history has been without discretionary power. None can be. Discretion is indispensable for individualised justice, for

---

[84] *Supra*, pp. 173–177. Reference may here be made to Mr Alex Lyon explaining the distinction between the different standards of proof to the Home Affairs Committee in 1981–1982. He said: "If somebody comes to me and says, 'Look this is my daughter', and they have to go and argue about whether they remember the date of the marriage and all the rest of it, that is a balance of probabilities situation, but if somebody comes to me with a birth certificate in Britain which says, 'This is your daughter', on the whole I would regard that as irrefutable evidence." See *Fifth Report, op. cit.*, Vol. II, p. 115, Q.332.
[85] Dicey, *The Law of the Constitution* (London, 1910), pp. 202–203.
[86] Hayek, *The Road to Serfdom* (Chicago, 1944), p. 72.

creative justice, for new programs in which no one yet knows how to formulate rules ... Eliminating discretionary power would paralyse governmental processes and would stifle individualised justice."[87]

The position now is that the legitimacy of discretionary power is acknowledged by Anglo-American legal theorists. In fact, it is perceived as falling squarely within the perview of the original Rule of Law model. How so, it may be asked? The answer lies in viewing the role and aim of such power as serving purposes that are consonant with those of the legal system. The purposes of the legal system — or in the words of another writer — its "purposeful enterprise"[88] was what Dicey sought to consecrate in his model of legal authority.[89] His purpose was to safeguard certain basic individual rights and freedoms from arbitrary official encroachment. He assumed that this purpose was best served by deprecating the use of discretionary power as this entailed the vagarious influences of personal inclination entering into the process of decision making. This made those processes arbitrary. If they were arbitrary they could not be fair and just. The revised model, however, acknowledged the simplicity of the original model by positing that those purposes of the legal system can be better served if decision making is "individualised" to meet those cases which cannot be covered by rules.

There is now, however, a further modification of the model — a third revision. This suggests that even if mandatory rules of law exist to prescribe the exercise of official power there is still room, in some cases, for officials to act in blatant disregard of those rules. The argument is that this model is a more realistic model of legal authority than either the first or the second. It finds its exponents in the writers M.R. Kadish and S.H. Kadish in their book, *Discretion to Disobey*.[90] Since there are already mandatory rules of competence the discretion in question here is "deviational discretion — the exercise of authority in ways or on the basis of considerations either unauthorised or prohibited by rules of competence".[91] Deviational discretion is exercised by officials in most spheres of law and administration:

"For example, the jury has a duty to reach its verdict in accordance with the judge's instructions on the law; the administrative agency, to give

---

[87] Davis, *Discretionary Justice* (Baton Rouge, 1969), p. 1.
[88] Fuller, *The Morality of Law* (Yale University Press, rev. ed., 1969), p. 4.
[89] This is seen in Dicey's second limb of his definition of the Rule of Law, particularly the emphasis on the exclusion of "the existence of arbitrariness".
[90] Kadish and Kadish, *Discretion to Disobey* (Stanford University Press, 1979).
[91] *ibid.*, p. 42.

controlling weight to one single factor or to disregard a certain factor entirely, or to consider some factor only in conjunction with other factors; the magistrate, to set bail on the basis of the need to ensure the defendant's presence at the trial; the judge to grant probation only in classes defined by law; the Court, to apply the law rather than follow its own inclinations.

But suppose the jury decides otherwise than in accordance with the judge's instructions. Suppose the administrative agency does not give proper weight to certain factors. Suppose the magistrate does not set the bail solely on the basis of the need to ensure the defendant's presence at the trial. Or suppose the judge, following his own inclinations grants probation to an offender who is not legally entitled to receive it. Granting the mandatory character of the rules of competence involved, does the legal system condemn all such actions as illegitimate?"[92]

Messrs Kadish and Kadish declare that in many cases such unlawful departures are often castigated as being illegitimate by the legal system, but there are equally many instances where there is no condemnation. This is because the legal system's "very organisation may at various critical points furnish the justification for officials taking upon themselves actions that depart from some rule of competence."[93] Thus the examples that the writers give in their book of official deviational discretions suggest that maverick conduct is only accepted within the context of the legal system because it is consonant with the basic purposes of the legal system — that is, they replenish the Rule of Law model by making the law conducive to greater individualised justice and the examples quoted above demonstrate this. In addition, however, the day-to-day functioning of the jury, the police, the public prosecutor and the judge is dependent, to no small degree, on the power to deviate from mandatory legal rules. All, however, find ready justification within the legal system itself.

These examples show then that deviational discretions do not derogate from, but merely up-date the original model. Kadish and Kadish state at the outset of their book that:

> "In order for citizens and officials to justify undertaking their actions in the context of a system of laws, they must argue toward a proposition of merit establishing that the action to be undertaken is, *in the context of the legal system, desirable or meritorious*, and they must argue toward a proposition of appropriateness establishing that the contemplated action is indeed appropriate for a citizen or official to undertake."[94] (Author's emphasis.)

---

[92] *ibid.*, p. 38–39.
[93] *ibid.*, p. 40.
[94] *ibid.*, p. 7.

But herein arises the difficulty for lawyers looking at immigration law. Discretionary power or "deviational discretion", where there are already existing rules of law, cannot always be explained in these terms in immigration law.[95] It cannot be explained in terms of the original Dicean model of the Rule of Law, because discretion figures so prominently here, but it cannot be explained in terms of any subsequent models either. It falls outside all three. Indeed, it is doubtful whether the justification for some basic immigration practices is sought under such a framework of legal authority at all, and this can be illustrated well by the case of *Manzoor Begum*.[96] To demonstrate this the facts here bear closer examination. In this case Mrs Begum made an application with her son Tamvir for an entry certificate in order to join her husband who was settled in the United Kingdom. This was in October 1977. Her status and the child's as wife and son of someone settled in Britain was established and her application was granted. However, as she was expecting another child she decided not to go to the United Kingdom until after the birth. In the meantime, however, the entry certificate, which is only valid for six months, expired. Her second child was born and she then made another application. The Visa Officer refused this application because he came to the conclusion, on the basis of certain discrepancies in answers to questions put by him, that the applicants were not related to someone resident in the United Kingdom. Mrs Begum appealed to an adjudicator. The adjudicator found from the explanatory statement that "nothing except the discrepancies" were against her. This seemed an insufficient basis to him for refusal. Nor could he find any evidence that "the first entry certificate was obtained by deception or concealment of material facts". Moreover, he believed, "it could well be argued that an estoppel arises in the circumstances."[97] On the basis of these considerations, the adjudicator allowed the appeal of Mrs Begum and her children.

The Visa Officer now appealed to the IAT. The IAT, notwithstanding the Court decisions in *Ex p. Alam Bi*[98] and *Ex p. Motahir Ali*,[99] reversed the finding of the adjudicator without investigating the Visa Officer's decision or whether the writing of the explanatory statement constituted a substantial error in the context of the

---

[95] See especially Chapters 4 and 5 above, where the wide disparities in the exercise of discretionary power is particularly noticeable and where, as in Chapter 4, the higher courts have regularly disapproved of this practice.

[96] *Visa Officer Islamabad v. Manzoor Begum* TH/83002/81 (2341) d. 10.5.82 (unreported).

[97] *ibid.*, p. 2.

[98] *Supra*, p. 137–138.

[99] *Supra*, p. 154.

decision. The Tribunal reached its decision on the basis that, "estoppel does not arise" in immigration. It held that "the doctrine of estoppel could not operate against the Secretary of State because he had power to change his mind". It went further to explain that, "similarly the doctrine of 'res judicata' has no application in immigration entry and immigration departments."[1]

A case such as this indicates that the *de facto* justification for some of the practices of immigration law lie rather in the *special context* of the *particular* laws that officials are enforcing, which are after all discriminatory and restrictive, rather than in any generally accepted model of law. In legal theory terms the process of rationalisation is arguably thereby inverted because role agents (*i.e.* immigration officials) in this area do not have to argue "toward a proposition of merit" as Messrs Kadish and Kadish would put it, in terms of their actions being "in the context of the legal system, desirable or meritorious."[2] They need only argue "toward a proposition of merit" within the narrow cadre of the law that they are enforcing. That is its justification. It also means that the traditional models of legal authority will have to be revised fairly drastically. As Nicola Lacey has said, this requires an "expansion of our intellectual horizons" so that we can "transcend the traditional boundaries" and thereby "develop a more context-sensitive and pluralistic approach than that generally offered by jurisprudence". As she explains:

> ". . . we must develop an approach which incorporates 'public' and 'private'; policy-formation and application; discretionary and other role-related power. We need to integrate empirical, interpretive, and normative questions in an attempt both to understand discretion and, ultimately, to ensure the legitimacy and effectiveness of the exercise of social power in particular contexts. Discretion must be taken, then, primarily as a *political* question . . ."[3]

According to Nicola Lacey, the search for legitimacy of discretionary decision making "calls for the concerted attention of a number of related and interdependent disciplines".[4] This suggests that there is room for a further reformulation of the Rule of Law model. We began this work at the outset by questioning the very concept of the Rule of Law as classically devised by A.V. Dicey and his

---

[1] *Op. cit.*
[2] *Supra*, n. 90.
[3] Lacey, "The Jurisprudence of Discretion: Escaping the Legal Paradigm" in *The Uses of Discretion* (ed. by K. Hawkins, Oxford, 1992), pp. 361–388.
[4] *ibid.*, pp. 387–388.

supporters. We argued against a formal recital of this concept. If equality in the law has to have a real meaning, it must involve substantive understanding of the effects of law, as interpreted and applied, on both the individual and the collective welfare of our society. This, after all, is the most noteworthy contribution of the New Public Law movement of this decade. In a sense, therefore, the Rule of Law notion has to be deconstructed and decentralised. It has to be seen less as a normative, and more as a social, empirical and interpretive device, against which the effects of the law can be properly judged. It is this that will in the future determine the legitimacy of the law. It is this that will make the concept of the Rule of Law meaningful to the discrete and diverse interests in our society by addressing their concerns on their terms. Cultural Jurisprudence then, is the essential modern artifact that fits the bill. It does not look to defining the law in terms of its theoretical and formal symmetry. It does not consider the law to be a neutral science. It sees the law as a cultural agent with clear cultural effects, and requires lawyers, courts and administrators to utilise social science information with a view to ensuring that the right cultural effects are secured in the application of the law. There is evidence that this is happening. Professor Jackson, for example, draws attention in his book, to three Tribunal decisions where there has been judicial recognition of the Muslim doctrine of "Ijbar", which imposes a duty upon a father to ensure that his daughter marries a man of good character and means of livelihood.[5] In the family re-unification cases that we have considered in this work it is both practically and theoretically impossible to avoid the implications of cultural jurisprudence.

More than 75 per cent of Britains non-white population are British nationals, but as everyone knows, the grant of citizenship *per se* does not solve the problem of integration, that is so essential to civic unity. Asians comprise three per cent of the British population. In 36 constituencies, the Asian vote in the 1997 British elections, was larger than the sitting M.P.s majority. In 12 of the top 60 seats that Tony Blair needed to win power, Asian voters determined the outcome.[6] The present immigration laws help divide families amongst these voters. Unless changed, they will help divide society too. No town, it is true, in Britain presently has an ethnic minority population of more than 50 per cent. This minority population makes up only 5.6 per cent of the total population. But the 1994 census shows that it is likely to double to six million in the next 40 years. It will, of course,

---

[5] See Jackson, *op. cit.*, p. 418.
[6] *The Times*, February 27, 1997.

still remain very much a minority and will still be less than 10 per cent of the total population.[7] However, this only means that this population's concerns about ethnic and cultural rights are likely to become more, and not less, pressing for governments to address. The New Public Law movement is based, in normative terms, on a dedication to the enhancement of the welfare of our society. The anachronistic laws and practices described in this work will not promote our general welfare as a society unless our laws and policies adopt a more culturally sensitive approach.

[7] See Ford, "U.K.'s Ethnic Minorities will Double in 40 Years". *The Times*, January 20, 1994.

Index